Complementary Democracy

Democracy in Times of Upheaval

Edited by
Matt Qvortrup

Volume 4

Complementary Democracy

The Art of Deliberative Listening

Edited by
Matt Qvortrup and Daniela Vancic

DE GRUYTER

ISBN 978-3-11-152923-3
e-ISBN (PDF) 978-3-11-074733-1
e-ISBN (EPUB) 978-3-11-074747-8
ISSN 2701-147X
e-ISSN 2701-1488

Library of Congress Control Number: 2022939567

Bibliographic information published by the Deutsche Nationalbibliothek
The Deutsche Nationalbibliothek lists this publication in the Deutsche
Nationalbibliografie; detailed bibliographic data are available on the internet at http://
dnb.dnb.de.

www.degruyter.com

Table of Contents

Matt Qvortrup and Daniela Vancic

Introduction: Complementary Democracy – The New Frontier in Theory, Research, and Practice

"The English People believe themselves to be free. They are gravely mistaken. They are only free once every five years." Thus wrote Jean-Jacques Rousseau in the 18th century – a statement more relevant now than ever before.[1] Yet, the misgivings with pure representative democracy are not new. Brexit, Trump, growing populism, and polarization suggest that the current form of democracy is being challenged and is outdated. Increasingly, people are turning away from democracy and opting for the promises of demagogues – who, when given the chance, turn into autocrats.

We have come a long way since the time when democracy was limited to merely electing representatives. In the middle of the 20th century, the Austrian-American economist, Joseph Schumpeter famously wrote,

> [Democracy does] not mean and cannot mean that the people actually rule in any obvious sense of the terms 'people' and 'rule.' Democracy means only that the people have the opportunity of accepting or refusing the men who are to rule them. But since they might decide this also in entirely undemocratic ways, we have had to narrow our definition by adding a further criterion identifying the democratic method, viz., free competition among would-be leaders for the vote of the electorate.[2]

But this model was predicated on the assumption that the parties represented individuals. This was never entirely the case, but in the age of class-politics, at the time when different parties corresponded to the major cleavages in society (as famously proposed by Stein Rokkan and Seymour M. Lipset[3]); workers' parties to cater for wage earners, agrarian parties to serve for rural communities, religious parties to represent the views of different denominational groups, and so on.

But this system no longer works as efficiently as it once did. Dealignment and the increased levels of electoral volatility are indications that the classic

---

1 Rousseau, Jean-Jacques (1964) 'Du contrat social.' In *Oeuvre III*. Paris: Pléiade, pp. 349–470, p. 429.
2 Schumpeter, Joseph (1942) *Capitalism, Socialism and Democracy*. London: Routledge, p. 242.
3 Rokkan, S. and Lipset, S. M. (1967) *Party Systems and Voter Alignments: Cross Sectional Perspectives*. Toronto: The Free Press.

https://doi.org/10.1515/9783110747331-001

model needs modification to fit a 21st century democracy. This type of indirect government by the people is still the main form for democracy, but it is not the only show in town. The idea that democracy is "the competitive struggle for votes" in a parliamentary system,[4] as was asserted in the mid-20th century, is no longer an accurate representation of the state of affairs. Elections of representatives – whether locally or centrally – will remain the norm. But this system can no longer stand alone. It therefore raises some questions: What are the issues in our democracies, and how can they be resolved? What can be done, and what is missing?

At the heart of the current malaise, as well as the ones before it, is a lack of legitimacy and a feeling that those in power no longer 'represent' the people For this to change, we need to find ways of adding to the 'supply' of democracy. Simply put, the lower the demand for democracy, the lower the levels of legitimacy are.

This can be illustrated using the familiar supply-and-demand curves of micro-economics. When the supply of direct democratic institutions is low (as under a system of pure representative democracy) there will be more demand for institutions that cater for individuals. For example, the legitimacy increases, all other things being equal, if we give people the opportunity to participate in citizens' juries. It increases to a higher level yet if we allow them to initiate referendums. Figure 1.1 shows this graphically. Each of the supply curves represents different levels of direct democracy. Thus, Supply Curve 1 represents different degrees of uses of citizens' juries (e.g. the number of juries held every year), and Supply Curve 2 represents different degrees of the use of popularly initiated referendums. Curves can continue to be added for additional institutions and democratic opportunities.

Needless to say, the analogy with economics can only be taken so far. However, to a degree, an increase in the supply of democracy will lead to greater legitimacy. This leads to a feeling of being in control, which will be conducive to greater stability and satisfaction.

In each of the chapters of this book we look at distinct institutions that add legitimacy to the political process and the system of governance. The institutions we look at are, among others,

- referendums (popular votes on distinct policies);
- the recall (on the revocation of the mandates of elected representatives);
- the increased use of citizens' juries (structured discussions of policies with a representative sample of voters to inform elected representatives);

---

4 Schumpeter, Joseph A. (1942) *Capitalism, Socialism, and Democracy.* London: Unwin, p. 269.

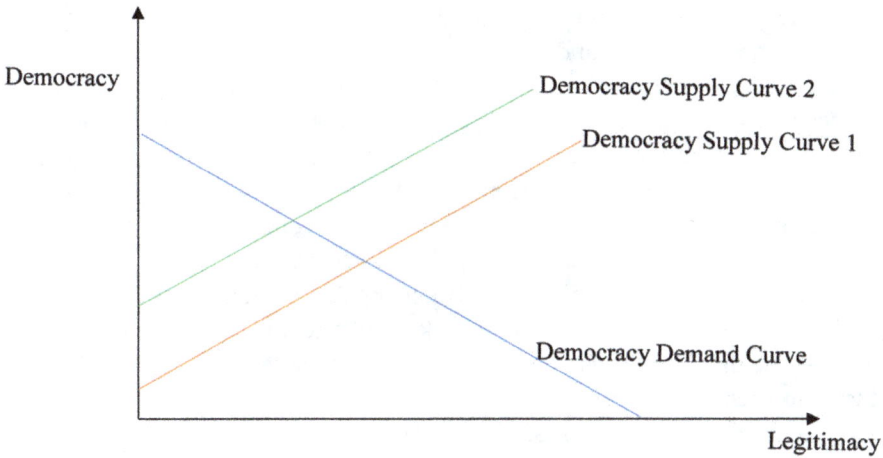

Figure 1.1: Supply and Demand Curves of Democracy.

- sortition (selection of advisory panels of citizens based on random selection);
- agenda initiatives (petitions submitted to parliaments);
- digital democracy (voting through formal and informal internet and digital platforms);
- participatory budgeting; and even
- citizens' movements (spontaneous action groups using performance and art).

Why are these institutions and practices of complementary democracy necessary? The political theorist Dennis Thompson has written that "Citizens and their representatives are expected to justify the laws they would impose on one another by giving reasons for their political claims and responding to others' reasons in return."[5] This is not happening now. To change this state of affairs – to build stronger democracies and increase trust – it is incumbent on both citizens and politicians to introduce institutions that reduce the current malaise.

But adding to the institutions of direct democracy is not just about constitutional change. Increasing the opportunities for participation is also not just about institutions adopting formal mechanisms, such as referendums, the recall,

---

5 Thompson, Dennis F. (2008) 'Deliberative democratic theory and empirical political science.' *Annual Review of Political Science* 11: 497–520, at 498.

and agenda initiatives. Nor is it merely about the experimentations with transnational citizens' initiatives and similar mechanisms.

Increasing legitimacy and adding "daring more democracy" (as German chancellor Willy Brandt called it[6]) is also about the informal ways in which individuals contribute to policy formulation – that is, social movements, citizens' groups, and even artistic expression (as in the case of the system envisaged by the German artist Joseph Beuys who, under the slogan "Demokratie ist lustig" ("Democracy is merry"), encouraged political activism as a form of artistic expression. (This is covered in Chapter Twelve by Andrea Adamopoulos.)

Each of the chapters that follows looks at different institutions and inquires whether the different forms of 'complementary democracy' are likely to be conducive to such a discourse.

The chapters are as follows:

In Chapter Two, regarding citizens' juries, Maija Setälä presents recent findings and introduces and evaluates the different practices of mini-publics. This is followed by Chapter Two on participatory budgeting. Pioneered in Brazil, participatory budgeting schemes allow citizens to deliberate with the goal of creating either a concrete financial plan (a budget) or a recommendation to elected representatives. In Chapter Three, Greta Ríos presents the institution with a special reference to recent developments in her native Mexico.

The philosopher Karl Popper once wrote that a democracy is a system where you can get rid of the government without bloodshed.[7] Of course, we can 'kick the rascals out' on election day, but there is a far more effective way: the recall. Practiced in California and several countries in Latin America, this mechanism allows citizens to revoke the mandates of elected representatives. Yanina Welp provides an expert overview in Chapter Four.

The traditional answer to the insufficient supply of democracy has been binding referendums and initiatives. In Chapter Five Matt Qvortrup presents an overview of the history, theory, and effect of referendums. The chapter covers both jurisdictions where these are a central part of democratic decision-making (e.g. California and Switzerland) but also polities where these provisions are used more sparingly, such as Uruguay and Italy. The chapter finds that while referendums are often held for less than idealistic reasons, the institution has overall positive effects. Indeed, statistically speaking, countries with more referendums are richer and live slightly longer.

---

6 He used the phrase in his inaugural address as chancellor of the Federal Republic of Germany in 1969: https://www.swr.de/swr2/wissen/archivradio/willy-brandt-rede-1969-mehr-demokratie-wagen-102.html.

7 Popper, Karl R. (2002) *The Open Society and Its Enemies*. London: Routledge, p. 118.

Citizen-initiated referendums are a radical solution for some. Not all countries have gone as far as introducing them. Thus, in some other countries, citizens put forward legislative proposals, which are then debated and voted on by their representatives – but not put to a popular vote. This type of mechanism is called the agenda initiative. As distinct from citizens' initiatives (like in the USA), which allow citizens to propose and directly vote on propositions, this type of indirect democracy seems weak. Yet, it has led to practical results – such as in Denmark, where the first climate law was a result of an agenda initiative. This and other examples are discussed by Fernando Mendez and Mario Mendez in Chapter Six.

So far, democracy has been a largely national affair. There are indications that this is changing. As the only transnational governmental organization in the world, the citizens of the European Union elect their own Parliament, and this body can even dismiss the European Commission in a vote of no confidence. But the EU also has more direct mechanisms for citizen engagement, namely the European Citizens' Initiative. In Chapter Seven, Daniela Vancic sums up the emerging practices and evaluates the pioneering projects that are inspiring a proposal for a United Nations World Citizens' Initiative.

In 2016 the Irish-Canadian academic Roslyn Fuller stood for election as an independent to the Irish parliament on a platform of *digital democracy*. While she did not win a seat, she nevertheless kept her election promise by conducting Ireland's first digital democracy experiment in the same year. In Chapter Eight she outlines the essence, promise, and pitfalls of digital democracy.

In ancient Athens and other Greek city-states, the government was chosen by lot. In modern times we have the same system for juries, but some have suggested that this system could be extended to other decisions. Gil Delannoi outlines in Chapter Nine recent practical examples of advisory panels of citizens based on random selection.

But sometimes democratic participation happens without a pre-established legislative framework. Social movements are an example of extra-parliamentary engagement. In Chapter Ten, on social movements in democracy, Donatella della Porta and Andrea Felicetti present an overview of social movements' contribution to democratic innovations. They provide a brief historical trajectory on the topic, and then focus on the ways movements are currently engaging in democratic life. This is done by looking at both internal practices and interactions with democratic institutions. The authors conclude by envisaging what challenges and opportunities lie ahead for social movements and democracy.

In a similar vein, Selen A. Ercan and Carolyn M. Hendriks in Chapter Eleven look at creative participation. The 'Knitting Nannas Against Gas' – or KNAGS as they style themselves – have been able to effect change merely through knitting. As they describe it:

We sit, knit, plot, have a yarn and a cuppa, and bear witness to the war against the greedy, short-sighted corporations that are trying to rape our land and divide our communities. Knitting Nannas happily support other anti-greed groups at their protests and meetings, or online.

These practices are not a million miles from the visions of artists. This is the theme in Chapter Twelve, in which Andrea Adamopoulos (using the example of the aforementioned Joseph Beuys) outlines examples of how artistic expression can support, facilitate, and deepen democratic participation.

In the final chapter, Daniela Vancic and Matt Qvortrup sum up the findings and present practical and theoretical ways forward.

We do not propose that we have squared the circle of governance, let alone the secret to saving democracy in a time of upheaval. We hope to inspire everyone across the political spectrum. The aforementioned KNAGS write on their website, "We are non-party political. We annoy all politicians equally." That could easily be the motto and goal of this book.

Maija Setälä
Functions of Deliberative Mini-Publics in Democratic Systems

Introduction

This chapter investigates different roles and functions of deliberative mini-publics in representative systems. Since Archon Fung's survey article on 'the recipes for public spheres,' the term 'deliberative mini-public' has become a part of the vocabulary of democratic theory and practice.[1] Nowadays, the term refers to designs such as citizens' juries, planning cells, consensus conferences, Deliberative Polls, and citizens' assemblies.[2]

The key design features of deliberative mini-publics are random selection of participants and systematic collection of evidence, for example through expert hearings, and moderated small-group discussions. Otherwise, deliberative mini-publics come in various sizes and lengths, and they produce different types of outcomes.

The first pilots of randomly selected citizen forums were conducted in the United States and Germany in the early 1970s. It seems therefore fair to say that the practices of deliberative mini-publics are now middle aged. The use of deliberative mini-publics has intensified during the past few years, not least because of the pressures to deal with complex and controversial policy issues related to climate change. At the same time, the formats and purposes of mini-publics have diversified.[3] This chapter points out that, after decades of experimenting, practicing, and studying randomly selected citizen forums, there is still no 'general theory' of deliberative mini-publics.

---

1 Fung, A. (2003) 'Survey article: recipes for public spheres: eight institutional design choices and their consequences.' *Journal of Political Philosophy* 11(3): 338 – 367.
2 For a review: Setälä, M. and Smith, G. (2018) 'Deliberative mini-publics and deliberative democracy.' In A. Bächtiger, J. Dryzek, J. Mansbridge, and M. E. Warren (eds.) *The Oxford Handbook of Deliberative Democracy.* Oxford: Oxford University Press, pp. 300 – 314.
3 See e. g.: OECD (2020) *Innovative Citizen Participation and New Democratic Institutions: Catching the Deliberative Wave.* Paris: OECD Publishing: https://doi.org/10.1787/339306da-en.

https://doi.org/10.1515/9783110747331-002

This argument is strongly inspired by the work of Gordon Smith,[4] who, in the mid-1970s, made an argument that there is no 'general theory of referendums.' Smith points out that the different circumstances called referendums have only superficial similarities with each other and that referendums have very different functions in political systems.[5] I will demonstrate that this is also the case – perhaps with some caveats – with deliberative mini-publics. While mini-publics are still typically advisory bodies that provide input for policy-makers, the practices of deliberative mini-publics and their functions in political systems have diversified during the past decades.

Moreover, while their contribution in terms of democratic renewal has been relatively modest so far, mini-publics continue to have much potential in this respect. This chapter aims to highlight better practices and ways of using mini-publics. From the perspective of deliberative democracy, the promise of mini-publics lies in their capacity to foster learning, reflection, and deliberation among policy-makers and the public at large. Obviously, this opens a range of new questions, especially when it comes to the circumstances in which mini-publics come about and how they are connected to elected representative bodies and the general public. To fulfill their democratic potential, mini-publics should not just give advice, but rather intervene and interact with collective will-formation in parliaments and the public at large.

What are Deliberative Mini-Publics?

A Brief History of Mini-Publics

The first citizens' jury was organized in 1974 in Minnesota on health care plans.[6] In the same year, Ned Crosby founded the Jefferson Center for New Democratic Processes in order to develop and spread the idea of the citizens' jury. A few years earlier, Peter Dienel at the University of Wuppertal had developed a randomly selected citizen forum called the planning cell. The Danish Board of Tech-

---

4 See Smith, G. (1975) 'The referendum and political change.' *Government and Opposition* 10(3): 294–305; Smith, G. (1976) 'The functional properties of the referendum.' *European Journal of Political Research* 4(1): 1–23.
5 Smith, 'The referendum and political change,' 294.
6 Crosby, N. (1995) 'Citizens juries: one solution for difficult environmental questions.' In O. Renn, T. Webles, and P. Wiedemann (eds.) *Fairness and Competence in Citizen Participation*. Dordrecht: Kluwer, pp. 157–174.

nology (Teknologirådet) developed a forum for citizen deliberation called the consensus conference. Consensus conferences were organized regularly in Denmark from 1987 to provide advice for parliamentarians on technically complex issues.[7]

In other words, models for citizen deliberation that we nowadays call deliberative mini-publics had already been developed and experimented with in the 1970s and 1980s.[8] In this respect, the ideas and practices of mini-publics surfaced before and independently of the so-called 'deliberative turn' in democratic theory, which took place in the 1980s and 1990s. What is more, the ideas and practices of deliberative mini-publics were not so much inspired by the classical texts in the theory of deliberative democracy, for example by Habermas and Rawls. Rather, forums for citizen deliberation were developed as a response to more general concerns among practitioners, activists, and scholars of democracy regarding the increasing complexity of decision-making and the growing distance between citizens and political elites.

Yet, there were some democratic theorists, most notably Benjamin Barber[9] and Robert A. Dahl,[10] who had an impact on the emergence of mini-publics. Barber and Dahl identified a set of problems in the existing representative systems and put forward ideas for participatory arrangements as a remedy. Both were inspired by the classical conception of democracy in the Ancient Greek and its idea of the selection by lot. Both argued for the use of randomly selected bodies to ensure that each citizen has an equal opportunity to participate in the democratic process, thus counteracting the elitist tendencies of electoral democracy.

In his 1984 book, *Strong Democracy*, Benjamin Barber argues for randomly selected forums for citizen deliberation as a part of his program for participatory democracy. Barber described the advantages of random selection in the following terms: "Since the nurturing of political judgment does not require that every citizen be involved in all decisions, the lot is a way of maximizing meaningful engagement in large-scale societies."[11] According to Barber, random selection would neutralize the skewing effects of wealth in the access to public office in

---

7 Joss, S. (1998) 'Danish consensus conferences as a model of participatory technology assessment: an impact study of consensus conference on Danish Parliament and Danish public debate.' *Science and Public Policy* 25(1): 2–22.

8 Floridia, A. (2017) *From Participation to Deliberation: A Critical Genealogy of Deliberative Democracy.* Colchester: ECPR Press.

9 Barber, B. (1984) *Strong Democracy: Participatory Politics for a New Age.* Berkeley: University of California Press.

10 Dahl, R. A. (1989) *Democracy and its Critics.* New Haven and London: Yale University Press.

11 Barber, *Strong Democracy*, p. 291.

electoral democracies, and help spread public responsibility in a more equitable manner across the whole population.

Dahl justifies democracy in procedural terms as a political system based on the principle of political equality. Dahl was especially concerned about the tendencies towards so-called 'quasi-guardianship' in contemporary complex societies. The risk is that a lack of relevant political information among mass publics leads to dominance by experts in public policy-making. In his classic book *Democracy and its Critics*, Dahl makes a proposal of so-called 'mini-populus,' which has been an inspiration for some of the current practices of deliberative mini-publics. It is notable that Dahl had developed the ideas regarding randomly selected deliberative forums already in the 1980s, inspired by then existing small-scale practices such as citizens' juries.[12]

In essence, Dahl's idea of the mini-populus entails a procedure where randomly selected citizens would deliberate on policy issues, possibly taking advantage of telecommunications. Dahl gave a detailed account of how mini-populus would work, including a description of the division of labor between the agenda-setting mini-populus and other mini-populus focusing on major policy issues.[13] However, he was not very specific when it came to the relationship between mini-populus and elected representative institutions. In fact, Dahl only said that they would complement existing representative democracy. On the legitimacy of mini-populus Dahl argued as follows: "Its verdict would be the verdict of the demos itself, if the demos were able to take advantage of the best available knowledge to decide what policies were most likely to achieve the ends it sought. The judgements of the mini-populus would thus derive their authority from the legitimacy of democracy."[14]

Dahl's idea of a mini-populus was clearly an inspiration for James S. Fishkin's views of what he calls "deliberative democracy."[15] For Fishkin, randomly selected deliberative bodies would create a possibility to combine the principles of political equality and deliberation. Fishkin echoes Dahl's idea that a randomly selected forum could give a representation of public opinion if citizens had an opportunity to make informed and reflected judgments. In 1991, James S. Fishkin proposed a model of a Deliberative Opinion Poll where a national sample of par-

---

12 Floridia, *From Participation to Deliberation*, p. 161.
13 Dahl, *Democracy and its Critics*, p. 340.
14 Dahl, *Democracy and its Critics*, p. 340.
15 Fishkin, J. S. (1991) *Democracy and Deliberation: New Directions in Democratic Reform.* New Haven: Yale University Press.

ticipants would be gathered together in intensive face-to-face debate. The first Deliberative Poll was actually organized in Texas in 1994.[16]

Theorists of deliberative democracy have not necessarily welcomed the ideas and practices of deliberative mini-publics. For starters, those having a 'systemic' perspective of deliberative democracy are highly critical of Fishkin's way of equating 'deliberative democracy' with Deliberative Polls. But this kind of 're-ductionism' is not the sole reason why theorists of democracy and deliberative democracy in particular have been critical of mini-publics. These issues will be dealt with later in this chapter.

The Design of Mini-Publics: Representation, Moderation, and Deliberation

Fishkin's counterfactual claim that a Deliberative Poll would provide a represen-tation of an informed and reflected public opinion is highly controversial. Most notably, it raises questions about the representativeness of a deliberative mini-public. The recruitment process of a mini-public usually begins with a random sample that is large enough to be representative of the whole population. How-ever, only a small proportion of those invited will eventually volunteer to partic-ipate. Because of self-selection in the recruitment process, even large-scale mini-publics such as Deliberative Polls include only some hundreds of participants. Only very few mini-publics have included more participants. In this respect, mini-publics cannot really be said to represent the wider public in a statistical sense.

But if mini-publics cannot be representative in a statistical sense, how should we interpret the claim that they should represent the public at large? There are many interpretations and disagreements related to representativeness of mini-publics. Some authors have argued that mini-publics should aim at rep-resentation of different societal viewpoints.[17] However, even representation of various societal viewpoints may be difficult to achieve in mini-publics. There are studies showing that highly educated citizens and those interested in politics

16 Fishkin, J. S. (2003) 'Consulting the public through deliberative polling.' *Journal of Policy Analysis and Management* 22: 128–133.
17 Brown, M. (2006) 'Survey article: citizen panels and the concept of representation.' *Journal of Political Philosophy* 14(2): 203–225, at 18.

are more prone to participate in mini-publics, and psychological factors such as willingness to avoid conflicts may affect people's readiness to participate.[18]

In other words, the processes of self-selection are likely to give rise to biases of representation in mini-publics. Such findings lend support to the argument that random sampling should be combined with stratification or quota methods in order to ensure descriptive representation of relevant societal groups. In fact, most mini-publics actually use stratification in the recruitment process in order to correct biases caused by self-selection and to ensure representation of different segments of society.[19] Stratification used in conjunction with random selection thus helps enhance representation of diversity of societal viewpoints, including those of marginalized groups. Sometimes specific quotas are reserved for particular affected groups such as ethnic minorities.[20]

But the representation of different viewpoints in a mini-public is not sufficient, and one should also pay attention to whether these viewpoints are voiced and considered in an equitable manner in the deliberative process. There is some evidence that men tend to be more active and influential than women in deliberative processes, although the decision rule and the gender balance in the forum make a difference in this respect.[21] Moreover, studies suggest that highly educated participants are more active in the deliberative process.[22] Such findings highlight the limits of deliberative mini-publics to enhance political equality and equity.

Yet, deliberative mini-publics entail certain procedural aspects that help level inequalities between participants. For example, trained moderators should be tasked to ensure that all participants have a voice and that deliberative norms such as mutual respect are followed in the process. Deliberative mini-publics also entail interaction with experts. In addition to enhancing the quality of the deliberative process, expert hearings can help level inequalities in participants' capacities to have a voice in the deliberative process.

---

18 Karjalainen, M. and Rapeli, L. (2015) 'Who will not deliberate? Attrition in a multi-stage citizen deliberation experiment.' *Quality and Quantity* 49: 407–422.
19 Farrell, D. M., Suiter, J., Harris, C., and Cunningham, K. (2020) 'The effects of mixed membership in a deliberative forum: the Irish constitutional convention of 2012–2014.' *Political Studies* 68(1): 54–73.
20 Warren, M. E. and Pearse, H. (2008) *Designing Deliberative Democracy: The British Columbia Citizens' Assembly.* Cambridge: Cambridge University Press.
21 Karpowitz, C., Mendelberg, T., and Shaker, L. (2012) 'Gender inequality in deliberative participation.' *American Political Science Review* 106(3): 533–547.
22 Himmelroos, S. (2017) 'Discourse quality in deliberative citizen forums: a comparison of four deliberative mini-publics.' *Journal of Public Deliberation* 13(1).

Obviously, there is a risk that experts have too much influence on mini-public deliberations. However, more interactive procedures for expert hearings can help avoid such risks.[23]

The Evaluation of Mini-Publics

The Positive Story: Mini-Publics as Correcting Flaws of Representative Democracy

From a purely normative perspective, deliberative mini-publics seem to have the capacity to correct certain dysfunctionalities of representative systems. Mini-publics have potential in terms of enhancing key democratic principles such as political equality and inclusion. Random selection gives each citizen an equal opportunity to be invited to a deliberative process, and is free from the skewing effects of money involved in the electoral process.

Mini-publics can also enhance the inclusion of the viewpoints of those affected in policy-making.[24] In order to counteract patterns of so-called 'external exclusion,' democratic systems should strive to identify those affected groups which are marginalized or underrepresented and to ensure their representation in the policy-making process. In addition to giving each citizen an equal opportunity to be invited, random selection can attract those citizens who are not particularly willing to participate in elections.[25]

Several studies show that electoral representative systems are to varying extents biased when it comes to the representation of different socio-demographic groups. Even in systems with proportional representation, there is often over-representation of men, well-educated, and high-income groups in parliaments.[26] Mini-publics could potentially help correct such biases in electoral representation and provide better descriptive representation of the public at large – including various marginalized groups. Biases of representation can be further counteracted if stratification and quotas are used in the recruitment process.

---

23 Roberts, J., Lightbody, R., Low, R., and Elstub, S. (2020) 'Experts and evidence in deliberation: scrutinising the role of witnesses and evidence in mini-publics.' *Policy Sciences* 53: 3–32.
24 See: Young, I. (2000) *Inclusion and Democracy.* Oxford: Oxford University Press.
25 Neblo, M., Esterling, K., Kennedy, R., Lazer, D., and Sokhey, A. (2010), 'Who wants to deliberate – and why?' *American Political Science Review* 104(3): 566–583.
26 See e.g.: Wägnerud, L. (2009) 'Women in parliaments: descriptive and substantive representation.' *Annual Review of Political Science* 12(1): 51–69.

In addition to counteracting patterns of external exclusion, mini-publics can potentially remedy internal exclusion, namely biases in the deliberative processes. Parliamentary institutions, especially committees, are expected to host deliberative processes where different viewpoints are voiced and evaluated on their merits. In reality, factors such as electoral accountability, party discipline, and the government–opposition divide constrain the prospects of parliamentary deliberation.[27] Deliberative mini-publics are designed to actually facilitate unconstrained deliberation among citizens representing different viewpoints. There are indeed some studies suggesting that the quality of deliberation in mini-publics can in some respects be better than that of parliamentary deliberation.[28]

Empirical and experimental studies on mini-publics seem to support these positive expectations at least to some extent. Participants in mini-publics learn a great deal about the issue at hand.[29] They also become more understanding of different viewpoints related to the issue[30] and more empathetic towards affected groups, including outgroups.[31] Deliberation can also alleviate polarization of opinions. What is more, participation in mini-publics increases civic skills and efficacy, and capacity and willingness to participate in politics in the future. In other words, there seems to be plenty of evidence of the capacity of mini-publics to host inclusive deliberative processes.

Therefore, it seems reasonable to expect that they can also enhance the quality of political decision-making by helping make more informed and reflected decisions that treat different groups of society in a fair manner. By providing a thorough consideration of different societal perspectives, mini-publics also have potential to resolve political deadlocks and counteract political polarization in a constructive manner.[32] This is the reason why mini-publics are increasingly used on contested issues related to climate transitions.[33]

---

27 Steiner, J., Bächtiger, A., Spörndli, M., and Steenbergen, M. R. (2004) *Deliberative Politics in Action*. Cambridge: Cambridge University Press.
28 See: Himmelroos, 'Discourse quality in deliberative citizen forums.'
29 Luskin, R. C., O'Flynn, I., Fishkin, J. S., and Russell, D. (2014) 'Deliberating across deep divides.' *Political Studies* 62: 116–135.
30 Andersen, V. N. and Hansen, K. M. (2007) 'How deliberation makes better citizens: the Danish deliberative poll on the Euro.' *European Journal of Political Research* 46: 531–556.
31 Grönlund, Kimmo, Setälä, Maija, and Herne, Kaisa (2010) 'Deliberation and civic virtue – lessons from a citizen deliberation experiment.' *European Political Science Review* 2(1): 95–117.
32 Luskin et al., 'Deliberating across deep divides.'
33 Devaney, L., Torney, D., Brereton, P., and Coleman, M. (2020) 'Ireland's Citizens' Assembly on Climate Change: lessons for deliberative public engagement and communication.' *Environmental Communication* 14(2): 141–146.

Mini-publics seem especially to be needed also on issues where elected representatives have difficulties in making judgments, for example due to strong vested interests or issues such as the design of the electoral system.[34] By enhancing inclusive deliberation in policy-making, mini-publics can enhance the legitimacy of public decisions and, moreover, the whole political system.[35] Yet, while there is already quite a lot of evidence on the effects of participation in mini-publics, there are fewer studies tackling their impact on policy-making and the democratic system more broadly. And this is where the critical story begins.

A Critical Story: The Risks of Mini-Publics

While much of the research on mini-publics has focused on their 'internal' characteristics, especially patterns of learning and opinion formation among participants, there are still gaps in understanding their potential 'external' impact on the wider political system. There are very different views on how mini-publics actually function or should function in the context of representative systems. Notably, there is an ongoing debate among theorists of democracy – and deliberative democracy in particular – on the risks and problems involved in the use of mini-publics in policy-making. By and large, this debate seems to revolve around three separate lines of argumentation highlighting potential weaknesses and risks of deliberative mini-publics.

First, scholars and other commentators have criticized mini-publics for being used by governments for instrumental reasons such as achieving particular policy goals. In this respect, there seems to be a risk that mini-publics, originally designed to enhance inclusion of different viewpoints in policy-making, may turn out to be exclusionary instruments that are used to suppress critical public discussion and voices from the opposition.[36] This argument seems to be

---

34 Thompson, D. (2008) 'Who should govern who governs? The role of citizens in reforming the electoral system.' In M. E. Warren and H. Pearse (eds.) *Designing Deliberative Democracy: The British Columbia Citizens' Assembly.* Cambridge: Cambridge University Press, pp. 20 – 49.
35 Suiter, J., Farrell, D., and Harris, C. (2016) 'The Irish Constitutional Convention: a case of "high legitimacy"?' In M. Reuchamps and J. Suiter (eds.) *Constitutional Deliberative Democracy in Europe.* Colchester: ECPR Press, pp. 33 – 52.
36 Hammond, M. (2020) 'Democratic innovations after the postdemocratic turn: between activation and empowerment.' *Critical Policy Studies*, DOI:10.1080/19460171.2020.1733629.

further confirmed by the fact that authoritarian governments like China are using mini-publics to enhance governmentality.[37]

Second, theorists of deliberative democracy have criticized mini-publics because they may arguably be used as 'shortcuts' that advise governmental policies and as 'cues' that shape public opinion. Such shortcuts and cues are not sufficient – the argument goes – since democratic legitimacy requires that public policies are subject to critical reflection and deliberation among the public at large. This argument is based on a normative view where democratic legitimacy is regarded in terms of informed and reflected consent by the public that can only be achieved in large-scale participation in public deliberation. For example, Lafont asks whether citizens outside a mini-public should just 'blindly defer' their judgments to the mini-public.[38]

As pointed out by Warren, participatory processes of public deliberation may not be feasible when it comes to most political decision-making in modern complex societies.[39] The cognitive demands related to policy-making are high, which calls for divisions of deliberative labor between citizens as well as different institutional actors such as experts and elected representatives. In fact, the idea of complexity of decision-making in modern societies was exactly the problem that Dahl wanted to address with his proposal of a mini-populus.

The third line of argument highlights the fact that the role of mini-publics in policy-making remains unclear. On the one hand, the advisory use of mini-publics leaves room for highly selective interpretations of those policy recommendations. On the other hand, authorizing mini-publics to make binding decisions would arguably give rise to problems of their legitimacy. Although mini-publics may be representative in the descriptive sense, they lack the mechanisms of authorization and accountability that are the key to the legitimacy of elected representative institutions such as parliaments.[40]

As a counterargument, one might point out that electoral authorization and accountability are not the only possible sources of democratic legitimacy of authority. Notably, democratic theorists, including Dahl (see above), emphasize that democratic legitimacy can be more directly based on democratic procedures

---

37 Woo, S. Y. and Kübler, D. (2020) 'Taking stock of democratic innovations and their emergence in (unlikely) authoritarian contexts.' *Politische Vierteljahresschrift* 61: 335–355.

38 Lafont, C. (2015) 'Deliberation, participation and democratic legitimacy: should deliberative minipublics shape public policy?' *Journal of Political Philosophy* 23(1): 40–63.

39 Warren, M. E. (2020) 'Participatory deliberative democracy in complex mass societies.' *Journal of Deliberative Democracy* 16(2): 81–88.

40 Parkinson, J. (2006) *Deliberating in the Real World: Problems of Legitimacy in Deliberative Democracy*. Oxford: Oxford University Press, p. 33.

such as inclusive deliberation. Moreover, while there are clearly risks related to the authorization of non-elected bodies such as mini-publics, it is important to keep in mind that electoral accountability alone is not sufficient for democratic legitimacy.

From the perspective of deliberative democracy, the delegation of powers to elected representatives requires deliberative accountability and 'warranted trust'.[41] Office-holder accountability to voters in regularly held elections needs to be accompanied by publicity of decision-making and public deliberation on policy alternatives. Otherwise, electoral accountability risks being 'blind', that is, based on uninformed and unreflected views among voters. In fact, there are already ideas that mini-publics could facilitate deliberative accountability, that is, processes of public justification, reflection, and feedback, which seems to have the capacity to enhance the quality of democracy (see below).

(How) can Mini-Publics be Compared with Referendums?

So far, most mini-publics have been initiated by governments on issues decided by them. In this respect, mini-publics seem to have some similarities with referendums, which are also typically initiated by governments. In what follows, I will compare mini-publics and referendums in order to highlight similarities and differences, especially when it comes to policy-makers' motivations to organize them and their impact on policy-making.

Obviously, referendums and mini-publics are very different types of participatory processes. Referendums require mass participation, whereas deliberative mini-publics are based on invited participation of a representative sample of citizens. Referendums are aggregative processes where all votes should have an equal weight, while the whole idea of a mini-public is to enhance a deliberative process where different arguments are weighted equally by their merits.

As 'top-down' processes involving citizens in policy-making, both referendums and mini-publics are manipulable. Obviously, risks of manipulation are even higher when authoritarian governments use these forms of citizen participation. In order to understand concerns regarding manipulation of participatory processes, it seems useful to refer to discussion on referendums. Gordon Smith makes the following remark: "There is almost no connection between the win-

---

41 Warren, M. E. (1996) 'Deliberative democracy and authority.' *American Political Science Review* 90(1): 46–60.

dow-dressing referendum operated by a dictator to bolster up his regime and the earnest deliberations which regularly take place in the Swiss cantons."[42]

Referendums may be manipulated, for example by providing (mis)leading questions or alternatives on the ballot paper, and perhaps biased or false information during the campaign. In addition, some groups of voters may be discouraged – or actively prevented – from turning out. Similarly, mini-publics can be manipulated by leading questions and alternatives, by biased representation of the public at large, or by allowing experts, witnesses, or individual participants to dominate the deliberative process.

These aspects pertain to the internal organization of participatory processes, and they may be explained by instrumental motivations by authorities who sponsor and organize them. Just like referendums, mini-publics may be used by governments for instrumental reasons; for example, for ensuring a particular policy outcome. The instrumental use of participatory processes is related to the distinction made by Smith between hegemonic and anti-hegemonic referendums based on whether they support or challenge those in power.[43] The hegemonic character of referendums depends to a large extent – although not entirely – on whether office-holders control the use of referendums.

While government-initiated referendums are likely to be hegemonic, it would be an oversimplification to argue that controlled referendums always turn out to be hegemonic, especially in the context of well-functioning representative democracies. First, in a democratic system with competitive, pluralistic political institutions, the government's intentions to achieve a particular outcome may actually backfire. People may not follow governmental voting recommendations, and even use the referendum to express their opposition towards governments more generally. Second, referendums are not necessarily motivated by policy goals, but, for example, by the need to resolve a divisive issue or to ensure the legitimacy of a major political decision. Of course, referendums held on such purposes may help governmental parties to remain in office and therefore be 'hegemonic' in a broader sense.

There may be similar instrumental motivations behind government-initiated mini-publics. Mini-publics may be organized in order to ensure a particular policy outcome. While mini-publics' outcomes cannot often be predicted, deliberative processes like those in mini-publics have sometimes been characterized by a

---

42 Smith, 'The referendum and political change,' 294.
43 Smith, 'The functional properties of the referendum.'

tendency towards so-called 'progressive vanguardism.'[44] This means that they are likely to bring about outcomes in favor of progressive goals such as citizens' equal rights, environmental protection, and so on.

Just as in the case of referendums, governments' decisions to organize a mini-public may be motivated by a more general aim to increase governmentality[45] – or for hegemonic purposes in the broader sense. Mini-publics may also be used to resolve divisive issues, especially those plagued with complexity, and in order to increase the legitimacy of governmental policies. Consider, for example, the recent Citizens' Assembly on Climate in France, which was organized to address the Yellow Vest protests.

Referendums can be either advisory or binding – although arguably even advisory referendums often turn out to be de-facto binding. With few exceptions, mini-publics are typically advisory. In this respect, mini-publics seem to be much lower than referendums on Arnstein's (1969) famous 'ladder of political participation.'[46] Compared with referendums, office-holders seem thus to have much more freedom in terms of how they interpret – or 'cherry pick' – mini-publics' outcomes. In this respect, mini-publics may be regarded as much less risky strategies of involving citizens in the political process than referendums. Moreover, mini-publics as deliberative bodies may help avoid some of the negative consequences that referendums might have since they do not polarize voters into competing camps of 'winners' and 'losers.'

The increasing use of mini-publics may thus suggest that they are, indeed, handy instruments for governments because they do not entail the risks of challenging their policy agenda or undermining their position of power. However, it is also good to remember that the 'hegemonic' impacts of deliberative mini-publics may not always be as sinister as they may at first sound. Increasing the capacity of political systems to make better-informed, reflected, and fair decisions on complex issues such as climate change should not be regarded a problem as such. The problem is rather that current instrumental usages of mini-publics that allow cherry-picking cannot live up to such expectations.

However, the instrumental use of referendums – or mini-publics – by governments can be avoided more or less entirely if they are not initiated by the government in the first place. For example, in the Swiss system of direct democracy, referendums are never initiated by governments. In fact, Swiss governments

---

44 Neblo, M. (2007) 'Family disputes: diversity in defining and measuring deliberation.' *Swiss Political Science Review* 13(4): 527–557.

45 Woo and Kübler, 'Taking stock of democratic innovations.'

46 Arnstein, Sherryl R. (1969) 'A ladder of citizen participation.' *Journal of the American Institute of Planners* 35(4): 216.

have relatively little control over referendum processes since they may be based on a constitutional requirement of a referendum on particular types of issues (mandatory referendums), popular initiatives including a new law proposal, or a popular request to repeal a particular law (rejective or abrogative referendums).

While such systems of uncontrolled referendums are relatively rare on a global scale, there is sufficient evidence to show that they are often used to challenge governmental policies or to bring new issues on to the political agenda – or for anti-hegemonic purposes. In addition, systems of rejective and abrogative referendums in particular make governments anticipate reactions by the opposition, thus enhancing the consideration of variety of viewpoints and consensual tendencies in policy-making.[47]

Similarly, like referendums, the potential functions of mini-publics in the political system depend not so much on the design of the mini-public itself, but primarily on how it interacts with other practices of policy-making. Exploring different ways of embedding mini-publics in representative systems seems to be the key in terms of their capacity to enhance the quality of democracy. This issue will be discussed in more detail in the following sections.

Towards Better Uses of Mini-Publics: Coupling and Institutionalization

The OECD report *Catching the Deliberative Wave* distinguished four possible roles of deliberative mini-publics in political systems.[48] First, mini-publics have been organized to provide considered opinions on individual policy issues, which has been the goal, for example, of Deliberative Polls. Second, mini-publics have been organized to provide considered policy recommendations. This has been the goal, for example, in many citizens' assemblies that have come up with policy recommendations on complex and divisive issues such as constitutional issues and climate policies.

Third, mini-publics have been organized in order to make informed citizen evaluations of policy measures. This is the goal, for example, of the citizens' initiative review process that is used to evaluate ballot initiatives. Similar measures could be used to evaluate governmental policy proposals or even for ex-post evaluations of actual policies.

---

47 See: Altman, D. (2011) *Direct Democracy Worldwide*. Cambridge: Cambridge University Press.
48 OECD *Innovative Citizen Participation*, pp. 34–35.

Fourth, there are some proposals and actual practices for permanent representative deliberative bodies that allow for representative citizen deliberation to inform public decision-making on an ongoing basis. Such systems are still quite rare, although there are some recent examples from local and regional government. One of the most interesting systems is the so-called 'Ostbelgien model,' which includes permanent mini-publics setting the political agenda and processes of collective will-formation.[49]

In what follows, I will discuss two dimensions that are crucial in terms of the functions and the impact of mini-publics, namely *coupling* and *institutionalization*.[50] Before explaining these dimensions in more detail, I will briefly discuss the normative standards applied in the evaluation of mini-publics' functions and impacts. Theorists of deliberative democracy have called for 'critical mini-publics' that can challenge governmental politics.[51] The point of critical mini-publics is that they should help enhance the deliberative norms – or perhaps rather actual processes of inclusive deliberation – in the wider political system.

In this perspective, the normative standards for evaluating mini-publics can be derived from the theory of deliberative democracy. The success of mini-publics is not measured directly by their policy impacts, but rather by their *deliberative impact*, that is, the extent to which they enhance the inclusion of different viewpoints and mutual justification in processes leading to public decisions. In addition, deliberative impact entails more individual processes of learning, reflection, and perspective-taking, which can be interpreted as forms of 'internal' or 'distributed' deliberation among policy-makers and the public at large.[52]

In terms of coupling of mini-publics, I will explore ways in which mini-publics could interact with decision-makers and the public at large. There are still relatively few – although an increasing number of – studies showing how mini-publics might affect policy-makers and the broader public. Often these studies focus on direct policy impacts of mini-publics rather than more subtle impacts on policy-makers' and citizens' reasoning or public deliberation.

---

49 Niessen, C. and Reuchamps, M. (2020) 'Institutionalising citizen deliberation in parliament: the permanent citizens' dialogue in the German-speaking community of Belgium.' *Parliamentary Affairs* 75(1): 135–153.

50 Hendriks, C. (2016) 'Coupling citizens and elites in deliberative systems: the role of institutional design.' *European Journal of Political Research* 55(1): 43–60.

51 Böker, M. and Elstub, S. (2015) 'The possibility of critical mini-publics: realpolitik and normative cycles in democratic theory.' *Representation* 51(1): 125–144.

52 Mansbridge, J., Bohman, J., Chambers, S., Estlund, D., Follesdal, A., Fung, A., Lafont, C., Manin, B., and Marti, J. L. (2010) 'The place of self-interest and the role of power in deliberative democracy.' *Journal of Political Philosophy* 18(1): 64–100. See also: Goodin, R. E. (2000) 'Democratic Deliberation within.' *Philosophy & Public Affairs* 29(1): 81–109.

Generally speaking, coupling refers to the frequency and the intensity of interactions between the mini-public and policy-makers, as well as the sequencing and the quality of these interactions. Even in cases of advisory mini-publics, it is possible to improve interaction, for example by organizing dialogues between mini-publics and policy-makers at different stages of decision-making.

In addition to coupling, the impact of mini-publics remains limited if they are initiated by governments on an ad-hoc basis. This leads to the second dimension of the analysis, namely the institutionalization of mini-publics. According to an OECD report,[53] there are three possible routes to the institutionalization of representative citizen deliberation. These include the following types of arrangements: i) the requirement for public authorities to organize deliberation under certain circumstances; ii) rules for citizens to demand a deliberative the following options possibility; iii) the establishment of a permanent or ongoing structure for citizen deliberation.

The OECD report mentions some examples of each form of institutionalization.[54] In terms of the requirement for mini-publics in particular conditions, there are examples such as the Mongolian Law that requires Deliberative Polls on constitutional laws. Citizen-initiated deliberative procedures exist, for example, in the Austrian state of Vorarlberg. As pointed out earlier, permanent structures for citizen deliberation can be found, for example in the government of the Ostbelgien region.

While some actual examples already exist, the question still remains whether institutionalization can and will actually boost the impact of mini-publics. It is possible that the requirement of a mini-public would actually weaken policy-makers' willingness to engage with the deliberative process, compared with mini-publics initiated by policy-makers themselves. In this respect, coupling and institutionalization are separate dimensions, which, however, are interrelated in a complex manner. In what follows, I will discuss these two dimensions in conjunction with different experiences or proposals for enhancing public deliberation through mini-publics.

Mini-Publics and Representative Deliberation

The problem with advisory uses of mini-publics is that they are particularly prone to 'cherry-picking,' which means that policy-makers use mini-publics' rec-

---

53 OECD, *Innovative Citizen Participation*, p. 126.
54 OECD, *Innovative Citizen Participation*, p. 126.

ommendations highly selectively to support their pre-established views. In this case, mini-publics may not be particularly likely to help deliberative processes, or learning and reflection among those who are responsible for decisions. Elected representatives, in particular, face a variety of external pressures, not least from their voters, and are likely to interpret the mini-public's recommendations selectively. In fact, civil servants and other non-elected public officials may actually be more open to the recommendations made by mini-publics than elected representatives.

It may therefore be necessary to go beyond purely advisory uses of mini-publics, and look for examples and ideas for more enhanced roles for citizen deliberation. A 'collaborative' model can entail hybrid or mixed deliberations in which policy-makers are directly involved in the deliberative process. Most notably, the Irish Constitutional Convention, convened in 2012–2014, included 66 randomly selected citizens and 33 members of the Irish parliament.

Studies on the Irish Constitutional Convention show that politicians did not dominate the discussion in the Constitutional Convention, which seems to be an encouraging example when it comes to the possibility of citizens and representatives deliberating together. The Irish Constitutional Convention deliberated on several constitutional issues ranging from electoral laws to same-sex marriage. It brought about certain important constitutional changes, most notably the legalization of same-sex marriage.[55] However, mixed deliberation did not help achieve policy changes on issues such as electoral systems where elected representatives had vested interests.[56] Nevertheless, the Irish example supports the view that mixed mini-publics can have quite a lot of impact even as one-off events. They could help policy-makers to consider a broader range of viewpoints and reduce the impact of party discipline and the government–opposition divide in parliamentary deliberation.

However, when organized as top-down procedures, they are vulnerable to the same kinds of criticisms of instrumental use as government-initiated referendums. The institutionalization of mixed deliberation would help dispel such doubts. In the model of 'directly deliberative democracy,' developed and investigated by Neblo and colleagues, members of the Congress engaged in regular online deliberations with a randomly selected cross-section of their constituents.

---

55 See: Suiter, Farrell, and Harris, 'The Irish Constitutional Convention.'
56 Farrell, D. M., Suiter, J., Harris, C., and Cunningham, K. (2020) 'The effects of mixed membership in a deliberative forum: the Irish constitutional convention of 2012–2014.' *Political Studies* 68(1): 54–73.

This model is expected to enhance ongoing deliberative accountability of elected representatives.[57]

Institutionalization could also mean, for example, a requirement to organize a mixed deliberation on specific types of issues such as constitutional issues or other far-reaching policy decisions that require thorough deliberative processes such as climate policies. Hybrid deliberation could also be institutionalized by allowing a certain number of citizens to require such procedures on a particular issue.

Mini-Publics Enhancing Distributed Deliberation among Mass Publics

Mini-publics can also be used as a source of information in mass participatory processes such as referendums. For example, the Citizens' Assembly in British Columbia in 2004 had an agenda-setting function since it was tasked to make a recommendation for a new electoral system for the province.[58] A large majority of the members of the Assembly voted in support of adopting Single Transferable Vote (STV) as a new electoral system. In addition to this agenda-setting function, studies show that the Assembly served as a cue or a shortcut for voters in the referendum on electoral reform. Voters had a lot of trust in the recommendation of the Assembly and many voters followed it when making their decision.

As pointed out already, scholars like Lafont have expressed concerns about using mini-publics as trusted proxies providing shortcuts or cues for voters.[59] The most important point to be learned from these critics is that the success of mini-publics should be evaluated by their capacity to foster processes of public deliberation in policy-making among those responsible for decisions and among the public at large.

Considering this critique of the use of mini-publics as trusted proxies, the Citizens' Initiative Review (CIR) seems to be a particularly promising model. The CIR has been developed and tested in Oregon, other US states, and, more recently, in Finland and Switzerland. The purpose of the procedure is to help voters make judgments on ballot initiatives. The CIR procedure entails a citizens' jury that formulates a statement on a ballot measure. The statement includes

---

57 See: Neblo, M., Esterling, K., and Lazer, D. (2018) *Politics with the People: Building a Directly Representative Democracy.* Cambridge: Cambridge University Press.
58 See Warren and Pearse, *Designing Deliberative Democracy.*
59 Lafont, 'Deliberation, participation and democratic legitimacy.'

key findings and the most important arguments for and against the measure, and it is sent to all voters before the ballot.

It is notable that the CIR statement does not provide a vote recommendation but just summarizes the most relevant and reliable facts and arguments related to the ballot measure. In other words, it is designed to help voters learn about and reflect on the pros and cons of the measure. As sources of information, CIR-type mini-publics are thus very different from partisan shortcuts. Indeed, Gastil argues that the CIR should be regarded as a voting aid rather than as a voting cue.[60]

There is some evidence that CIR-type mini-publics can help voters make informed judgments and enhance learning, reflection, and perspective-taking in direct democratic campaigns.[61] Moreover, a study by Már and Gastil indicates that by reading a CIR statement, voters learn information that is not supportive of their views based on partisan identification, which suggests that the CIR process could counteract the effects of partisan-motivated reasoning.[62] In addition, reading a CIR statement induces learning and reflection on arguments supporting different viewpoints even in polarized contexts where trust in all public institutions is low.[63] Reading a statement including arguments from both sides can actually increase voters' trust in political actors on the 'other side.' The systemic impact of the CIR may, however, remain modest unless it is institutionalized and systematically used. Although there is a legal provision for the CIR in the Oregon law, it is still quite weakly institutionalized. There is no guaranteed funding for the procedure or a requirement for organizing the CIR procedure on all initiatives. The institutionalization of the CIR could mean that it is required on all popular votes or referendums or that it is routinely used to evaluate arguments made in electoral campaigns.

---

60 Gastil, J. (2014) 'Beyond endorsements and partisan cues: giving voters viable alternatives to unreliable cognitive shortcuts.' *The Good Society* 23(2): 145–159, at 156.

61 Knobloch, K. R., Gastil, J., Reedy, J., and Cramer Walsh, K. (2013) 'Did they deliberate? Applying an evaluative model of democratic deliberation to the Oregon Citizens' Initiative Review.' *Journal of Applied Communication Research* 41(2): 105–125.

62 Gastil, J. and Wright, E. O. (2018) 'Legislature by lot: envisioning sortition within a bicameral system.' *Politics and Society* 46(3): 303–330.

63 Setälä, M., Serup, C. H., Leino, M., and Strandberg, K. (2021) 'Beyond polarization and selective trust: a Citizens' Jury as a trusted source of information.' *Politics*, 02633957211024474.

Scrutinizing Mini-Publics

Deliberative mini-publics could be used systematically to scrutinize governmental policies. Mini-publics would add to the public scrutiny of legislation and enhance the deliberative accountability of policy-making by encouraging policy-makers to provide justifications that would be acceptable, not just to their own voters, but also to a mini-public representing a variety of societal perspectives.

The capacity of mini-publics to scrutinize legislation could be limited to particular policy domains or particular aspects of policy-making. For example, MacKenzie has made a proposal in which randomly selected citizens would routinely review any law from the perspective of its long-term impacts.[64] The task of mini-publics would be to scrutinize laws based on the mandatory posteriority impact statements that summarize the anticipated long-term consequences of legislation.

To be an effective method of public scrutiny, mini-publics should be institutionalized as a regularly used element of the policy-making process. Or, alternatively, mini-publics could be demanded, for example, by a number of citizens or by parliamentary opposition groups. There are also proposals to take a further step and establish randomly selected second chambers.[65] The powers of randomly selected chambers in the legislative process could be strengthened by giving them powers to delay legislation. As MacKenzie suggests, such a system could be used to counterbalance the tendencies towards short-termism in electoral representation.[66]

In this respect, scrutinizing mini-publics and randomly selected second chambers could have some similarities to rejective or mandatory referendums, which are used as ex-post checks on policy-making. Such procedures can be expected to have an anticipatory effect on governmental policy-making. Public scrutiny by mini-publics or randomly selected second chambers would incentivize governments to ensure the quality of law proposals and proper consideration of viewpoints by various affected groups.

---

64 MacKenzie, M. (2020) 'There is no such thing as a short-term issue.' *Futures:* https://doi.org/10.1016/j.futures.2020.102652.
65 MacKenzie, M. K. (2016) 'A general-purpose, randomly selected chamber.' *Institutions for Future Generations*, 282–298.
66 MacKenzie, 'A general-purpose, randomly selected chamber.'

Conclusions

While deliberative mini-publics are designed to foster inclusive deliberation, their functions and impacts on the democratic system are increasingly varied. In this respect, it is unlikely that there will be a general theory of mini-publics. But in all too many cases, mini-publics are still used on an ad-hoc basis on issues defined by governmental actors, and their impact on policy-making remains vague and undetermined. The fact is that mini-publics are still typically initiated by political actors in power, which makes them vulnerable to accusations of instrumental use. Moreover, it remains all too easy for governments to 'cherry pick' mini-publics' recommendations.

There seems to be some instrumentality, for example in the ways in which democratic governments have recently organized high-profile citizens' assemblies in order to seek legitimacy for important societal changes required to mitigate climate change. In these cases, instrumental motivations may be well meaning, and mini-publics may support democratic climate governance. The democratic credentials of mini-publics are obviously more debatable when the instrumental goals behind them are not as benign as climate change mitigation or when they are used by authoritarian governments. In other words, there remain good reasons to be critical of mini-publics from a democratic perspective.

At the same time, we have witnessed not just a proliferation of different types of mini-publics, but also their use in different roles and functions. In this respect, the academic and public debate on mini-publics could benefit from the analysis of the functions of different types of referendums. As highlighted in this chapter, mini-publics can, for example, facilitate deliberation on policy problems together with elected representatives, help voters make more informed and considered choices in referendums, and scrutinize governmental policies.

From the normative perspective of deliberative democracy, mini-publics could improve democracy if they facilitate inclusiveness and quality of public reasoning among policy-makers and the public at large. Instead of general theories of deliberative mini-publics, there is a need for theory-guided empirical research to explore potential functions and develop better practices of mini-publics.

Greta Ríos

Participatory Budgeting: A Brief Introduction

The concept of participatory budgeting (PB) was a gift from the global South to the world. It emerged as part of a series of policy experiments conducted in the Brazilian city of Porto Alegre in the late 1980s, intended to improve governance conditions in the region, as well as rebuilding citizen confidence in the government through participation.[1] At that time, the newly elected progressive party had just won an election based on the premises of citizen participation and a new focus on spending (public money) priorities. The materialization of this promise was seen as a way of redistributing public income and making sure that those who needed it most were getting a bigger share of the pie.

The idea behind PB was quite simple: getting people involved in deciding how to distribute public funds would not only increase literacy on public spending among the general public, but also raise and retain citizen engagement in public matters. When this hypothesis proved true, PB started growing and replicating throughout the world, with amazing results.

As Wampler describes it, "Participatory Budgeting is a decision-making process through which citizens deliberate and negotiate over the distribution of public resources."[2] As it expanded through time and territory, the initial model received some tweaks, but the general concept prevailed: having regular folks collectively decide how to spend (a part of) the money raised through taxes. This novel and simple idea has not only changed the way people understand public spending, but has also contributed to democracy in unforeseen manners throughout the world.

This article will provide readers with a general overview on how PB works and how it has proved to have positive effects on both the things it most wants to influence: the ability of governments to increase tax collection and the levels of citizen engagement. It will also point out some of the challenges that implementing PB poses and how some governments have overcome them. The case of Brazil's Porto Alegre will also be further analyzed, followed by a section dedicated to the effects of COVID-19 in the implementation of PB.

---

1 Wampler, B. (2007) *Participatory Budgeting in Brazil*. Philadelphia: Pennsylvania University Press.

2 Wampler, *Participatory Budgeting*, p. 21.

https://doi.org/10.1515/9783110747331-003

What is PB?

The concept of PB arose in Brazil, at the very end of the 1980s. It was run for the very first time in 1989, in the City of Porto Alegre. According to Porto Alegre's authorities, PB "is a dynamic process that has to be adjusted periodically to local needs, working always through participatory, amplifying and debate-oriented formats that include both the municipal government and the population."[3] PB has been recognized by several international organizations as one of the top best practices when it comes to urban management in the world.

The Porto Alegre model has served as a basis for many different PB experiences around the world, having already reached all continents. According to the Participatory Budgeting World Atlas, there were at least 11,000 documented PB experiences throughout the world in 2019.[4]

One of the main challenges – and opportunities – related to the concept of PB has to do with the fact that it is highly adaptable and has thus taken many different shapes in many different places. In Portugal, for instance, there is a national Participatory Budgeting, a Participatory Youth Budgeting, and a Participatory Budgeting for Schools. Each of these has its own rules and its own participants.[5] In most parts of the world, PB is implemented at the local (municipal or state) level within a country.

In general terms, for a PB experience to exist, there are only two main elements that need to be present: a certain amount of money and the possibility of deciding how to spend that money in a public and democratic way. Every other detail about the process is to be tailor-made for the particular experience. I have encountered several different ways of conducting a PB experience and will describe the most common ones below, emphasizing that this is not an exhaustive list.

The Regular PB Model: Local PB Mechanisms

Based on the Porto Alegre prototype, enacting a regular PB mechanism would require for the government (most of the time the City or local authorities) to de-

---

3 Prefeitura Municipal de Porto Alegre, (2015) *Regimento Interno: Critérios Gerais, Técnicos e Regionais – 2015/2016*, p. 62.
4 Dias, N. et al. (2019) 'Participatory Budgeting world atlas 2019': https://www.pbatlas.net/pb-world-atlas-2019.html.
5 Dias et al., 'Participatory Budgeting world atlas,' 31.

vote a certain amount of public money and set rules for how the voters could gain access to the said resources. In that set of rules, the government would decide, for instance, the types of projects that the citizens are allowed to present before the mechanism, which citizens are allowed to vote,[6] what the voting procedure is, and so on.

While there is no official definition of what PB is, there is consensus on the basic elements any PB mechanism should have. "Basically, PB allows the participation of non-elected citizens in the conception and/or allocation of public finances. However, five further criteria need to be added …:

1. Discussion of financial/budgetary processes; …
2. The city level has to be involved, or a (decentralized) district with an elected body and some power over administration and resources (the neighborhood level is not enough);
3. It has to be a repeated process over years (if it is from the outset planned as a unique vet, it is not a PB process);
4. Some forms of public deliberation must be included with the framework of specific meetings/forums (the inclusion of ordinary citizens into the institutions of "classic" representative democracy represents to PB process);
5. Some accountability on the results of the process is required."[7]

Let us take a closer look at every element presented above. To begin with, the mere idea of having citizens involved in discussing budgetary matters is so revolutionary, yet simple, that it proves surprising how many centuries it took humanity to even put it into consideration. Not a single soul would question today the importance and benefits of having citizens involved in public matters, but opening the door to giving citizens a taste of how public expenditure works is a whole new paradigm.

One of its immediate results is budget literacy, a very important tool in building stronger citizens in a democratic context. Nevertheless, in less democratic environments, having citizens understand how public spending works is not only undesirable but also a liability. In that sense, the mere idea that governmental bodies exist that are willing and able to bring these exercises into existence is a good sign that the whole world is becoming inexorably more democratic. PB

---

6 Some PB exercises require, for instance, that all voters show proof of having complied with their fiscal obligations prior to voting. This is the case of the PB mechanism in Jalisco, Mexico.
7 Sintomer, Y., Yves Sintomer, Herzberg, C., and Röck, A. (2014) 'Transnational Models of Citizen Participation: The Case of Participatory Budgeting.' In Días, N. *Hope For Democracy: 25 Years of Participatory Budgeting Worldwide*, p. 29. Available at: https://democracyspotdotnet.files.wordpress.com/2014/06/op25anos-en-20maio20141.pdf.

mechanisms throughout the world have been contributing to this greater goal – deliberately or not – for the past 30 years.

The second element, involving the city authorities, is indeed a must. Any individual citizen may have dreams and desires about using public funds to solve the problems in their neighborhood, but without the willingness and active participation of a governmental entity, those aspirations would remain forever in a fantasy world. Regarding this particular requisite, Sintomer (and his co-authors) is quite explicit in mentioning that PB with only neighborhood-level authorities does not qualify as PB. This has to do with the fact that city authorities are the lowest-level governmental entities with authority over the use of public resources. Some neighborhoods may have special funds with particular rules on how to use them, but let us keep in mind that the basic concept of PB involves the spending of public money that has been obtained through tax collection. As such, these funds have to be subject to the broader rules of public spending, which do not apply to neighborhood authorities or budgets.

As to the third condition (the need for PB to be repeated over the years), this seems evident but may not necessarily be so. The recurrence of this kind of exercise is a must for several reasons. The first is that devoting public resources to PB requires a certain level of complexity. For instance, legislation has to be created to regulate and bring certainty to the mechanism, lest it become an instrument for populism or worse. It is true that there may arise one-time mechanisms based on the rules and principles of PB, but they would not create the long-term effects that PB was intended to create: increasing citizen engagement, public budget literacy, and governance. Running a one-time participatory exercise may be motivated by reasons not compatible with those just described. It could provide political figures a fast track to popularity prior to an electoral process, for instance.

The repetitive factor has also given rise to very interesting phenomena around the world. In Mexico City, for example, PB has been enshrined in the local Constitution as a right of all citizens. This would certainly not be the case if PB were not held every year with the same rules and expectations. While one-time mechanisms may bring some benefits, I concur with Sintomer et al. in the need for regular repetition for these exercises to be considered PB.

The element of public deliberation also plays a very important part. As I mentioned earlier, every PB mechanism has its own ways of unfolding, but all must include the element of public deliberation. The deliberation process is decided on a case-by-case basis. Some are done digitally (and generally throughout a period of several days), while others require an in-person participation at a specific time and place. What really matters is that there has to be a mechanism for expressing the popular will and a mechanism to enforce it once it has been expressed. This mechanism should be objective and the rules must be set before citizens can activate their right to express their will.

To this point, Sintomer et al. make a very important qualification: including citizens in the regular budget decision-making processes is not, *per se*, conducting a participatory budgeting exercise. Creating citizen observatories, councils, and other budget-monitoring mechanisms is a good idea and helps build citizen budget literacy and greater accountability on the part of the authorities, but it is not equivalent to setting a participatory budgeting mechanism in motion. For one, none of the examples above allows all citizens to have a say on how public funds are being spent, either by proposing projects or by voting for them. In all these mechanisms, the organs of the state have the protagonist role, while a group of citizens merely accompanies the process. It is true that these citizens may have some degree of influence on how decisions are taken along the process of deciding expenditures, but the scope and the amount of power for doing so are way more limited than those which citizens experience when participating in a PB exercise.

The last requisite, according to these authors, is that every PB must have some sort of accountability mechanism included, to make sure that the projects elected by the people are actually set in motion. This comes as no surprise, since one of the main theses behind PB lies in the idea that people are going to become more observant of how public resources are spent once they get involved in PB mechanisms. This means that governments instituting PB processes must be particularly attentive to the different ways in which the elected projects are being developed and how these results are communicated to the general public. If we want PB to be a truly democratizing tool, we need to make sure that projects are shaped to the demands of the public who designed and voted for them. Accountability is one of the main areas of opportunity when it comes to evaluating the state of PB processes throughout the world. Bearing in mind that these processes are recurrent, and that public expenditure usually requires intricate systems to be set in motion, it proves hard for citizens to be able to track the progress of projects.

In my personal experience, I have been in contact with several individuals who manifested their desire to have more information on how the winning projects were being run but had to go through highly specialized and long processes in order to obtain the data that allowed them to understand the level of advancement of a given project. Talking from the perspective of the PB mechanism in Mexico City, this lack of accountability arises from the fact that there is no one authority charged with providing this information to the public. While the local electoral authority is charged with organizing everything related to the referendum where citizens vote for projects, the execution of the projects is conducted by the municipal authorities, who are indeed obliged by law to provide information on their expenditures, but not necessarily to provide specific information on how PB projects are faring. In this sense, in order to obtain this information, one must dig into several confusing databases, which is time-consuming and extremely confusing.

Participatory Budgeting in Mexico City

To provide a concrete example, let's have a look at the Mexico City participatory budgeting mechanism. It was provided for by a Citizen Participation Law in 2004, but only came into full force in 2011. In Mexico City, 4 percent[8] of public expenditure is subject to being collectively decided by PB. The institution in charge of receiving and classifying the project proposals as well as conducting the voting process is the local electoral authority, the Instituto Electoral y de Participación Ciudadana de la Ciudad de México. This brings certainty to the whole process.

In Mexico City's PB mechanism there are few restrictions as to who is entitled to proposing ideas, which means that in practice almost everyone can do it. This includes children, and it has given the world several amazing case studies of truly awe-inspiring projects conceived and proposed by children. One of my favorite examples is a music academia that provides a whole neighborhood with free music lessons, as proposed by a 13-year-old girl who happened to love music and heard about PB. This project has successfully helped improve the social fabric in her neighborhood, while providing this child with the music lessons she craved.[9]

According to the governing law, all projects presented before the PB mechanism must fall into one of the following categories: public space improvement, urban infrastructure, public works and related services, sports-related activities, or cultural activities. This classification is quite restrictive, but creative neighbors have been able to justify why their projects fall within one of these categories, even when the link is not so obvious.

---

8 According to the 2019 Mexico City Citizen Participation Law, the amount of money devoted to PB would gradually increase from 3 to 4 percent in yearly 0.25 points. As such, in 2020, the percentage devoted to PB was 3.25 percent; in 2021 it was 3.5 percent; in 2022 it will be 3.75 percent; and finally, in 2023, it will reach and stay at 4 percent.
9 For more information about this project, kindly refer to: https://www.youtube.com/watch?v= jL-HxNkLKHs.

Once proposals are submitted via the local electoral authority, each municipal government sets up an eligibility committee that reviews all proposals and decides which ones are viable. These committees have been criticized in the past for being too subjective (or even biased) about the kinds of projects that are considered viable. Undoubtedly, work needs to be done in order to improve and make these committees' determinations more transparent and objective. Nevertheless, they also bring certainty and a sense of fair play to the whole process.

With the 2019 reform to the applicable law, these committees became a bit more solid because they now include five academics, while in the past they were composed of public servants only. I believe this addition will yield much better options of projects that are deemed viable in the years to come. In 2020, the first year this new element was brought into play, there was some resistance on the part of the municipalities, but, in the end, they had no choice but to yield. The process of deciding which projects are viable and which are not has a lot of areas of opportunity, and I am sure it will have to be adapted in the years to come to become less bureaucratic and, above all, more objective. One of the main problems related to this figure is the lack of objective and uniform criteria to decide on feasibility of the projects. Each committee decides its own parameters and sometimes even these are not applied evenly to all projects, due to the process being extremely long and exhausting for everyone involved.

Citizens who proposed the projects deemed viable get to campaign to promote their projects. In trying to convince their neighbors to vote for their projects, these people also get to know each other and listen to their neighbors' wants, needs, and points of view. I believe this is one of the most important outcomes of the whole process because, aside of bringing people together, it is a very easy way to get a grasp of what things are perceived as areas of opportunity for a certain community and how to solve these issues from a citizen perspective. It also opens dialogue as to what others see as problems in the neighborhood so that new proposals can be built upon this information in the following years.

In the Mexico City PB process, only city residents over 18 years of age may vote. The voting stations used are the same as those used for regular elections. The only difference is that for the PB process only a fraction of the voting stations is set, so it can prove a bit difficult (and sometimes even confusing) to find yours. Another particularity of the PB process in Mexico City is that it is one of the few processes in Mexico in which citizens may vote digitally. People may register for voting online some weeks before the election. Those who do so receive a series of codes and have to comply with some verification steps, but in turn they are allowed to vote before the physical voting takes place and have a full week to enter their choices in the system. I believe this is a great way of getting more people to experience and trust digital voting and might be paving the way for digitalizing elections in Mexico (in the very long term).

After the voting concludes and winners are announced, the process is managed by municipal authorities. They are the ones in charge of exercising the budget for the projects that have won. This process is done hand in hand with the citizens, but on many occasions lacks transparency and accountability. There are several documented cases of winning projects that have been modified, or even cancelled, by the municipal authority after the PB process has concluded. This, of course, is a great area of opportunity for Mexico City's PB mechanism.[10]

One big problem with Mexico City's PB is all the legal loopholes and uncertainties that the current legal framework allows. While there is a Mexico City Citizen Participation Law[11] that regulates PB, this instrument lacks the specific tools to govern the actual execution of the PB process. My hypothesis is that there needs to be a secondary law that regulates PB in particular, and that provides for any eventualities that may arise at any stage during the process. This would, for instance, reduce the number of arbitrary decisions to modify projects that have already been selected and provide for better accountability mechanisms. In this manner, citizens would possess better tracking tools that would in turn increase citizen engagement and trust in the whole process.

I used Mexico City as an example of a 'regular PB process.' Please note that this does not mean that every PB process in the world follows this same formula. While the concept is the same, there are several tweaks that come with every PB process, such as the participation of an electoral authority or the manner in which the voting is conducted.

National PB Mechanisms

As mentioned in the sections above, most PB mechanisms are designed to work at the local level. Nevertheless, there is at least one very interesting case of a national PB mechanism – that of Portugal. This country started implementing PB at the local level in the early 2000s with great results.

---

10 If you wish to know more about the implementation of PB projects in Mexico City, kindly refer to www.presupuestoparticipativo.org, where you can track the winning projects by neighborhood and the status of completion of each one.
11 This lay may be consulted online here: http://www.contraloria.cdmx.gob.mx/docs/1908_LeyParticipacionCiudadanaN.pdf.

In 2017, Portugal decided to conduct an experiment and start a national PB exercise, becoming a world pioneer in doing so. This experience is relevant because, aside from being the first of its kind, it allowed for regional projects to exist. The lack of such projects has been one of the most common obstacles that PB implementation has at the local level. While it is true that most problems can be solved at the hyper local level, sometimes geographical divisions can become obstacles. For example, valuable projects may be unable to be implemented only because their geographical scope would spread over more than one municipality. Most local PB mechanisms lack provisions for making these projects actionable.

The national PB mechanism in Portugal started in 2017 with a three million euros budget, which was increased to five million euros in 2018. Regarding participation, in the first round, nearly 80,000 citizens took part in the process. This figure increased to 120,000 the following year.[12] These numbers are indeed meager, but one of the main challenges that PB mechanisms have around the world relates to active citizen engagement and even awareness of their existence. This topic will be discussed later in this chapter.

As per design, national PB projects could be focused on four policy areas: culture, agriculture, science and education, and adult training. In 2017, 599 projects were submitted to the mechanism, of which 38 were selected for implementation.[13] The national PB projects that were selected in Portugal included a 35 kilometer educational, cultural and ethnographic route, and Livrar, a national online donation platform for books.[14]

Unfortunately, in 2019 the national PB mechanism in Portugal was paused because the projects elected in 2017 and 2018 were still underway, and it was decided to focus all efforts (and budget) in the implementation of these rather than having new projects elected. Many PB processes have also been deeply affected by the COVID-19 pandemic. Getting back on track is going to be one of the main challenges that PB mechanisms will have to face worldwide in the near future. This topic will be addressed more thoroughly later in this chapter.

Besides the national PB mechanism, Portugal also possesses a special PB process for young people only. The intention of having a youth PB exercise is precisely to expose young people to democracy in a very direct way and thus convince them that their participation is not only desirable, but also necessary for

---

12 Politics Reinvented: 'Portugal – the world's first national Participatory Budgeting': https://politicsreinvented.eu/model/portugal-the-worlds-first-national-participatory-budget/.
13 Kuenkel, L. (2018) 'Participatory Budgeting – Portuguese style': https://www.centreforpublicimpact.org/insights/participatory-budgeting-portuguese-style.
14 The Livrar platform can be visited at http://www.livrar.pt.

transforming society. This particular PB mechanism also started in 2017 and is open to young people from 14 to 30 years of age, who may present proposals to the process and vote on the proposals presented.

This PB mechanism is also implemented at the national level. As such, the rules for implementation are the same as those for the national PB mechanism. The total budget allocated to Youth PB in Portugal is 500,000 euros. This mechanism works on specific themes, which are: education (formal and non-formal), employment, housing, health, environment and sustainable development, governance and participation, equality, and social inclusion. All projects must fall within one of the aforementioned themes.

To be eligible, projects presented to this mechanism may have a maximum value of 100,000 euros each, must not involve the construction of infrastructure, must benefit more than one municipality, must be technically feasible, and must be located within the territory of Portugal. They must also not be contrary to any ongoing public program or piece of public policy. Voting for these projects is done online through a special website created for the purpose. Voting may also be conducted via SMS.

Having been implemented for the first time in 2017, it is still impossible to elicit information on how this Youth PB is having positive effects on the Portuguese youth and on strengthening democracy. It will undoubtedly be a great source of information for analysis in the years to come.

PB in Schools

PB mechanisms have inspired several adaptations that have been adopted by smaller – and more controlled – scenarios. One of these adaptations is the PB at schools model. As described by Mogilevich: "Participatory budgeting is a democratic process in which community members decide how to spend a part of a public budget. In this case, the community members are students and the budget is the school budget."[15] In this model, students assess the community's needs, create projects to tackle them, and campaign for getting their peers' support.

There are cases, such as Portugal, where schools are obliged by law to implement PB processes. In the case of Portugal, there was a particular focus on high school students, so that they could learn about public budgets and decide to-

---

15 Mogilevich, V. 'A guide to Participatory Budgeting in schools,' Participatory Budgeting Project, p. 5. Available at: https://www.participatorybudgeting.org/what-is-pb/pb-in-schools/.

gether how to spend the funds. In most other cases, PB in schools has been developed on a case-by-case scenario and therefore has a lot of manifestations, different rules, and conditions. In all of them, however, the purpose is the same: bringing democracy to every corner of everyone's lives and making sure that students of all ages learn how to solve their community problems through joint ideation, negotiation, campaigning, and exercising civic and political rights. The idea behind this is brilliant: how can children who have already experienced the power of democracy later turn their backs on it? Hopefully they will not.

PB in schools is currently happening throughout the world at every level of education. The Participatory Budgeting Project, a US-based non-governmental organization (NGO), is one of its most renowned advocates. They recently launched a *Guide to Participatory Budgeting in Schools*, available for consultation for free.[16] There is an increasing tendency towards the implementation of PB mechanisms in schools around the globe. This in turn has opened new business opportunities for several companies, ranging from contractors to perform the improvements chosen by the PB mechanism inside the schools, to software developers who have created platforms and apps for managing the whole PB process inside the school community. It is my belief that PB in schools will continue growing, and it will permeate other realms, such as private companies.

So far, the concept of 'participatory budgeting in companies' is a bit different from the main idea behind PB. While PB processes require communal decision-making regarding the expenditure of public funds, private companies have created the concept of participatory budgeting (or bottom-up budgeting) to describe a process in which people from different ranks within a company intervene in the creation of their departments' budgets. This process shares some of the main principles of PB, such as deliberative decision-making, sharing information with all participants, creating dialogue, and joint responsibility. However, it lacks the part where this budget is actually used for improving life in the community. It is true that budget allocation within companies can prove tricky and a big source of trouble, and this new approach to budgeting is very welcome. Nevertheless, it lacks key elements for it to be deemed PB.

I believe there is fertile ground within private companies to undertake PB in its literal sense. They could, for instance, run PB mechanisms within their unions to decide where to invest their corporate responsibility efforts or decide how to allocate the money they have raised in the company's annual fundraiser. This kind of exercise has demonstrated its capacity for community-building within

---

16 You may consult and download the guide here: https://www.peoplepowered.org/resources-content/pb-in-schools-guide.

schools and municipalities. I am sure it could be exported into the corporate world with equally good results.

Participatory Grantmaking

Participatory processes are taking place more and more in all realms of society. In the world of non-profits, the idea of democratizing fund allocation strategies has become increasingly popular. Funders are beginning to change their approaches towards priority-setting, which, in turn, defines their budget allocation mechanisms. This new practice has given way to the creation of a novel approach called participatory grantmaking that resembles PB in many senses. According to Gibson, "participatory grantmaking cedes decision-making power about funding – including the strategy and criteria behind those decisions – to the very communities that funders aim to serve."[17]

This process includes consultation sessions with grantees and beneficiaries so that projects and budgets can be collectively decided upon, changing the role of funders as the sole decision-makers regarding these important considerations. This allows funders to get a much deeper understanding of the objectives and indicators of the projects they are willing to fund. At the same time, it empowers grantees and gives them invaluable elements to understand more deeply how budget allocation takes place, how to better fundraise, and how to defend their priorities vis-à-vis those of their funders.[18]

The model of participatory grantmaking has become very popular, particularly in the United Kingdom and the United States of America. I am sure that this horizontal way of decision-making will very soon permeate other countries and that it will yield very interesting results. It is indeed a practice to keep an eye on.

Is PB actually working? I hear this question often in my line of work as a PB advocate. Yes, PB sounds like a dream come true, but after some 30 years of implementation, has it really made situations better when it comes to tax collection and citizen engagement? The short answer to both questions is yes, although, of course, there are caveats. I will devote the following section to providing the

---

17 Gibson, C. (2018) *Deciding Together: Shifting Power and Resources through Participatory Grantmaking*. Foundation Center, New York, NY, p. 7.

18 For more information about participatory grantmaking, kindly refer to Camden Giving's 'What we stand for' video, available on YouTube: https://www.youtube.com/watch?v=tRSx6segQIE&t=76s.

reader with some information that may be valid for responding to these very important questions.

PB, Tax Collection and Citizen Engagement

Nobody likes paying taxes. Moreover, nobody likes paying the government money and seeing how it is spent on things that, in the best of cases, may not be a priority for the individual taxpayer, and, at worst, may be allocated to support projects and programs contrary to their individual beliefs. I cannot help but think of the absolutely hilarious scene in the film *Stranger than Fiction*, where the tax collector conducts an audit on the baker and finds she has not been paying her complete taxes. She, in turn, explains to him that the missing part of her taxes is precisely the percentage the government has been using to finance war and violence and, thus, she is not willing to pay for that.

One of the main theses behind PB mechanisms is that people will be more willing to pay their tax share if they participate actively in deciding how (at least a part of) their taxes will be used and have better information on exactly how this money will be spent. The fact that PB happens mostly at the hyper local level brings a new perspective into the equation: it is not only decided by the community, but by the neighbors themselves. Who could be a better advocate for a much cleaner and peaceful neighborhood than the actual folks who inhabit the place?

On paper, it should work very easily: local people are getting better incentives to pay their taxes and participate in community decision-making. They should almost instantly spring into action and at least reduce their reticence towards sharing their hard-earned money with the government. Let us dig a bit deeper to find out whether this proves true.

The general theory behind improving tax collection techniques has been centered in the punitive perspective that the higher the risks of getting caught and the higher the possible punishment, the less tax evasion a country will experience. "Governments following this logic seek to optimize enforcement regimes to increase their revenue."[19]

Nevertheless, the novel PB approach yields interesting results, while not being punitive at all. "At the broadest level, we would expect that citizens' perceptions of having a say in the political system conditions their attitudes toward

---

[19] Touchton, M. et al. (2019) *Of Governance and Revenue: Participatory Institutions and Tax Compliance in Brazil.* World Bank Group, Washington, D.C., p. 6.

government, especially surrounding accountability and legitimacy."[20] The mere idea of being able to have and exercise one's opinion on public expenditure changes the entire narrative. We move from a know-it-all kind of governmental body that gets to decide how to allocate and spend part of our individual earnings, to a system where our voice and ideas are important and taken into consideration when planning and deciding how to use this hard-earned money for something that, in my individual view, will bring more benefits to the community where I live, and, in addition, to me and my family. I will not only be able to have and express my opinion on this, but will also get to experience the winning proposal's coming into being. In some cases, it will be brought to life by my own neighbors and friends.

This whole new idea will not only change my perception of the whole tax system, but will also influence my perspective of the government. If the government is open enough to have the common folk participate in these processes, then it will become a more legitimate and trustworthy government in my eyes. This will, in turn, make me more likely to become engaged in more collective actions and follow the government's actions more closely, and not only on PB-related matters.

These are, of course, assumptions on how systems must change if participatory mechanisms become available in places where they did not previously exist. There seems to be a consensus among scholars regarding the lack of a long-term observational study that allows the experts to draw solid conclusions regarding this train of thought. Nevertheless, there is documented evidence that points towards proving both theses discussed to be true.

For instance, in 2019 three practitioners published a policy research working paper under the auspices of the World Bank. In this work, called *Of Governance and Revenue: Participatory Institutions and Tax Compliance in Brazil*, Touchton et al. analyze data from almost 6,000 municipalities in Brazil covering a 13-year period, trying to find the effects (if any) on tax collection of the implementation of participatory practices. According to them, "our analysis demonstrates a connection between the presence of participatory institutions and municipal revenue collection."[21]

To cite some of their results, they concluded that municipalities where PB mechanisms exist have tax outcomes that are 34 percent greater than those in municipalities without PB. They also found that this ratio increases as time pass-

---

20 Putnam, R. D., Leonardi, R., and Nanetti, R. Y. (1994) *Making Democracy Work: Civic Traditions in Modern Italy.* Princeton, NJ: Princeton University Press. Quoted from Touchton, 2019, p. 6.
21 Touchton et al., *Of Governance and Revenue*, p. 7.

es. For instance, municipalities with eight years or more of PB implementation reported a 39 percent greater tax outcome than those without PB.[22]

This alone could be reason enough to implement PB everywhere. Nevertheless, there are further interesting findings when it comes to the effects of PB on communities. For example, in Brazil indicators as important as child mortality have seen a decrease in communities with PB, while they have stayed the same in communities that are not implementing PB.[23] Nowadays, there are several research projects dealing with how PB could play an important role in facing the effects of climate change around the world. This mechanism would provide those most affected by this phenomenon with a powerful mechanism for creating the much-needed joint solutions at the local level for a worldwide problem of devastating magnitude.

In conclusion, it is true that more research needs to be conducted on this subject, but so far PB seems to be having very positive effects on the two things it aims to change: tax collection and citizen engagement. As this mechanism continues to spread throughout the world, we will be able to attain more precise information on how this is happening and how to catalyze it so it can benefit more people in a shorter time span.

PB is not free of problems. Its implementation can become chaotic and, for lack of proper legislation, can even bring about more trouble than positive results. In the next section we will analyze some of the challenges of PB implementation, in hopes that they will be resolved before replicating faulty PB mechanisms elsewhere.

Bumps in the Road: The Challenges of PB Around the Globe

One cannot discuss the development of PB and its spread around the globe without talking about Brazil and, in particular, about Porto Alegre. Some 30 years after this novel idea was introduced for the first time in this Brazilian city, PB has actually been suspended in Porto Alegre, although there have been some efforts to bring it back.

22 Touchton et al., *Of Governance and Revenue*, p. 22.
23 Wampler, B., Touchton, M., and Kumar, N. (2021) 'How Participatory Budgeting can improve governance & well-being,' People Powered Research Board: https://www.peoplepowered.org/news-content/how-participatory-budgeting-can-improve-governance-well-being.

To better understand what happened in Porto Alegre, one must keep in mind that Brazil has been struggling for years with large corruption scandals and the rise of right-wing political parties that have deeply polarized the country. In addition to this, the COVID-19 pandemic has presented several new implementation challenges, not only in Brazil but also throughout the globe.

When the pandemic hit, there were already implementation problems in the Porto Alegre PB, to be honest. In 2017 a new government was elected. By then, there were already more than 2,000 projects elected by PB that had not come to a conclusion. These projects spanned from 1994 onwards and were the reason why the government proposed that, for the first time in almost 30 years, no additional PB projects should be presented that year. The idea behind this proposal was to devote time and money to evaluate the more than 2,000 unfulfilled projects and decide whether they were still actionable and, if so, how this should be done. Seven hundred of them were discarded after this process.

In 2018, the government alleged lack of funds for running a PB process. In 2019, voting resumed. Nevertheless, there was great discontent when the government presented the winning projects along with the budget they were planning on devoting to their implementation. For instance, in a municipality that had received a governmental pledge for 17.8 million BRL (Brazilian reals), the proposed budget the government came up with was 149,000 BRL.[24]

This was not the first year with discrepancies between the promised budget and the budget actually spent on making PB proposals come true. For instance, in 2016 the winning projects' budget amounted to 80 million BRL, but only 300,000 BRL were executed. Between 2013 and 2017, the total budget was almost 500 million BRL, with a real expenditure of less than 1 percent devoted to the winning proposals.[25]

Brazil's PB is plagued with obstacles. The lack of transparency and the actual rate of projects that come to life has direct effects on how many citizens have trust in the process and how many of them decide to take part in this mechanism. According to Nelson Dias, the only way to bring it back to life would be to incorporate two new elements to the process. The first would be decreasing the decision power of the PB Committee, a governmental entity that decides what kind of proposals are to be submitted each year. The second would be having certainty on the size of the available budget before submitting proposals and voting

---

24 Wenzel, F. (2020) 'Pandemia pode enterrar de vez o OrÇamento Participativo em Porto Alegre,' Matinal Jornalismo: https://www.matinaljornalismo.com.br/parentese/pandemia-pode-en terrar-de-vez-o-orcamento-participativo-em-porto-alegre/.
25 Wenzel, 'Pandemia pode enterrar.'

on them. Under the current model, proposals are voted without a budget, and only after they have been selected by the public does the government decide how much money to allocate to each of them.[26]

The COVID-19 emergency did nothing to alleviate the tension with the Brazilian PB. In 2020, public assemblies were suspended due to the pandemic and many people feared that would be the end of PB. Nevertheless, PB has helped to create strong community leadership that will be put to a big test in years to come. While many people are big skeptics of the return of PB, many others are already trying to solve the structural problems it is facing. For instance, there is talk about moving the public assemblies to open spaces with strictly distanced chairs. In Dias's words: "We have to adapt the participation processes to the new health safety standards so that they are never used as an excuse for these processes not to be resumed."[27]

Brazil was not the only place where PB implementation was threatened by the COVID-19 pandemic. For instance, in Mexico City there was a proposal from the City Mayor for cancelling the implementation of PB projects in 2020 and 2021. Fortunately, this would have required the local Congress to change the Citizen Participation Law and, given the public uproar following the proposal, the Congress changed it to a mere suspension instead of cancelling the entire exercise.

While this is a temporary win and demonstrates the power of citizen engagement, it does set a precedent that citizens' rights[28] may be subjected to interpretation and suspension when there is public money tied to them. Furthermore, according to the new plan approved by the Congress, PB winning projects in Mexico City for the years 2020 and 2021 will be implemented jointly in 2021.

---

26 Wenzel, 'Pandemia pode enterrar.'
27 Wenzel, 'Pandemia pode enterrar.'
28 According to Article 26 of Mexico City's Constitution, PB is a right of all citizens:
"Artículo 26
Democracia Participativa
[...]
B. Presupuesto Participativo
1. Las personas tienen derecho a decidir sobre el uso, administración y destino de los proyectos y recursos asignados al presupuesto participativo, al mejoramiento barrial y a la recuperación de espacios públicos en los ámbitos específicos de la Ciudad de México. Dichos recursos se sujetarán a los procedimientos de transparencia y rendición de cuentas." [People have the right to decide on the use, administration and destination of the projects and resources assigned to the participatory budget, neighborhood improvement and the recovery of public spaces in the specific areas of Mexico City. These resources will be subject to transparency and accountability procedures.]

This determination has brought major chaos and severe delays as well as overlaps on projects that were planned to be implemented one after the other over a timeframe of at least six months each.

At the time this chapter is being written in October 2021, a small number of projects have started implementation, but the vast majority are still on the verge of becoming non-viable. If all 2020 winning projects were properly contracted by the beginning of November, they would be facing an implementation time of less than a third of their original schedule, as well as the need to run in parallel with the selected projects for 2021. This, of course, will affect the final outcome of these projects, as well as their capability to provide accountability and citizen participation in their implementation.

Nevertheless, the alternative to this looks even more dangerous. There is an ongoing discussion as to whether these projects should be moved to 2022 for implementation. This would undoubtedly provide more time for their implementation, but poses two fundamental problems. The first is the technical impossibility of exercising public funds pertaining to one year in a different year. This would require the Congress to allocate funds for these projects in 2022 (which would not necessarily be the funds that the city had allocated for these projects in 2021). The second problem, as mentioned earlier, is that this opens a door for governments to decide when and how a PB proposal may be implemented or not, using excuses such as the COVID-19 pandemic to justify arbitrary decisions that threaten citizens' rights and the rule of law.

The Future of PB: A Case for Citizen Engagement

The future of PB in the world depends on a series of factors that range from political openness of governments for the implementation of participatory and direct democracy mechanisms to the rate of citizen empowerment that will actually allow common citizens to make this mechanism truly actionable. We are facing severe circumstances that could prove lethal to PB. Fortunately, the final result can be deeply influenced by how citizens respond to these challenges.

There are several examples of how empowered and coordinated citizens have changed the status quo in the past. One of the main features of PB is that we can clearly trace its origins back to the global South. I believe this is particularly symbolic and that it brings hope to those willing to have everyone's voices heard. For the first time, countries facing the biggest development challenges have come up with a win–win solution so powerful that the so-called 'mature democracies' could do nothing but adopt and cherish the idea.

The world is a better place because of PB. It is the role of citizens throughout the world to learn about this mechanism, but also to nurture and defend it against those whose interests are opposed to it.

Yanina Welp
Recall Elections

Introduction

According to the notion of 'imperative mandate,' an elected delegate is expected to transmit and/or to implement the instructions of his or her electors without further intervention, and a non-compliance of such mandate would make him or her subject to recall. On the other side of the spectrum, political representation implies that a representative is elected on the basis of her proposals and/or personal attributes, but has to govern for all and not only for those electing her. Thereby, the authority would have the power to make decisions with a degree of discretion, within the rule of law. Laurence Whitehead defined this as bourgeois democracy,[1] in the sense that the incumbent has acquired a set of rights and duties that constitute a personal status (or property) held according to the relevant terms of the constitutional order. This seemed to work in practice and as an ideal, but the bourgeois model of democratic representation is facing challenges in the 21st century.

The widespread citizen disenchantment with professional politicians has, among many other trends, promoted the spread of recall regulations and an increasing number of recall activations, as well as a claim to regulate it where it is not available. However, imperative mandate and recall elections are not the same, opening room for a debate on the reconfiguration of political representation. "With an imperative mandate, elected officials commit to implement specific measures and can be removed if they depart from this original agreement. In contrast, recall election leaves greater room of interpretation for citizens who can remove their representatives when they feel that they are not meeting their obligations."[2] Thus, what kind of incentives do recall elections offer and to what extent could they reinforce democracy or, the opposite, further erode trust and confidence? Recall elections might provide a 'safety valve' that could help to

---

[1] Whitehead, Laurence (2018) 'The recall of elected office holders: the growing incidence of a venerable, but overlooked, democratic institution.' *Democratization* 25(8): 1341–1357.

[2] Egger, C. and Magni-Berton, R. (2020) 'The debate on the recall in France: imperative mandate or political irresponsibility under the Fifth Republic?' In Y. Welp and L. Whitehead (eds.) *The Politics of Recall Elections*. London: Palgrave, pp. 49–72, at p. 49.

https://doi.org/10.1515/9783110747331-004

re-legitimize democratic politics in an era of dissatisfaction and fatigue on the one hand, and mobilization on the other, as well as social upheaval.

The heightened sensitivity of the public towards pressing political issues in times of a governability crisis leads to demand for more tools for accountability. But does it work like that? Is it a good idea to introduce recall in increasingly fragile and fragmented polities? Even more, in times of growing polarization and fake news, is more personalization of politics a good idea? This chapter seeks to provide answers to these questions by offering an overview of recall in history, regulation, and practices – sections in the text are organized along these topics –, in order to finally bring conclusions.

The Spread of Recall Elections in Time

Recall elections (also known as recall referendums) have historical roots that go back to Ancient Rome and have appeared several times in history until their most recent spread and discussion after the fall of the Berlin Wall. In 1787, a more modern mechanism with similar goals to the Roman one, that is, to get rid of an unpopular authority, was discussed within the American Convention. It was never introduced at the federal level in the US nor was it discussed again, but it did spread at the subnational level from the end of the 19th century. Interestingly, it was introduced in the French Constitution in 1793 but never entered into force.

The path of recall in modern states started at the subnational level in the Swiss cantons, the American states,[3] and some Argentinian provinces in the 19th and early 20th centuries. Thus, in the 21st century, despite being considered a 'democratic innovation,' it opens up longstanding debates on the meaning of representation and the exercise of power. Recall elections are supported by many movements-based parties campaigning for a 'real democracy' in which people should retain the power temporarily in the hands of a delegate.

There is a discussion about how to classify the mechanism within the set of participatory devices. There is discussion about the features of mechanisms, oriented to collective deliberation or to decisions taken by an elector, where recall

---

3 In 1892, the Socialist Labor Party and the Populist Party reintroduced the claim for recall and succeeded in in getting it included in the new Charter of the City of Los Angeles in 1903. Within a decade, the Los Angeles example had been taken up by some 200 cities as well as by three states. After a century, it had spread to the 26 states that provided some legal means to activate it. See: Cronin, T. (1989) *Direct Democracy: The Politics of Initiative, Referendum and Recall.* Cambridge and London: Harvard University Press.

would fit among the second group, that is, the Mechanisms of Direct Democracy (MDDs). For some scholars from the Swiss tradition recall does not fit in the group, given that its target is a representative and not a policy. However, following the American tradition, (see Cronin 1989), we assume that if MDDs are mechanisms that allow the citizenry to keep being a player (veto player or law promoter) in policy-making through a vote, recall needs to be considered as a tool of direct democracy.

Democratic innovations are the result of institutional change processes in which political actors struggle over two different things: different ideas concerning the value of citizen participation (and democratic legitimacy) and also the very balance of power between actors in a political system. Thus, any institutional change is shaped in a process of negotiations, bargaining, and competition in which advocates and opponents for including more mechanisms for political participation struggle over rival concepts (e.g. about what constitutes democratic legitimacy) as well as for power.

Meanwhile, opportunity structures play an important role in explaining outcomes in the short and middle terms because there is no lineal connection between the expected outcomes of an institution and the effective ones. Any institutional change oriented to increasing political participation, and especially those oriented to increasing the number of 'veto players' in a given system, touches upon the power balance between political actors and their influence in the political decision-making process, and, therefore, entail high stakes.[4] For example, bottom-up referendums activated by signature collection can be directed against the policies that a government might be pursuing, thus increasing citizens' capacities of veto, control, and agenda-setting. But innovations could also reinforce executive power (e.g. in what O'Donnell has qualified as 'delegative democracy'[5]). Different devices would lead to different outcomes. For example, the consequences of promoting or vetoing laws through a referendum or an initiative are not equivalent to the systemic consequences of activating recall referendums to remove authorities before the end of their term, given that the latter do has a stronger impact on governance and eventually on governability, as happened in many Peruvian municipalities between 1997 and 2015.

The recall is quite specific in this sense, or, in other words, it is well known that turkeys do not vote for Christmas. Why should politicians be interested in

---

4 Hug, Simon and Tsebelis, George (2002) 'Veto players and referendums around the world.' *Journal of Theoretical Politics* 14(4): 465–515; and Scarrow, Susan (2001) 'Direct democracy and institutional change: a comparative investigation.' *Comparative Political Studies* 34(6): 651–665.

5 O'Donnell, Guillermo (1994) 'Delegative democracy.' *Journal of Democracy* 5(1): 55–69.

introducing a mechanism that could play against them? And there is evidence of such a challenge: just to mention a prominent one, it happened to Hugo Chávez in 2004. But sometimes turkeys may vote for Christmas if they believe that another animal may be the one slaughtered. Historical examples could help to identify the circumstances in which recall was regulated, whether the promoters faced strong social pressure and the survival of their parties was challenged, or alternatively whether they perceived that their opponents were more vulnerable than themselves. However, the literature does not provide any single or systematic explanation of the conditions under which recall has been introduced. Moreover, it has appeared in both the liberal tradition and in the communist one.[6]

In Japan, elite discussions about direct citizen participation can be traced back to more than a century ago with the establishment of the Meiji Constitution in 1889. The Japanese Social Democratic Party was a staunch defender of direct democratic institutions, as shown by its electoral program of 1901. Shortly after, the party was banned and only after the Second World War did the topic return to the public debate. Under the supervision of the US military occupation, the Japanese were required to democratize the country. The Social Democrats became the strongest party in 1947 and then promoted the introduction of a series of direct democratic rules, including not only the right to dissolve the assembly (as in Switzerland), but also to remove assembly members and mayors (the three types of recall regulated in Japan) (Okamoto and Serdült 2020). Was it part of the Japanese interrupted political tradition or imitation of the US political system? Probably a bit of both. The cases of Germany and Poland could be related to the *zeitgeist* (spirit of the time) of the fall of the Berlin Wall as well as to their specific trajectories. In Germany, recall has only been introduced regionally by some Länder, acting under their decentralized powers,[7] while in Poland it was introduced through the Local Referendum Act of 1991.[8] In both, the discourse in the promotion was related to revitalizing local democracy and increasing accountability.

---

6 The recall referendum certainly received considerable attention from prominent writers on the left in the early part of the 20th century. It was championed by Harold Laski, Antonio Gramsci (1978: 50) Vladimir Lenin (2004: 36), Rosa Luxemburg (2004: 306) – and the institution was even used in the early years of the Soviet Union (White and Ronald 1996).

7 Geissel, Brigitte (2017) 'Direct democracy and its (perceived) consequences: the German case.' In S. P. Ruth, Y. Welp, and L. Whitehead (eds.) *Let the People Rule? Direct Democracy in the Twenty-first Century.* Colchester: ECPR Press, pp. 155 – 167.

8 Piasecki, A. (2011) 'Twenty years of Polish direct democracy at the local level.' In Theo Schiller (ed.) *Local Direct Democracy in Europe.* Germany: Springer, pp. 126 – 137.

Transitions to democracy, peace processes, or huge political crises are quite often conditions for institutional reform. Contrary to some expectations, social pressure appears sometimes, but not always. In Latin America, recent developments in the Andean countries offer a pattern of regional diffusion. From the 1990s onwards, several republics replaced (or even 'refounded') their constitutions, and some introduced recall referendums together with various other mechanisms of direct and participatory democracy. This happened in Colombia in 1991, in Ecuador in 1998 and in 2008 (two constitutions were approved in this period, both including recall at the local level and the second also at national level), in Peru in 1993, in Venezuela in 1999, and in Bolivia in 2009. While in Ecuador and Bolivia the demand for more participation was on the cards, in Peru the social pressure to introduce recall was much less evident.[9]

By 2021, I had identified 77 cases in which direct recall (i.e. activated by the people through signature collection or bottom-up initiatives) is regulated, some at the national level and some at the state, cantonal, or provincial level.

Regarding practices, experiences are mainly registered at the subnational level. Recall has been intensively used in such diverse settings as Japan (Okamoto and Serdült 2020), Peru,[10] and the US.[11] Meanwhile, there have been a number of cases that generated hot debates and media coverage, such as those in California (2021, against Governor Gavin Newsom, and 2003, against Governor Gray Davis), Venezuela (2004, against President Hugo Chávez), Romania (2012, against President Traian Băsescu), Lima (2013, against Mayor Susana Villarán), and Chişinău (2017, against Mayor Dorin Chirtoacă), among others, exemplifying the growing incidence of recall.[12]

Institutional Designs Matter

Recall is expected to provide a 'safety valve' that could help to re-legitimize democratic politics in an era of dissatisfaction. However, the empirical evidence at hand highlights substantial differences in institutional design, both between

---

9 Welp, Yanina (2016) 'Recall referendums in Peruvian municipalities: a political weapon for bad losers or an instrument of accountability?' *Democratization* 23(7): 1162–1179.

10 Welp, 'Recall referendums in Peruvian municipalities.'

11 Spivak, J. (2020) 'Recall elections in the US: its long past and uncertain future.' In Y. Welp et al. (eds.) *The Politics of Recall Elections*. Basingstoke: Palgrave Macmillan, pp. 73–93. See also: Qvortrup, Matt (ed.) (2014) *Referendums Around the World: The Continued Growth of Direct Democracy*. Basingstoke: Palgrave Macmillan.

12 Welp, Y. and Whitehead, L. (2020) *The Politics of Recall Elections*. London: Palgrave.

and within countries, while evolving episodes of reform over time, which affect the performance of the institution. Institutional designs diverge over which authorities can be removed by recall, for what reasons, the period during which activation is allowed, the number of signatures required, the time given to collect signatures, and the actions taken if the authority is removed. Recall can be activated against all elected authorities in only six countries, five of them in Latin America (Bolivia, Ecuador, Mexico, Venezuela, and Cuba, which regulates it, despite not being a democracy) and in Taiwan RC. In Cuba, only the delegates at the bottom level can be removed by referendum (as this is the only level that is elected), so the device has a very insignificant impact.[13]

In Liechtenstein the whole council can be removed. The same applies for Switzerland but on the cantonal level. In some cases, it is the national constitution that provides recall rules at the subnational level, as in Cuba, Bolivia, Colombia, Peru, Poland, Ecuador, Venezuela, and Japan. In Colombia, only local executive authorities can be removed by recall. In Peru, both executive and legislative representatives (mayors and councilors) can be removed by a recall vote. In contrast, in federal countries, the rules are determined by subnational units, and vary among units within the same country, as happens in Germany, Argentina, the United States, Switzerland, and Mexico, where Länder, provinces, states, or cantons offer differing procedures for the recall of mayors and/or legislatives authorities (Welp 2018). All these considerations (in combination with other variables) affect which of the attempted recalls end in a vote. One should also add partisan motivation into the mix.[14]

The frequency of activations is conditioned by citizen discontent, the emergence of scandals, the ease of activation (like a low number of signatures), partisan motivations (losers against the party in government), and the role of electoral management bodies in allowing or preventing attempts, in an exercise conditioned by the law and the level of autonomy of the institution.[15] For the German case, Geissel and Jung suggest that since higher signature requirements and

---

[13] Guzmán Hernández, Y. (2014) 'Cuba: deudas pasadas y retos presentes desde la norma.' In Y. Welp and U. Serdült (eds.) *La dosis hace el veneno: la revocatoria del mandato en Suiza, Estados Unidos y América Latina*, Serie Ciencia y Democracia. Quito: Consejo Nacional Electoral, pp. 187–205.

[14] Welp, Yanina and Milanese, Juan Pablo (2018) 'Playing by the rules of the game: the partisan use of recall referendums in Colombia.' *Democratization* 25(8): 1379–1396; and Mișcoiu, S. (2019) 'Never just a local war: explaining the failure of a mayor's recall referendum.' *Contemporary Politics* 25(1): 47–61.

[15] Welp, Yanina and Castellanos, Ana Sofía (2020) 'Understanding the use of recall referendums: evidence from Ecuador.' *International Political Science Review* 41(3): 335–348.

shorter time limits increase the costs of a successfully initiated recall, such rules could be expected to cause less frequent recall challenges, while lower signature thresholds and more campaigning time would incentivize citizens to initiate more recalls.[16] Peru, where more than 5,000 recall referendums were activated between 1997 and 2013 against democratically elected authorities from 747 Peruvian municipalities (45.5 percent of all municipalities), is the world's most intensive user of recall. This high frequency of activations has been explained by a combination of the institutional design of these procedures giving ease of activation and the low degree of party system institutionalization. This combination creates unexpected incentives for political losers and their parties to gain power beyond regular elections.[17]

The key role played by institutional designs is exemplified by the cases of Colombia and Ecuador, where changes in regulation had an almost immediate impact in launching or preventing activations. In Colombia, a new law approved in 2015 reduced the number of signatures required to activate a recall referendum (from 40 percent to 30 percent of the total votes obtained by the elected authority), reduced the threshold for success (dropping from 50 percent to 40 percent of valid votes originally cast), and also sped up the registration of promoters. This led to an abrupt increase in the number of recall attempts, which in only five months doubled the total recorded over the fifteen previous years.[18]

In Ecuador, in its first introduction into the Constitution of 1998, recall activations were allowed only against acts of corruption and failure to accomplish the electoral program. Surprisingly, in corruption cases a judicial sentence was required (i.e. accordingly, the authority is removed by a judicial process and recall is not required). From 1998 to 2007, no referendums took place. Then, the Constitution of 2008 reformulated the recall referendum as a political and participatory right (i.e. loss of confidence in the elected authority was enough to trigger a recall) and reduced the number of signatures required to 15 percent. Soon, the number of attempts jumped to almost 1,000 (784 were officially registered between 2010 and 2011). The institution was reformed again, and in May 2011 requisites became higher, having an evident effect on reducing the number of attempts, which fell drastically, to less than a hundred. New reforms changed patterns again.[19]

---

16 Geissel, B and Jung, S. (2018) 'Recall in Germany: explaining the use of a local democratic innovation.' *Democratization* 25(8): 1358–1378.

17 Welp, 'Recall referendums in Peruvian municipalities.'

18 Welp and Milanese, 'Playing by the rules of the game.'

19 Welp and Castellanos, 'Understanding the use of recall referendums.'

The Devil is in the Detail: Outcomes of Recall Activations

The idea of 'common people' or individuals activating direct democracy has been challenged by empirical research[20] and also applies to recall activations that might not necessarily reflect the unfiltered will of the 'people.' The activation of a recall process requires organization and resources. In this regard, organized political parties (and other well-structured vested interests) will usually have the edge in activating direct democratic procedures and may also have more incentives to do so. Recalls are particularly likely in a climate of scandal and/or in the context of extreme political polarization, both of which can be expected to motivate strong elite mobilization as well as popular engagement. Latin America presents an abundance of such situations. Currently the erosion of traditional political party systems and the spread of social digital networks add to the factors triggering direct recall campaigns where the law allows them, and also prompts interest in establishing this option where it is not yet available.

Recall arrangements may provide a limited and partial 'safety valve' for specific sources of discontent, but they cannot supply an overall corrective to generalized citizen dissatisfaction with an entire 'political class' of professional office-holders. Moreover, such patchy recall provision is likely to disturb the balance of power between levels of government that are placed at risk of a foreshortened mandate and those office-holders whose positions are not in play. For instance, when the mayor of a capital city could be targeted for recall but not the president of the republic, as happens in Colombia and Peru, the effective 'leader of the opposition' becomes an opponent to the president, who can react, incentivizing a recall against the mayor.

But where this procedure is on offer at all levels throughout a national electoral system, bad design choices can be both far more consequential and also much harder to diagnose and then reverse. Too many powerful actors have too much at stake to allow consensual fine-tuning. Nationwide direct recall arrangements are both more resistant to revision and more prone to powerful backlash

---

20 Kriesi, Hanspeter (2006) 'Role of the political elite in Swiss direct-democratic votes.' *Party Politics* 12(5): 599–622; Garret, E. (2004) 'Democracy in the wake of the California recall.' *University of Pennsylvania Law Review* 153: 239–284; Serdült, Uwe and Welp, Yanina (2017) 'The levelling up of a political institution: perspectives on the recall referendum.' In Saskia Ruth, Yanina Welp, and Laurence Whitehead (eds.) *Let the People Rule? Direct Democracy in the Twenty-first Century.* Colchester: ECPR Press.

than earlier scattered 'safety valve' experiments. The consequences of defenestrating a serving head of state are of a different order of magnitude from other recalls, and the potential for governance dysfunctionality is considerable. Since the political interests at stake are so high, the incentives to game the system are magnified accordingly. Both the promise and the pitfalls of direct recall are redoubled when it is made universal.

At a more general level, outcomes have been assessed in case studies but leave gaps for the understanding of the consequences of recall in a more general way. The classic work of Cronin summarizes arguments in favor of and against recall.[21] Advocates advance the following arguments: i) recall provides for continuous accountability so that voters need not wait until the next elections to get rid of an incompetent, dishonest, unresponsive, or irresponsible public official; ii) it helps to check the undue influence of narrow special interests; iii) it enables jurisdictions to permit their officials to serve long terms; iv) it gives the average person a reason to stay informed about civic developments between elections; v) recall offers a safety valve mechanism for intense feelings; and vi) it provides a sensible alternative to impeachment. Opponents affirm that: i) the very premise of recall is antagonistic to republican principles, especially to the idea of free mandate representation; ii) it makes public office less attractive to the most able individuals; iii) recall votes are divisive, disruptive, polarizing, and subject to myriad abuses and unintended consequences; iv) recall votes are confusing, often unfair, and place too much burden on the voters to keep informed between elections; and v) recall referendums are costly, unnecessary, and directed against the wrong target. Most of these arguments, whether in favor or against, are still unproved by empirical evidence or only related to specific cases.

In the case of Switzerland, Serdült has suggested that recall is a 'dormant institution' because the availability of other mechanisms of direct democracy, such as initiatives and veto referendums, make the activation of these more efficient than the former.[22] In their study of Japan, Okamoto and Serdült (Okamoto and Serdült 2020) define recall as an example of imbalance institution. In their view, the mechanism has been intensively activated in some periods because recall is binding and its activation mandatory if the requirements are fulfilled, while initiatives are consultative, and the call for a veto referendum depends on the agreement of the council. This would explain why recall is identified

---

21 Cronin, *Direct Democracy.*
22 Serdült, Uwe (2015) 'A dormant institution – history, legal norms and practice of the recall in Switzerland.' *Representation: Journal of Representative Democracy* 51(2): 161–172.

there as working for indirect accountability (addressing a policy despite being formally oriented to removing an authority).

The recall of Governor Gray Davis (Democratic Party) in 2003 in California is a well-studied case which highlights some of the issues that arise when recall is in place. Davis, who had come to power in 1999 with a clear victory (58 percent of the vote), was accused of corruption in his second term. Quickly after his re-election, members of the Republican Party led by Ted Costa formally initiated a process accusing Davis of gross mismanagement of California finances. Recall proponents gathered signatures through a volunteer effort that combined the forces of conservative radio shows and the internet (25,000 hits for the pro-recall website 'Rescue California'). However, only when representative Darell Issa from the Republicans provided hundreds of thousands of dollars towards the effort did the process reach the number of signatures required.

The role of money in the process has been well studied. California's process has an exceptional feature, given that the recall election takes place together with the election of an eventual successor. It opened a door for Arnold Schwarzenegger, the former movie star turned political activist (who shortly before the election had promoted a ballot initiative to introduce after-school activities for students). Davis was ousted with 55.4 percent in favor of recall. Schwarzenegger received 48.4 percent support as a replacement among a total of seven viable candidates in a vote that split mostly along party lines.[23] More case studies show the role of interests in promoting recall: this was the case in Chișinău, Lima, Warsaw, and Bogotá.[24] Venezuela in 2004 and the attempt of 2016 also show to what extent the rule of law is key in allowing or preventing activations as well as in conditioning the results.[25] A clear research gap emerges from the lack of case studies developed under similar analytical models. These would help identify paths and make generalizations.

Finally, the formation of public opinion needs special attention. Recall referendums are somehow an extension of a normal campaign and many variables

---

23 For detailed case studies see Garret, Elizabeth (2004) 'Democracy in the wake of the California Recall.' *University of Pennsylvania Law Review* 153: 239–284; Kousser, Thad (2004) 'The California governor's recall.' In Keon Chi (ed.) *The Book of the States, 2004 Edition*, vol. 36. Lexington: The Council of State Governments, pp. 307–315; Miller, K. P. (2005) 'The Davis recall and the courts.' *American Politics Research* 33(2): 135–162.

24 See Uribe Mendoza, Christian (2016) 'La activación de la revocatoria de mandato en el ámbito municipal en Colombia: lecciones del caso de Bogotá.' *Estudios Politicos* 48: 179–200; and Welp, Yanina and Rey, Julieta (2014) 'Revocatoria de mandato y democracia: análisis de las experiencias recientes en Lima y Bogotá.' *Democracias* 2: 189–208.

25 Kornblith, Miriam (2005) 'The referendum in Venezuela: elections versus democracy.' *Journal of Democracy* 16: 124–137.

can influence the fairness of the process. The caveat here refers to the campaigns and the expected levels of polarization behind such controversial cases. In some states of the US, the increase in the number of activations has also been related to low levels of electoral participation because this reduces the number of signatures required to start a recall process (given that in most of the US cases, this is a percentage of the votes cast in the election of the authority[26]), while digital media diffusion facilitates fast and cheap campaigning.

Conclusions

Recall elections might provide a 'safety valve' that could help to re-legitimize democratic politics in an era of dissatisfaction, fatigue on the one hand, and mobilization on the other, as well as social upheaval. But does it work like that? Recall elections could be seen as a good mechanism when politicians are poorly evaluated. However, they can also produce more disadvantages without resolving the problems for which they were introduced. This could happen if the actors activating them frequently create a situation of 'permanent campaign,' or if elite power struggles diminish governability and erode the capacity for policy-making and management. The balance between such positive or negative outcomes depends partly on the underlying legitimacy and robustness of the system in question, partly on the precise design features of the recall mechanism itself, and partly on the particular context in which it was first adopted and then adapted. As regards pre-existing legitimacy, the crucial issue is whether the result of the recall is accepted by the losers as well as the winners, and that depends not only on whether the process is procedurally correct and generates a public benefit, but also on whether the electorate is inclined to demand institutional compliance from all its political operators. Context matters when determining the effectiveness and acceptability of any given procedural rule, since each society develops its own traditions and collective understandings about the rightness of claims to political authority. So, the question is never just does recall work well, but also does it mesh with our expectations and assumptions, and how well is it understood and approved by our people?

That said, this chapter has highlighted some design problems arising from the weakness of the epistemic community that would be needed to flag pitfalls and encourage best practice. One simple suggestion might provide a valuable design improvement compared with most existing practice. It would surely be both

---

26 Zimmerman, J. F. (1997) *The Recall: Tribunal of the People*. New York: Praeger Publishers.

more democratic and easier for losers to accept if there were two thresholds that must be passed to make a recall effective, rather than just one. In addition to securing a majority of the votes cast, a recall could also require that more voters oppose the continuance in office of the representative than the number cast in his or her favor in the first place. It has also drawn attention to other design features that might reduce the risks of unintended or de-legitimizing consequences.

The best-organized actors will invariably try to game the new system before the general public has learnt how to make good use of it. But more systematic comparative study and greater public education into the merits of well-structured recall might shift the balance back towards a more positive pattern. One suggestion implicit in several of the case studies is that recall may work better when it is embedded in a broader process of public deliberation and policy debate, rather than simply operating as a device available to be used for the purpose of partisan aggression.

On the other hand, another theme requiring more attention is the possibility that some (more radical) variants of recall may be so entangled with more far-reaching programs of social transformation that they can be overused to undermine the status quo, but then get entirely set aside once the radicals are in the ascendant and might be vulnerable to the same sanctions that they had favored before their ascent (Venezuela's Bolivarian Republic and the Mexican experiment of Andres Manuel López Obrador currently exemplifies this risk).

In empirical terms there is still much to be discovered about the various channels through which recall episodes may impact upon the quality and stability of contemporary democracies. The broad fan of recall procedures surveyed here can serve a wide variety of purposes and is capable of delivering both short- and long-run outcomes that are highly consequential for the nature and quality of the democratic regimes that adopt them.

Comparative experience can be useful as a source of guidance to minimize unintended or damaging effects and to increase the chances of successful institutional design. In view of the broader forces at work challenging classical models of political representation (which include the instantaneous citizen responses facilitated by advances in information and communications technology, the reduced authority of national parliaments, and traditional hierarchical political parties, etc.), it would be unrealistic to expect that the direct democracy surge can simply be blocked or disregarded, but it should be a claim to redirect it to policies in place of keeping it attached to individuals.

Representation and participation are fundamental to the proper functioning of democracy, but the current balance between the two dimensions needs to be changed. It seems that recall is not the best institution to find a better equilibrium, and, on the contrary, could increase trends towards polarization and permanent campaign while not producing good incentives for feeding a public debate. The goals would be not weakening parties, but making them more rooted and responsible. For this to happen, citizens must have a voice and a vote in public affairs.

Politics must be depersonalized and placed in the programmatic sphere. Let's talk more about common good and less about the leaders!

Matt Qvortrup
Referendums as Complementary Democracy

The referendum is not an alternative to representative government; it's an adden-
dum. This was summed up by the Liberal politician Lord Rosebery,[1] who briefly
served as prime minister of the United Kingdom (1894–1895). He said, "I am
strongly for the referendum ... but not for daily bread, only for rare and exceptional circumstances."[2] As such, the referendum is almost the quintessential institution of complementary democracy. Or, as the political theorist Dennis F.
Thompson has put it recently, "representative government with referendums ...
is superior representative government without them."[3]

Referendums are controversial. Once they were championed as 'the nation's
veto,' which is intended to keep elites in check, and the embodiment of the principle "that behind and above parties lies the will of the nation."[4] But critics say
that they sow division, are held to cater for the interests of populist leaders, and
that they lead to suboptimal outcomes. This chapter analyzes when referendums
have been held (using mainly statistical and historical data) and examines their
effect on macro-economic performance. It is hoped that this dispassionate analysis will provide a sober starting point for those who contemplate their use – and
that those who remain skeptical will have better grounds on which to base their
opinions.

It is shown that referendums tend to be held in countries with less proportional electoral systems and in countries that are ideologically dominated by the
center-right. The research also shows that the number of referendums is positively correlated with increased wealth. In statistical terms, for every referendum
held, the average citizen gains an additional $800.

1 Lord Rosebery quoted in Vernon Bogdanor (1981) *The People and the Party System: The Referendum and Electoral Reform in British Politics.* Cambridge: Cambridge University Press, p. 81.
2 Lord Rosebery quoted in Bogdanor, *The People and the Party System*, p. 81.
3 Thompson, Dennis F. (2022) 'Why representative democracy requires referendums.' In James
A. Gardner (ed.) *Comparative Election Law.* Northampton: Elgar, pp. 191–209, at p. 207.
4 Dicey, A. V. (2019) *Lectures on Comparative Constitutionalism.* Oxford: Oxford University Press,
pp. 147–148.

https://doi.org/10.1515/9783110747331-005

Introduction

There is something odd about referendums (here defined as a popular vote on policy propositions). To its supporters, the referendum is the most eminently democratic of institutions. In the words of one academic writer, "In the last resort, the arguments against the referendum are also arguments against democracy, while acceptance of the referendum is but the logical consequence of accepting the democratic form of government."[5] Yet, to its detractors it is the recipe of untamed mob-rule. Clement Attlee (the Labour prime minister 1945–1951) dismissed Winston Churchill's call for a referendum by saying that he would "not consent to the introduction into our national life of a device so alien to all our traditions as the referendum, which has only too often been the instrument of Nazism and Fascism."[6]

How is it that an institution such as this can be equated with the worst kinds of totalitarian regimes, and yet by others be lauded as the most democratic of instruments? How can this constitutional device be equated with mob rule as well as be seen as a vehicle of democratic deliberation?

In some way this apparent paradox is as old as democracy itself. As far back as 350 BCE, Aristotle famously wrote that all forms of government had a positive and a negative form. That is, monarchy was contrasted with tyranny, aristocracy with oligarchy, and *Politeia* – a positive word for government by the people – was the opposite of *demokratia*[7] – a negative version of legislation by the citizens themselves.

Maybe the current debates could do with an injection of Aristotelian common sense? Maybe current debates could be enlightened if we were to see the referendum the way the Ancient Greek philosopher viewed the similar institution in his day, namely as a system of government that can be both a positive and a negative. In the spirit of Aristotle, the empiricist, what we will do in this chapter is to present a largely empirical assessment of the way referendums are being used.

After some initial thoughts on the political theory (or philosophy) of referendums, we look at the patterns of their use and on why referendums have tended to be held. This is followed by mainly quantitative section on the consequences of referendums.

---

5 Bogdanor, *The People and the Party System*, p. 93.
6 Attlee quoted in Bogdanor, *The People and the Party System*, p. 35.
7 Aristotle (1944) *The Politics*. Cambridge MA: Harvard University Press, p. 1279b.

What are Referendums?

First, a bit of terminological clarification. A referendum is a vote taken by the whole of a people on a policy issue. Etymologically the word comes from the Latin *referre* – 'to refer back.' The referendum is often, if mistakenly, seen as an example of pure direct democracy and is seen as detrimental to representative government.

Referendums are not very radical really. It is simply a vote on a policy by the people, typically on an issue that has already been debated by the elected representatives. Thus, under the referendum, the voters do not have the right to initiate legislation (as under citizens' initiatives, which exist in some American states[8]); they can merely approve or reject proposals put forward by the legislature. For some, the referendum is thus a small first step towards more democracy, but that is not the issue to be debated here.[9]

The referendum, consequently, is fundamentally a conservative institution. It allows the people – or a legally specified part of them – to veto a proposal or a law already adopted by the legislature.

The Political Philosophy of the Referendum

The idea that the people should have the final say on the most important matters is almost as old as Western civilization itself. The Roman historian Tacitus observed that, "on matters of minor importance, only the chiefs decide; on major matters, the whole community decides."[10]

The idea that the people ultimately have the last word was also an axiomatic position of our earliest political philosophers. In the wake of the so-called 'Glorious Revolution,'[11] the English philosopher John Locke noted in *The Second Treatise of Government* published anonymously in the same year that

---

8 Matsusaka, J. (2004) *For the Many or the Few: The Initiative, Public Policy and American Democracy.* Chicago: University of Chicago Press.

9 For a more radical view of democracy, including the use of modern technology, see: Becker, Ted (2001) 'Rating the impact of new technologies on democracy.' *Communications of the ACM* 44(1): 39–43. For a general overview of the mechanisms of direct democracy (including the initiative), see my book: Qvortrup, M. (2021) *Democracy on Demand: Holding Power to Account.* Manchester: Manchester University Press, pp. 178–221.

10 Tacitus (1970) *The Agricola and Germania.* London: Penguin, p. 110.

11 In 1688 Catholic King James II of England was deposed by a humanitarian intervention by the Dutch William of Orange and James's daughter, Mary.

> If a controversy arise betwixt a Prince and some of the people, in a matter where the law is silent, or doubtful, and the thing be of great consequence, I think the proper Umpire in such a case should be the Body of the People.[12]

This supremacy of the people in the last resort has been the justification of referendums.[13] No less a figure than the poet Percy B. Shelley wrote in his 'Declaration of Rights,'

> Governments have no rights; it is a delegation from several individuals for the purpose of securing their own. It is therefore just, only so far as it exists by their consent, useful only so far as it operates to their well-being.[14]

The referendum was not just a theoretical construct. Indeed, in some ways the theoreticians were justifying the use of the referendum *ex post*. Thus, there were a relatively large number of popular votes in the 17th century and even before. Indeed, as early as 1527 a vote had been held in Burgundy on whether to transfer sovereignty of the region from the French to the Spanish king.[15] But it was only in the wake of the War of Independence that many American states adopted referendums before their constitutions could be changed. (Though, to date, no referendum has been held at the federal level.)

That the referendum could be used to resolve policy matters grew out of the dual events of the American and French revolutions. Henceforth the "consent of the governed" – to use the words of the Declaration of Independence – became the gold standard of legitimacy.

This was a change from the earlier age of absolutism. As a prominent scholar of referendums wrote in a classic study,

> The French Revolution proclaimed the dogma that we now term self-determination. ... The mental and logical process was simple. The people are the state and the nation; the people are sovereign. As such they have the right to decide, as the ultima ratio, by popular vote and simple majority, all matters affecting the state and the nation.[16]

---

12 Locke, J. (1988) *Two Treatises of Government*. Cambridge: Cambridge University Press, p. 427.
13 Though Locke himself did not draw this conclusion, and maintained that when the legislative power had been placed "in any assembly of men ... the legislative [power] can never revert to the people." Locke, *Two Treatises of Government*, p. 428.
14 Shelley, Percy B. (1906) 'Declaration of rights.' In *The Prose Works of Percy Bysshe Shelley*. London: Chatto & Windus, p. 284.
15 Wambaugh, Sarah (1919) *The Doctrine of Self-Determination Vol. 1: A Study of the Theory and Practice of Plebiscites*. Oxford: Oxford University Press, p. xxiii.
16 Mattern, J. (1921) *The Employment of the Plebiscite in the Determination of Sovereignty*. Baltimore: Johns Hopkins University Press, p. 77.

This idea of the referendum as the ultimate expression of popular sovereignty was also central to the political theory of the referendum.

A. V. Dicey, who is famous – or infamous – among lawyers for firmly establishing the doctrine of parliamentary sovereignty, had a side interest: he was the first theoretician to develop a rounded and coherent political theory of the referendum. In a series of articles and papers, including in the 6th edition of his influential treatise *An Introduction to the Law of the Constitution* and in the article 'Ought the Referendum to be Introduced into England?'[17] Dicey made a case for the referendum as an "alternative second chamber."[18]

Dicey was a conservative – albeit with a small 'c.' He was opposed to, what he considered, hasty and ill-considered change. But, like Alexis de Tocqueville, he realized that it was impossible to stem the tide of democracy and political equality.[19]

Unlike the House of Lords, the referendum was – in Dicey's opinion – "the one available check on party leaders" and the only institution that could "give formal acknowledgement of the doctrine which lies at the basis of English democracy – that a law depends at bottom for its enactment on the consent of the nation as represented by its electors."[20] Concerned about irreversible and possibly revolutionary changes to the British Constitution, Dicey advocated the use of referendums on major political issues He wrote:

> The referendum ... prevents legislation which goes much beyond popular opinion. ... Secondly, the referendum brings clearly before the nation that the law is the decree of the people for which they are responsible and not the rule made by oppressors of the people. ... Thirdly, the referendum makes it possible for statesmen honourably and honestly to conduct the affairs of the country even though on some point the policy of the nation does not agree with the views held by the executive.[21]

For Dicey, therefore, the referendum was a strictly negative political instrument. It was an assertion of the principle that "the sole body which in a modern state

17 Dicey, A. V. (1981) [1915] *Introduction to the Study of the Law of the Constitution*. Indianapolis: Liberty Fund.
18 On this see: Qvortrup, M. (1999) 'A.V. Dicey: the referendum as the people's veto.' *History of Political Thought* 20(3): 531–546.
19 On Tocqueville, see: Tocqueville, A. (2003) *Democracy in America*. London: Penguin. Interestingly, Dicey wrote an article about Tocqueville, see: Dicey, A. V. (1893) 'Alexis de Tocqueville.' *The National Review* 21(126): 771–784.
20 Dicey, A. V. (1911) *A Leap in the Dark*, 2nd edn. London: John Murray, pp. 189–190.
21 Dicey, *Comparative Constitutionalism*, p. 272.

such as England, which carries greater moral weight than Parliament itself is the people, or, in other words, the majority of the electorate."[22] For Dicey, the people had assumed the role once held by the monarch:

> The essence of the referendum ... is that the passing of important laws and especially laws touching the constitution needs the sanction of the electors. It places the electorate in the position once occupied in England by the Crown. ... It establishes the only conservative check on legislation which is clearly in harmony with those democratic principles which in a modern world form the moral bases of government.[23]

Before we look at how the referendum might be improved, we need to look at some descriptive facts about its use.

The Use of the Referendum: A Historical Overview

In the 19th century there were few referendums; 21 to be exact. This figure was surpassed in the first two decades of the 20th century, when no less than 27 nationwide votes were held. The beginning of the 20th century marked something of a watershed in the use of the referendum – and in the perception of referendums. The referendums held at the beginning of the new century in Australia (on conscription in 1917), or a couple of years before the turn of the century in the Canadian vote on prohibition (1898), were not held for idealistic reasons but to deal with practical issues. In the Australian case, the vote was held to paper over cracks within the Labor Party.[24] And in Canada the vote on prohibition was arguably a way to hinder a split within Prime Minister Wilfried Laurier's Liberal Party.[25]

Earlier, such strategic considerations had not been necessary. But with an enlargement of the electorate, controversial decisions could no longer be taken without concern for the opinions of the majority of the people. Rather than risk electoral defeat, the referendum was arguably an effective mechanism for defusing controversial issues.

---

22 Dicey, *Comparative Constitutionalism*, p. 270.

23 Dicey, *Comparative Constitutionalism*, p. 147.

24 Gilbert, A. D. (1969) 'The conscription referenda, 1916–17: the impact of the Irish crisis.' *Australian Historical Studies* 14(53): 54–72.

25 Dostie, Benoit and Dupré, Ruth (2012) '"The people's will": Canadians and the 1898 referendum on alcohol prohibition.' *Explorations in Economic History* 49(4): 498–515.

As Figure 5.1 shows, there was a steady growth until the high watermark in the 1990s, when a number of independence and constitutional referendums were held in the former communist countries, and this accounts for the total rise seen in the figure. After that the average number of referendums dropped, though to a higher level than before the 1990s. To wit, there were 281 referendums in the 1990s, and after that the number dropped to 208 in the first decade of the 21st century, with a further drop to 176 in the period 2010 – 2020. In the same period, there were 650 nationwide referendums in Switzerland (see Figure 5.2).

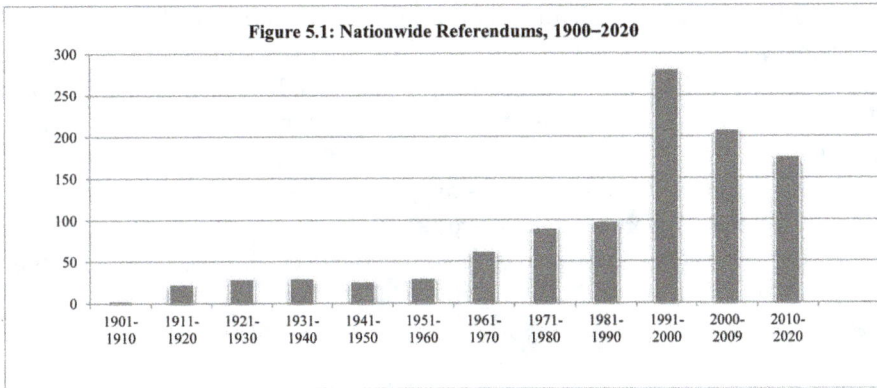

Figure 5.1: Nationwide Referendums, 1900–2020

Figure 5.1: Nationwide Referendums, 1900 – 2020.
Source: Based on data compiled by the author for this article.

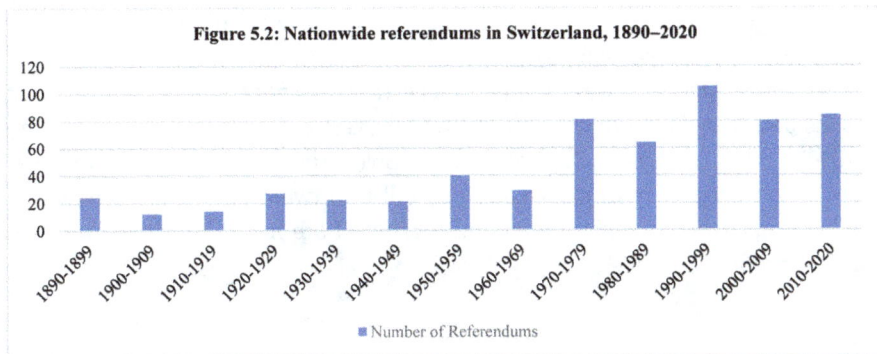

Figure 5.2: Nationwide referendums in Switzerland, 1890–2020

Figure 5.2: Nationwide referendums in Switzerland, 1890 – 2020.
Source: Bundeskanzlei.ch 2021.

We shall shortly look at the statistical factors associated with the occurrence of referendums, but overall it seems that the propensity to hold them increased as more and more countries became democratic or felt the need to appear to heed the 'will of the people.' This also explains the explosion in the number of referendums after the fall of the Berlin Wall. Countries that had hitherto held very few referendums (such as the communist countries) felt a need to show their democratic credentials and to be responsive to the people after the fall of the dictatorships. The referendums held in the 1990s were testament to this.

There is nothing that suggests that referendums have been systematically used (or abused) by populist politicians. To be sure, the likes of Erdoğan in Turkey and Orbán in Hungary have held referendums. But the countries that have held the highest number of votes have been small countries without notorious strongmen. The countries that held more than ten referendums in the period 2000–2020 were Italy (25), Slovenia (18), Ireland (17), Taiwan (15), and Slovakia (12). Only one semi-authoritarian regime has held more than five referendums, namely Venezuela (6).

Thus, the charge that referendums are held by dictators, as alleged by Clement Atlee, is not supported by evidence.

So, what are the more specific factors correlated with the use of referendums? Above all, when are they actually held?

Why Are Referendums Held?

Political scientists have been skeptical regarding the possibilities of finding general patterns of referendum use. To wit, Arend Lijphart concluded that "the question of why referendums occur more frequently in some countries than in others cannot be answered satisfactorily."[26]

One of the problems with referendums is that they are called for a number of reasons and that they differ significantly. However, generally most countries are relatively alike. Thus, with the exception of Switzerland and a handful of other countries, referendums in most countries fall into two categories: referendums that are constitutionally mandated and those that are held to resolve an urgent political problem.[27]

---

26 Lijphart, A. (1984) *Democracies: Patterns of Majoritarian and Consensus Government in Twenty-one Countries*, vol. 203. New Haven: Yale University Press, p. 197.
27 In Switzerland 50,000 citizens can demand a referendum on any bill before it becomes law if they can gather signatures demanding this within 100 days of the third reading of the bill. See: Serdült, Uwe (2014) 'Referendums in Switzerland.' In Matt Qvortrup (ed.) *Referendums around the World*. Basingstoke: Palgrave, pp. 65–121, esp. p. 72. Similar provisions exist in some US states. In Italy 500,000 citizens can demand a referendum requesting a repeal of any law on

In the case of the former, governments are occasionally forced to submit issues to the voters due to constitutional requirements. The Republic of Ireland is a prime example of this. Since the High Court's decision in *Crotty v An Taoiseach* in 1987, it has been the established legal position that all constitutional changes must be submitted to the voters.

That Dicey's ideal of a constitutional safeguard has had some impact is evident from the historical record. For example, in the period 1945–1989, 29 out of the 85 referendums held in Europe (with the exception of Switzerland) were constitutional votes. That countries were bound by the requirement that constitutional changes must be submitted and approved by the voters shows that the mechanism has worked as a brake on change.

Apart from legal necessity, referendums are generally held for less than idealistic reasons. Not, mind you, because politicians are devious and scheming (though they can be that too!) but because referendums provide a practical solution to an immediate problem. "Referendums are held infrequently, usually only when the governments think that they provide a useful ad hoc solution to a particular constitutional or political problem or to set the seal of legitimacy on a change of regime."[28] And David Butler and Austin Ranney again, this time in their seminal *Referendums Around the World:* "Universal judgements about their nature and impact must, for the most part, be avoided. ... There are no universal rules."[29]

Well, you are not likely to find them unless you look for them. And the problem with these earlier studies was that they failed to look at general statistical trends and tendencies, and based their conclusions on a small number of comparisons.

Political scientists have increasingly moved away from behavioral models and have focused on the effect of political institutions such as federalism, proportional representation, second chambers, and presidential systems (and their opposites).[30]

---

the statute book. See Uleri, P. V. (1996) 'Italy: referendums and initiatives from the origins to the crisis of a democratic regime.' In M. Gallagher and P. V. Uleri (eds.) *The Referendum Experience in Europe.* Basingstoke: Macmillan, pp. 106–126.

28 Butler, D. and Ranney, A. (1978) 'Summing up.' In David Butler and Austin Ranney (eds.) *Referendums: A Comparative Study in Practice and Theory.* Washington, DC: American Enterprise Institute, p. 221.

29 Butler, David and Ranney, Austin (1994) 'Conclusion.' In David Butler and Austin Ranney (eds.) *Referendums Around the World: The Growing Use of Direct Democracy.* London: Macmillan, pp. 258–263, at p. 258.

30 See e. g.: Persson, Torsten (2002) 'Do political institutions shape economic policy?' *Econometrica* 70(3): 883–905.

Why might some of these institutions have an impact on the number of referendums held? We can begin by looking at the case of federalism.

In a federal system, it is necessary to keep a delicate balance between individual states. As a result of this, politicians at the central level have to do their utmost not to appear to override the concerns of the units of the federation.[31] This might explain why Switzerland, the perennial exception to the rule, is the only federal state to use referendums on this scale.

Referendums are rare in federations like Mexico and Canada. None has been held at the central level in Germany and the USA. Even Australia, that used to have a relatively high number of referendums, has not held a single one in the 21st century, although a nationwide vote was held in 2017.[32]

Yet, as the figures below show, this hypothesis (that referendums are common in federal states) is not supported by the facts. Indeed, the occurrence of referendums is significantly lower in states with this constitutional arrangement.

What about electoral systems? Is there a reason why referendums are more likely to be held in countries with, for example, majoritarian electoral systems? It would seem so. Referendums can be divisive. For this reason, we would expect the countries with majoritarian systems to have more of them. The reason for this, so might we speculate, is that majoritarian systems tend to be two-party duopolies that follow Downs Voter Theorem.

In plain English, in order to attract the 'median voter' the two parties become ideologically indistinguishable.[33] As a result of this, they submit issues that are 'too hot to handle' to the voters.[34] Does this explanation hold true? As the figures in Table 5.1 show, it largely does. The more proportional the electoral system, the less likely it is that it has referendums. Conversely, there is nothing to suggest that constitutional provisions for popular votes have any effect on the number held.

31 On this see: Mendez, F., Mendez, M., and Triga, V. (2014) *Referendums and the European Union: A Comparative Inquiry.* Cambridge: Cambridge University Press, pp. 157 ff.

32 The *Australian Marriage Law Postal Survey* was not a referendum but in effect a large-scale consultation. See: Hegarty, B., Marshall, D., Rasmussen, M. L., Aggleton, P., and Cover, R. (2018) 'Heterosexuality and race in the Australian same-sex marriage postal survey.' *Australian Feminist Studies* 33(97): 400–416.

33 Downs, A. (1957) *An Economic Theory of Democracy.* New York: Harper & Row.

34 Matsusaka, J. (1992) 'The economics of direct legislation.' *Quarterly Journal of Economics* 107(2): 541–571, at 543.

Table 5.1: Institutional Factors and the Occurrence of Referendums
(Standard Errors in Brackets).

Variable	B
Ideology (Right)	.323**
	(.106)
Federalism Dummy	−6.356*
	(3.347)
Provisions for Referendums	−1.640
	(2.016)
Proportional Representation	−3.121*
	(1.527)
Parliamentary System Dummy	−.131
	(2.552)
Presidential	−1.348
	(2.259)
Senate Index	1.389
	(1.467)
Constant	−8.200
	(5.538)

Dependent Variable: Total number of Referendums 2010 – 2018, N: 257
R-Squared: .82*** <p,0.01, **p<0.05, *p< 0.1

Another curious factor is that referendums tend to be held in nations that are ideologically more conservative. If we use the data for the Manifesto Project,[35] which used content analysis to code political parties' manifestos on a scale from 0 – 100, with a higher score meaning that the country's political parties are to the right, we find a statistically significant tendency that countries where the bourgeois parties are strong are more likely to hold referendums. In fact, this correlation is very strong; R=.80, statistically significant at the 0.01 level (2-tailed), N: 174. Perhaps this is not coincidental.

Political parties on the left have always had an uneasy relationship with referendums. In the United Kingdom, the Fabian Society (a group within the Labour Party) published a pamphlet entitled 'The Case Against the Referendum.'[36] By

---

35 For a general introduction to the Manifesto Project see: https://manifesto-project.wzb.eu/down/data/2019b/codebooks/release_notes_MPDS2019b.pdf.
36 Sharp, Clifford (1911) *The Case Against the Referendum*, Fabian Tract, No. 155. London: The Fabian Society.

contrast, on the other side of politics, the referendum was "mooted repeatedly throughout the [20th] century ... by conservatives who saw it as a brake on change."[37]

However, it should be noted that the referendums studied here were held in the period 2010 – 2020, during which time most governments were of the center-right in democratic societies. The data thus might overestimate this tendency towards a greater use of referendums in conservative countries, especially if we bear in mind that most referendums are initiated by the government in office.

This finding seems to be supported by quantitative studies by Laurence Morel.[38] She found three different types of referendums. These are as follows:

– *Referendums as Mechanisms for Managing Disagreement:* These are held to keep a party or a coalition together. When parties are split down the middle on an issue, they can 'agree to disagree' by holding a referendum. This is what happened in 1975 when the UK Labour Party was split over the EU. This use of the referendum was also the main reason the Conservative–Liberal coalition government held a vote on electoral reform.

– *Referendums as Negotiating Tactic:* Referendums can also, though more rarely, be used as part of a bargaining or negotiating process. This is arguably why the Spanish government held a referendum on the European Constitution in 2005. By informing the negotiating partners that the fate of the treaty would depend on the consent of the Spanish voters, the Madrid government was able to get concessions for fear that the voters in Spain would reject the whole treaty. It was arguably also the logic behind the referendum held in Greece in early July 2015, though it is debatable whether the Syriza government was successful in using the referendum to get a better deal.

– *The Plebiscitary Referendum:* Political leaders can bypass a legislature by calling a referendum. In the 1960s the French president Charles de Gaulle submitted the issue of Algerian independence to the voters when he couldn't win endorsement for his policy in the National Assembly. He used the same tactic in 1969, when he organized a referendum on regional government and reform of the Senate. But this failed and de Gaulle resigned. In addition, the referendum has been used as a mechanism to mobilize supporters, some-

37 Butler, David (1978) 'United Kingdom.' In David Butler and Austin Ranney (eds.) *Referendums: A Comparative Study of Practice and Theory.* Washington. DC: American Enterprise Institute, pp. 211–219, at p. 211.
38 Morel, L. (2007) 'The rise of "politically obligatory" referendums: the 2005 French referendum in comparative perspective.' *West European Politics* 30(5): 1041–1067.

thing which in large measure explains the rise of the number of referendums in Slovakia. As two country specialists have written, "in Slovakia ...political parties use the employment of this tool solely for their own purposes. ... either as a way to mobilize their own supporters for upcoming national elections or to harm their opponents. Hence, a referendum in Slovakia serves as a tool for expanding the power of political parties rather than as a way of increasing the public engagement of citizens in the democratic system".[39]

That referendums are often held for these practical reasons does not mean that they are part of a sneaky plot and political calculation. Granted, politicians normally follow what we might call the 'logic of consequentiality';[40] they consider what is in their rational self-interest and act accordingly. But there are also examples of referendums which are held out of a political sense of appropriateness. For example, there was nothing that forced the British government to hold a referendum on the Good Friday Agreement in 1998.[41]

So, if referendums are not held for idealistic reasons, might we dismiss their use? And might they be opportunistic instruments that result in suboptimal public policies?

The Policy Effects of Referendums

It is an open question if referendums have any effects on public policy.[42] Given the relative paucity of them, it has been argued that it is difficult to test their effects with empirical accuracy.[43] The annual number is simply, so it might be argued, too small.

This might have been true before the 1970s. It is no longer so. Given the increase in the number of referendums in recent decades, we are now able to use statistical methods to determine the effect of their use.[44]

---

39 Nemčok, M. and Spáč, P. (2019) 'Referendum as a party tool: the case of Slovakia.' *East European Politics and Societies* 33(3): 755–777.

40 March, J. G. and Olsen, J. P. (2010) *Rediscovering Institutions.* New York: Simon and Schuster.

41 Atkinson, L., Blick, A., and Qvortrup, M. (2020) *The Referendum in Britain: A History.* Oxford: Oxford University Press, p. 178.

42 Though see: Freitag, M. and Vatter, A. (2006) 'Initiatives, referendums, and the tax state.' *Journal of European Public Policy* 13(1): 89–112.

43 This was the position taken by Ranney, A. and Butler, D. (eds.) (1978) *Referendums: A Comparative Study of Practice and Theory.* Washington, DC: American Enterprise Institute.

44 Indeed, there have already been single-country studies of the effect of initiatives. See Gerber, E. R. and Phillips, J. H. (2005) 'Evaluating the effects of direct democracy on public policy: Cal-

Popular policy is about many things, but economic policy is arguably the most important. Without sound macro-economic performance nothing much can be achieved.

So, what is the relationship between referendums and economic success? This is, admittedly, difficult to measure, but one way of gauging the effect of referendums is to look at the total number of votes held in a decade and then contrast and correlate that figure with social and economic indicators.

If we look at the total number of referendums held since the beginning of 2010, we get a total of 257. Of these, Switzerland, the perennial *sui generis*, accounted for 73. Including Switzerland, the average number of referendums per country was 2.9 per decade.

So, does this correlate with policy developments? Can we detect an effect of referendums? Overall, as shown in Figure 5.3 there is a positive correlation between the number of referendums and GDP per capita, with R=.433** (statistically significant at the 0.01 level 2-tailed, N= 172). Though, as shown in Figure 5.4 the band within which these findings hold is relatively wide, so the relationship is not a simple and straightforward one. Not unexpectedly there are other factors and outliers, but the overall trend is there, more direct democracy is correlated with greater prosperity.

Of course, there are other institutional factors that might conceivably play a role. For example, presidentialism and semi-presidentialism might be conducive to better economic performance. Further, it has often been argued that Senates (or second chambers) result in moderation and hence better thought-through policies.[45] And federal constitutions are believed to create competition that leads to better economic outcomes.[46]

On the other hand, it is conceivable – though democrats do not want to admit it – that one-party states (like China or Vietnam), or even traditional monarchies (like Saudi Arabia and Brunei), do better. Indeed, it is possible that having a democracy is not good for economic well-being.

Actually, democrats need not worry.

When we added the Freedom House score for the country in question and correlated it with GDP per capita, the result was encouraging – except for Xi Jinp-

---

ifornia's urban growth boundaries.' *American Politics Research* 33(2): 310 – 330, and, more generally, Matsusaka, J. G. (2020) *Let the People Rule*. Princeton: Princeton University Press.

45 Mughan, A. and Patterson, S. C. (1999) 'Senates: a comparative perspective.' In S. C. Patterson and A. Mughan (eds.) *Senates: Bicameralism in the Contemporary World*. Columbus: Ohio State University Press, pp. 33 – 49.

46 Inman, R. P. and Rubinfeld, D. L. (1997) 'Rethinking federalism.' *Journal of Economic Perspectives* 11(4): 43 – 64.

Simple Scatter with Fit Line of GDPCap by TotalRef

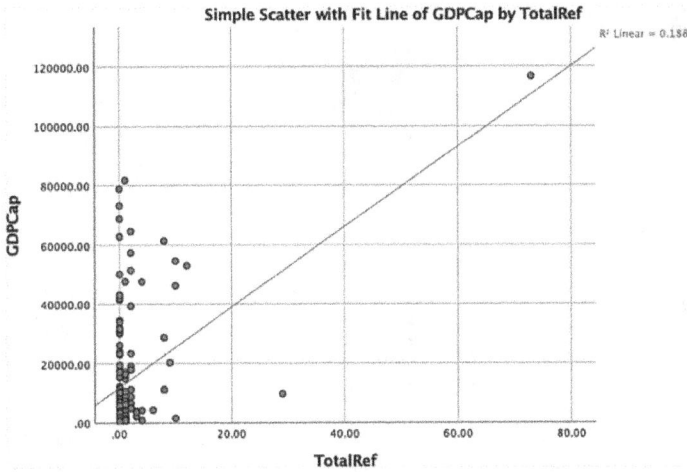

Figure 5.3: Total Number of Referendums (Own figures and World Bank Data on GDP per Capita).

ing and Vladimir Putin. For every notch up the 100-point Freedom House scale, the average citizen gains nearly US $300. On mere utilitarian grounds, democracy works.

Overall, we find that the most statistically significant correlation with a strong economy is having a democracy. This is by a considerable distance the best predictor of wealth. The self-assured claims regarding the supposed benefits of authoritarianism – as espoused by the likes of the Chinese Communist Party – are simply not supported by statistical evidence. There were no data that suggest that authoritarianism is good for the economy.

But what about other factors, such as presidentialism, parliamentarism, semi-presidentialism, and monarchies, and, finally, the number of referendums held in the past ten years? The findings corroborate the earlier pattern that referendums are positively associated with a high average GDP per capita. Federalism, according to political theorists such as Montesquieu, is an ideal form of government, one that, in the view of the French sage, has "all the internal advantages of republican government and the external force of monarchy."[47]

---

47 Montesquieu, Charles (1989) *The Spirit of the Laws.* Cambridge. Cambridge University Press, p. 131.

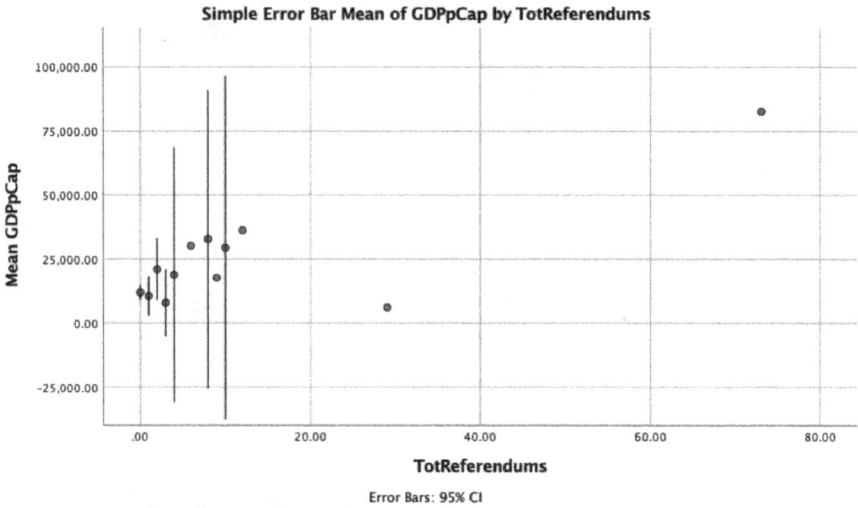

Figure 5.4: Error Bars: Total Referendums and Mean GDP Per Capita (Own figures and World Bank Data).

This is based on the same reasoning that modern economists believe that federal constitutions are efficient. They create competition, which in turn leads to better economic outcomes.[48]

Except in the past ten years, this factor has been statistically absent. Federal states come in many shapes and sizes, and there are poor ones (e. g. Nigeria and Ethiopia) as well as rich ones (Canada, USA, and Germany, for example). But having this particular system is not in itself a good predictor of a high GDP per capita.

The same is true for the dummy variable for Senates. The proposition that second chambers are good for the economy is not supported statistically. But at least it is not directly negative. Other institutional factors are statistically harmful to the economy.

Thus, having a presidential system (as in the United States and Brazil), where the president is independent of Congress, has, statistically speaking, a negative effect on the economy. The same is true for a semi-presidential system (like the French model with both a prime minister and a president), which, statistically, is also directly detrimental to prosperity, as shown in Table 5.2.

---

48 Inman and Rubinfeld, 'Rethinking federalism.'

Table 5.2: Institutional Factors and GDP per Capita (Standard Errors in Brackets).

Variable	B
Presidential	−7570.8* (4536.6)
Parliamentarism	815.391 (4988.4)
Semi-presidentialism	−10348.2** 5230.329
Federalism	6837.9) (4574.1)
Senate Dummy	523.664 (2651.8)
Total Number of Referendums 2010–2018	884.1** (427)
Democracy	284.041*** (.000)
Constant	−1124.601 (5058.3)

Dependent Variable: GDP per Capita R-Squared: .33; N:173 *** significant at p<0.001, ** significant at p<0.05, * significant at p<0.1.

In contrast to these absent or negative effects, the number of referendums has positive effects. Quantitatively speaking, there is a significant relationship between the number of votes and average wealth. In purely numerical terms, for every referendum held, citizens become US \$884 richer. This is an important finding, and one that corroborates earlier single-country studies showing that "allowing the general public to participate in law-making often seems to improve the performance of government."[49]

49 Matsusaka, J. G. (2005) 'Direct democracy works.' *Journal of Economic Perspectives* 19(2): 185–206, at 185.

Table 5.3: Institutional Factors and Life Expectancy (Standard Errors in Brackets).

Variable	B
Presidential**	−4.740**
	(1.672)
Parliamentarism	−2.148
	(1.838)
Semi-presidentialism**	−5.886
	(1.928)
Federalism	.586
	(1.686)
Senate Dummy	.183
	(.977)
Total Number of Referendums 2010–2018	.367**
	(.158)
Democracy	.130***
	(.021)
Constant	67.368***
	(1.864)

Dependent Variable: Life Expectancy, R-Squared: .33; N:173 *** significant at p<0.001, ** significant at p<0.05, * significant at p<0.1.

Public politics is not just about money, of course. You also want to live a long life. Referendums, statistically, will help you. Statistically speaking, for every referendum held, you live a few months longer. By contrast, as the data in Table 5.3 shows, those living have a life expectancy that is five years shorter than the average. That presidential and semi-presidential systems are directly harmful to your life expectancy might have many explanations – above all, gridlock and the inability to get things done in these systems. These correlations, of course, do not prove causation, and in many cases it is difficult to see what the links could be.

Not everything can be measured by statistics, but quantitative data are a good place to start. Overall, there are many positive effects of having referendums. The doomsayers who hold that people are too stupid to vote rationally are not vindicated. If anything, the opposite is true. Indeed, there are far better arguments against presidential systems than against systems that allow a modicum of direct democracy. Though, as we shall see in the next chapter, not all issues can be resolved through referendums.

Conclusion

Referendums can be a democratic safety-valve, and a last resort for those who want to block changes enacted by governments that are out of sync with the population. In 2021, for example, a majority of the voters in Slovenia. They were against the so-called Water Law, which would have allowed construction of flats in coastal areas, which, they claimed, would have detrimental environmental effects[50]. The government tried to delay the vote, but to no avail. The vote was held, and 86 percent voted against the law, which was thereby invalidated. This was a rare case of a citizen-initiated referendum that resulted in a binding decision. But this is a rare example, this is not how most successful referendums are held.

So, why are referendums held? What are their consequences? And are they a genuinely positive mechanism of complementary democracy?

To answer the first question first, referendums are not generally held for idealistic reasons. Qualitative studies suggest that they are held for tactical and party-political reasons. But overall, referendums tend to be held in countries with majoritarian electoral systems (possibly because homogeneous parties need to distinguish themselves in a Downsian two-party system that is often a result of first-past-the-post electoral systems).

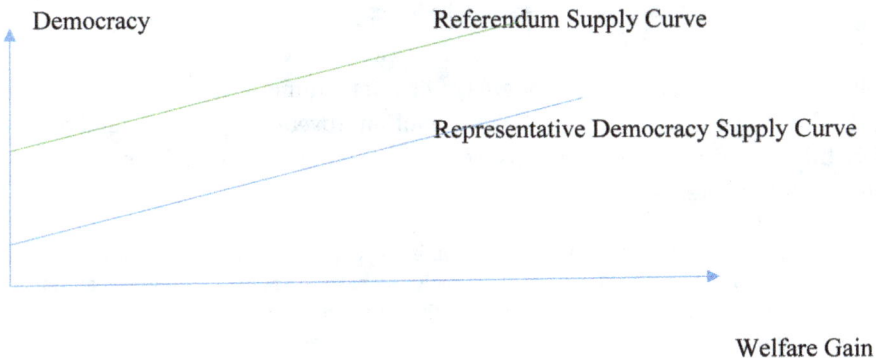

Figure 5.5: Complementary Democracy: Supply and Legitimacy.

This chapter has found evidence that people who live in countries that are more democratic, all other things being equal, are better governed, slightly richer, and

---

50 https://sudd.ch/event.php?lang=fr&id=si012021, Accessed 18th May, 2022.

have fewer social ills. Figure 5.5 above summarizes this. The higher the supply of democracy, the greater the level of welfare. For every notch up the Freedom House scale, you earn another $300. But when we add referendums to the mix, we get even higher levels of democracy and concomitantly welfare gains. In straight numbers, just over $800 for every additional referendum held.

Of course, direct legislation by the people is not a cure-all. There are concerns about populism and polarization that cannot be ignored. But most of the countries that have held a high number of referendums in past decades have not been the ones that have experienced democratic back-sliding or have regressed into semi-authoritarianism. There have, of course, been examples of referendums that led to polarization and debates that were a far cry from the ideal of deliberative democracy (the British Brexit referendum is often cited). But there have also been examples of referendums that have been preceded by deliberative discussions. The Irish referendums on marriage equality in 2015, and on, respectively, abortion and blasphemy, were all held after a representative sample of voters had deliberated in a citizens' jury. The evidence from this suggests that such a process can remedy some of the negative effects referendums can have in a society with deep divisions and 'culture wars':

> The establishment of assemblies in advance of the referendum has an impact on the deliberative nature of the referendum in the wider community. In both referendums in [2018], there [was] a positive and statistically significant effect on the probability of voting Yes by those who felt they fully understood the issues.[51]

Given the overall positive policy effects of referendums, tweaking them in line with the Irish experience might be the small improvement that is needed to perfect this tool. If that is so, perhaps we can still entertain the high hopes for the referendum expressed by Dicey:

> The referendum is, or may be, an education in the application of men's understandings to the weightiest of political concerns – namely the passing of laws – such as is absolutely unobtainable by voters who are trained to think that their role or duty as citizens consists in supporting the conservative or radical party, and their blind acceptance of every proposed enactment which happens to form part of the party platform.[52]

---

51 Jane Suiter quoted in Renwick, A. and Palese, M. (2019) *Doing Democracy Better: How Can Information and Discourse in Election and Referendum Campaigns in the UK be Improved?* London: Constitution Unit, p. 196.
52 Dicey, A. V. (1890) 'Ought the referendum to be introduced into England?' *Contemporary Review* 57: pp. 489–511, at p. 508.

Fernando Mendez and Mario Mendez
Agenda Initiatives in Comparative Context

Introduction

The agenda initiative (AI) is a bottom-up democratic instrument that allows a defined number of individuals to submit a request to (ordinarily) the legislature for
legislative action following a signature-gathering exercise. It offers a channel for
direct citizen participation and potentially increased policy responsiveness to the
citizenry. Agenda initiatives originally emerged in several European constitutions
in the interwar period and proliferated very slowly until the late 1980s, by which
point the instrument had been adopted in primarily European and Latin American countries as well as at the transnational level of the European Union (EU).

Despite AIs existing for over a century and having diffused rapidly in recent
decades, the instrument continues to remain surprisingly little known and little
studied, especially from a comparative perspective. Ultimately, we still know little about AIs, whether that be the specific drivers for their emergence and diffusion, how their design varies across different constitutional systems, or their actual usage and effects within political systems. This chapter contributes to
redressing the scholarly neglect from a comparative perspective of these valuable tools of 'complementary democracy.'

We begin in a first section by exploring the origins and diffusion of these instruments while touching on some of the academic debate to which they have
given rise, as well as some shortcomings apparent in the extant literature. A second section maps AIs from a comparative perspective across the 27 Member
States of the EU. A third section takes a different approach and provides three
brief case studies of AIs in two EU countries and at the EU level with a view
to drilling down into how these tools of complementary democracy were born,
designed, and work in specific systems. A final section offers brief concluding
remarks.

Origins, Features, and Diffusion of the Agenda Initiative

The AI at the nation state level emerged in the Austrian Constitution of 1920. Article 41 expressly provided for electorate-initiated legislative proposals, requiring
either 200,000 eligible voters or half the eligible voters in three federal states to

https://doi.org/10.1515/9783110747331-006

put forth the legislative proposal. It has been asserted to be the brainchild of the distinguished jurist Hans Kelsen,[1] who played a central role in drafting the Austrian Constitution and wrote contemporaneously, albeit very briefly, about the instrument.[2]

The Austrian instrument is to be distinguished from its forerunner in the Weimar Constitution of the preceding year (1919). This Constitution provided that 10 percent of the electorate could seek the passage of a law to be submitted to a referendum, but if the law were adopted unamended, no referendum would be needed. Thus, the Weimar Constitution provided a route for a portion of the electorate to put a proposal on the legislative agenda that could expressly culminate in legislation without the necessity for approval in a referendum. This can, however, clearly be differentiated from the Austrian instrument under which there is simply no role for a referendum. And it is relatively minor variations on the Austrian AI, with no place for the referendum, that have spread, and rapidly so, in recent decades.

The AI was included in at least three more constitutions, all short lived, of the interwar period. First, in the 1921 Constitution of Georgia; however, Georgia was occupied by Russia that same year and its Constitution was suspended.[3] Second, in the 1922 Constitution of Lithuania, though following a 1926 coup it was not included in the Constitution of 1928. Third, the Spanish Constitution of 1931, inspired by the earlier Austrian AI, empowered a minimum of 15 percent of the electorate in order to submit legislative proposals. However, the required implementing law was never passed, and the Spanish Civil War began in 1936 culminating in a long-lasting military dictatorship. The instrument then made its first appearance in a Latin American constitution, being included in the 1940 Cuban Constitution, albeit never going into effect. A coup then took place in 1952. The instrument was next included in the 1947 Italian Constitution and the 1961 Constitution of Venezuela. The 1978 constitutions of Ecuador and Spain also included the AI, the latter in effect reinstating the AI provision of its 1931 Constitution. In sum, by the mid-1980s, the AI which had first emerged over sixty years earlier in Austria had still only been included in the constitutional texts of fewer than ten states: primarily in Europe, with a few Latin American

---

1 See e.g.: Biglino Campos, P. (1987) 'La iniciativa legislativa popular en el ordenamiento jurídico estatal.' *Revista Española de Derecho Constitucional* 19: 75–130; Ferro, M. S. (2007) 'Popular legislative initiative in the EU: alea iacta est.' *Yearbook of European Law* 26, 355.
2 Kelsen, H. (2013) *The Essence and Value of Democracy.* New York: Rowman & Littlefield.
3 Papuashvili, G. (2012) 'The 1921 Constitution of the Democratic Republic of Georgia: looking back after ninety years.' *European Public Law* 18(2): 323–350.

examples, and in the majority of which the instrument was either never given effect or no longer existed.

Diffusion however took place rapidly in the decade between 1988 and 1997, for the AI was included in over 20 constitutional texts, two of which were reinstating an instrument provided for in a prior constitution.[4] This rapid diffusion can largely be explained by democratization in Latin America and the transition from communism to democratic regimes in Central and Eastern Europe. However, the AI was now also included in both an African and Asian constitutional text for the first time, namely Burkina Faso (1991) and Thailand (1997). Cape Verde followed suit in 1999, and since the turn of the century the AI has been included in over 15 additional constitutional systems, primarily in constitutional texts, including at the transnational level of the EU (2009).[5] This incorporation at EU level has itself been an important spur for its diffusion in – and potentially beyond – other EU states.

The AI that was born over a century ago via its inclusion in the seminal Austrian Constitution now exists in over 40 national constitutional texts – as well as at the EU-wide level – in primarily European and Latin American countries. And yet, despite this enticing context for comparative scholarship, there has been a scarcity of it in relation to this mechanism of 'complementary democracy.' There are also notable shortcomings apparent in existing literature. For example, we have identified inconsistencies, omissions, and mistakes relating to the diffusion of the instrument. To give only some examples from the literature: the emergence of the instrument in Hungary has been attributed to its 1949 Constitution,[6] when it was provided for some 50 years later; similarly with the 1976 Portuguese Constitution,[7] when it was actually provided for via a constitutional amendment 21 years later; asserting that the Netherlands does not have the instrument,[8]

---

4 Lithuania (1992) and Georgia (1995). Other examples include: Albania (1991); Andorra (1993); Argentina (1994); Belarus (1994); Brazil (1988); Burkina Faso (1991); Colombia (1991); Hungary (1989); Kyrgystan (1993); Macedonia (1991); Nicaragua (1995); Paraguay (1992); Peru (1993); Poland (1997); Portugal (1997); Romania (1991); Slovenia (1991); Thailand (1997); Yugoslavia (1992).
5 Angola (2010); Azerbaijan (2002); Bolivia (2002); Bulgaria (2009); Costa Rica (2002); Denmark (2017); Dominican Republic (2010); Estonia (2014); Finland (2012); Greece (2019); Latvia (2012); Mexico (2012); Montenegro (2007); Morocco (2011); Netherlands (2006).
6 Krunke, H. and Dalsgaard, J. C. (2016) 'Towards increased citizen participation in Europe: impact of current developments on political decision making and democracy.' *International Journal of Open Governments* 5: 135–158.
7 Suárez Antón, O. (2019) *Iniciativa Legislativa Popular: Análisis de la iniciativa de agenda en América Latina y la Unión Europea*. Valencia: Tirant lo Blanch.
8 Krunke and Dalsgaard, 'Towards increased citizen participation in Europe.'

when it had long existed; tracing diffusion and referencing Lithuania as 1928,[9] when it was introduced in 1922 and actually abolished in 1928; inaccurately referencing its existence in a range of African countries;[10] providing definitions of an AI that excludes citizen-initiated referendums while giving national examples that in some cases are actually instruments for citizen-initiated referendums;[11] and providing comparative analysis of usage over time while using 'active years' that reflects the year the AI was included in constitutional text,[12] rather than when it actually became active via legislative implementation. In short, we get an inaccurate picture of diffusion, where the instrument exists, and usage, from existing literature.

Some of the aforementioned shortcomings may be linked to the considerable terminological variation relating to the instrument, including in constitutional and legal texts. While the nomenclature of AI has been used in the manner we propose,[13] a non-exhaustive list of other labels used either essentially synonymously with our earlier definition of an AI, or encapsulating that and instruments leading to referendums, includes: "citizens agenda initiatives";[14] "citizens initiatives";[15] "citizens legislative initiatives";[16] "indirect popular initiatives";[17] "legislative initiatives";[18] "popular initiatives";[19] "popular motions";[20] and even "petitions."[21]

9 Ferro, 'Popular legislative initiative.'

10 IDEA (2008). Of the ten African countries listed, we can only confirm it being constitutionally provided for in Burkina Faso and Cape Verde.

11 Ferro, 'Popular legislative initiative'; IDEA 2008.

12 Krunke and Dalsgaard, 'Towards increased citizen participation in Europe.'

13 Schiller, T. and Setälä, M. (2012) 'Introduction.' In M. Setälä and T. Schiller (eds.) *Citizens' Initiatives in Europe*. Basingstoke: Palgrave.

14 Moeckli, D. (2021) 'Introduction to the legal limits of direct democracy.' In D. Moeckli et al. (eds.) *The Legal Limits of Direct Democracy*. Cheltenham: Edward Elgar.

15 Krunke and Dalsgaard, 'Towards increased citizen participation in Europe.' IDEA (2008) uses this label exclusively to refer to citizen-initiated referendums.

16 The Bolivian Constitution since 2002.

17 Fatin-Rouge Stefanini, M. and Dumont, H. (2019) 'L'initiative citoyenne européenne à la lumière du droit constitutionnel comparé.' In E. Dubout et al. (eds.) *L'Initiative Citoyenne Européenne*. Brussels: Bruylant.

18 Qvortrup, M. (2012) 'The legislative initiative: a comparative analysis of the domestic experiences in EU countries.' In M. Dougan et al. (eds.) *Empowerment and Disempowerment of the European Citizen*. Oxford: Hart.

19 Spanish Constitution (1931/1978), Brazilian Constitution (1988). Terminology others reject absent a referendum, e.g. Auer, A. (2005) 'European Citizens' Initiative.' *EUConst*, 1: 79.

20 Auer, 'European Citizens' Initiative.'

Crucially, these labels are being used in different ways to encapsulate different instruments. Some authors have used different labels in the same contribution,[22] as have different authors within the same volume.[23] This terminological variation, and even disagreement, sows confusion, helps account for some of the discrepancies in existing literature, and impedes mapping the diffusion of the instrument. Furthermore, inconsistencies and omissions tend to become replicated over time.[24]

Another dimension of conceptual and terminological confusion relates to what type of instrument the AI actually is. For many it is "direct democracy,"[25] others insist it is not;[26] some call it a form of "semi-direct democracy,"[27] some "participatory democracy,"[28] and for others it is "participatory direct democracy."[29] Again, this can sow further confusion and impede comparative analysis. Moreover, it can result in the instrument being associated with criticism traditionally directed at referendums (e.g. that it can be demagogic, that it bypasses representative democracy, and the like) that has limited applicability to the AI where legislative outcomes depend on the legislature. This can discourage adoption of the instrument. This conceptual and terminological confusion need not be resolved for the purposes of this chapter. Suffice to note we do consider the AI a form of direct democracy, and it clearly falls within the definition of a mechanism of 'complementary democracy' provided by the editors of this volume.

Another notable shortcoming apparent in the limited comparative literature is non-assessment of the actual usage of the AI. Some seek to map the properties of the instrument and its inclusion in constitutional text without mentioning

---

21 Suksi, M. (1993) *Bringing in the People*. Leiden: Martinus Nijhoff. Burkina Faso Constitution (1991).
22 Krunke and Dalsgaard, 'Towards increased citizen participation in Europe,' alternate between "citizens' initiative" and "popular initiative."
23 See case studies in Setälä, M. and Schiller, T. (eds.) *Citizens' Initiatives in Europe*. Basingstoke: Palgrave.
24 For an example in a different context, see Mendez, F. and Germann, M. (2018) 'Contested sovereignty: mapping referendums on sovereignty over time and space.' *British Journal of Political Science* 48: 141.
25 See e.g.: Moeckli, D. et al. (eds.) (2021) *The Legal Limits of Direct Democracy*. Cheltenham: Edward Elgar; Krunke and Dalsgaard, 'Towards increased citizen participation in Europe.'
26 Biglino Campos, 'La iniciativa legislativa.'
27 Qvortrup, 'The legislative initiative.'
28 Biglino Campos, 'La iniciativa legislativa.'
29 Cuesta-López, V. (2008) *Participación Directa e Iniciativa Legislativa del Ciudadano en Democracia Constitucional*. Madrid: Thomson.

whether it has been implemented, much less engage with the use of the AI in the practice.[30] When practice has been engaged with, there has also been a tendency to view legislative action as a proxy for the success of the instrument, which risks promoting an impoverished account of its value.[31] Ultimately, a more nuanced and comparatively sensitive approach encourages a richer conception of AIs' value to emerge not least as mechanisms that can clearly promote deliberative listening, including when legislative outcomes are not forthcoming.

Mapping the Agenda Initiative across the EU-27

For the purposes of mapping the AI across the EU, we draw on the LIDD dataset.[32] Our objective is two-fold: first, to situate the AI against the backdrop of other direct democratic (DD) instruments; and, second, to map some basic features of how the AI is 'regulated.' By 'regulated,' we are mostly interested in the limitations that could constrain the usage of the AI. These regulatory constraints take two main forms: a set of formal limits and substantive limits on the one hand, and the criteria regulating the signature-gathering process on the other.

The Agenda Initiative and Other Instruments of Direct Democracy

The LIDD typology distinguishes between seven types of DD instruments, of which the AI is one. For the purposes of simplifying the analysis, we will combine the LIDD categories into three basic types of DD instruments:

1. *Top-down instruments:* mainly refers to the legislature-initiated and the executive-initiated referendum.
2. *Bottom-up instruments:* refers to citizen-initiated referendums. The LIDD typology distinguishes between two main forms of citizen-initiated referen-

---

30 Examples include Ferro, 'Popular legislative initiative,' and Hernández, T. Y. G. (2019) 'La iniciativa legislativa popular en América Latina – un análisis comparado en clave axiológico-procedimental.' *Revista de Investigações Constitucionais* 6: 35.

31 Comparative works focusing on legislative outcomes include Qvortrup, 'The legislative initiative'; Suárez Antón, *Iniciativa Legislativa Popular*; Krunke and Dalsgaard, 'Towards increased citizen participation in Europe.'

32 The LIDD dataset covers the provision of direct democracy instruments among Council of Europe Member States. It is available at: http://lidd-project.org/data/.

dum: a proactive variant, where citizens can put issues to a vote, and a rejective version, where citizens can challenge particular laws. The AI is also a bottom-up form of DD, albeit mediated by representative institutions, and does not lead to a referendum.

3. *Law-initiated:* refers to the mandatory referendum. Such referendums are triggered if certain conditions specified by law (i.e. the constitution or a legislative act) are met. The law may determine the topic (e.g. transfer of sovereignty) or the type of legal act (e.g. constitutional amendment) triggering the referendum process.

Table 6.1: EU Member States without AI Provisions at National Level.

Country	Top-down	Bottom-up	Mandatory
Croatia	Yes	Yes	Yes
France	Yes	No	Yes
Germany	No	No	Yes
Hungary	Yes	Yes	No
Ireland	Yes	No	Yes
Luxembourg	Yes	Yes	No
Malta	No	Yes	Yes
Sweden	Yes	No	No

Source: LIDD database.

In mapping the EU-27, we begin with those that do not provide for the AI. Three EU Member States – Belgium, Cyprus, and the Czech Republic – are coded as not providing for DD instruments.[33]

Of the 24 EU Member States with provisions for DD, eight do not provide for the AI (see Table 6.1). Four of these eight Member States – France, Germany, Ireland, and Sweden – do not provide for any form of bottom-up DD at national level. The other four – Croatia, Hungary, Luxembourg, and Malta – provide for bottom-up DD but do not have the AI (see bottom-up column in Table 6.1). This trade-off may seem intuitive. If these four states already possess the more powerful instrument of the citizen-initiated referendum, is an AI unnecessary? This raises the question of whether such a pattern can be detected among the countries that do provide for the AI. In other words, is there an inverse relationship between providing for the AI on the one hand and providing for other bottom-up instruments on the other?

---

33 In Cyprus and the Czech Republic referendums have been held via ad-hoc legislative acts.

Table 6.2 lists the 16 EU Member States that provide for the AI. The table also includes information on whether referendums are provided for. The second column in Table 6.2, showing the provision of top-down instruments, suggests that in every country, with the exception of the Netherlands, the AI is complemented by a top-down instrument of DD. The more interesting variable is the third column of Table 6.2 that shows the existence of the bottom-up citizens' initiative. Half of the cases possess both the AI and the citizen-initiated referendum (the bottom-up instrument). It thus appears that the putative inverse relationship between the two types of instruments does not exist. However, the AI may be 'regulated' differently from the citizen-initiated referendum.

Table 6.2: Provisions for referendums among EU member states with an AI instrument.

	Country	Top-down	Bottom-up	Mandatory
1	Austria	Yes	No	Yes
2	Denmark	Yes	No	Yes
3	Estonia	Yes	No	Yes
4	Finland	Yes	No	No
5	Greece	Yes	No	No
6	Netherlands	No	No	No
7	Romania	Yes	No	Yes
8	Spain	Yes	No	Yes
9	Bulgaria	Yes	Yes	No
10	Italy	Yes	Yes	No
11	Latvia	Yes	Yes	Yes
12	Lithuania	Yes	Yes	Yes
13	Poland	Yes	Yes	No
14	Portugal	Yes	Yes	No
15	Slovakia	Yes	Yes	Yes
16	Slovenia	Yes	Yes	No

Source: LIDD database.

How the Agenda Initiative is Regulated

We outline three main aspects of how the AI is regulated. Two of the limitations are related to formal limits (e.g. wording requirements) and substantive limits (i.e. prohibited topics). Of the two limitations, the substantive one has by far the greatest impact. A third dimension, the rules governing the signature collection process, can also make the AI more (or less) onerous for citizens.

Table 6.3 provides information on how the AI is regulated. As we can see, most Member States do not impose formal constraints (9 out of 16). For those imposing formal limitations on the wording of a proposal, this can include the need to submit a draft legal text (Italy and Spain), a clarity requirement (Denmark, Netherlands, and Romania), or a unity of substance requirement (Finland). Denmark is distinctive in imposing both a clarity and unity of substance requirement.

Table 6.3: How the AI is Regulated across EU Member States.

Country	Substantive	Formal	Electorate (%)	Time (days)	Territory	ID required	E-signature
Austria	No	Yes	1.56	8	No	Yes	Yes
Bulgaria	No	No	0.001	90	No	Yes	No
Denmark	Yes	Yes	1.18	180	No	Yes	Yes
Estonia	Yes	No	0.11	No limit	No	Yes	Yes
Finland	No	Yes	1.11	180	No	Yes	Yes
Greece	Yes	No	5.02	No limit	No	No	No
Italy	No	Yes	0.11	180	No	Yes	No
Latvia	Yes	No	0.65	No limit	No	Yes	Yes
Lithuania	No	No	2.01	60	No	Yes	Yes
Netherlands	Yes	Yes	0.31	No limit	No	No	Yes
Poland	Yes	No	0.33	90	No	Yes	No
Portugal	Yes	No	0.19	No limit	No	Yes	Yes
Romania	Yes	Yes	0.55	180	Yes	Yes	Yes
Slovakia	Yes	No	0.23	No limit	No	No	No
Slovenia	No	No	0.29	60	No	Yes	No

Table 6.3: How the AI is Regulated across EU Member States. *(Continued)*

Country	Substantive	Formal	Electorate (%)	Time (days)	Territory	ID re-quired	E-signa-ture
Spain	Yes	Yes	1.36	9 (months)	No	Yes	Yes

Source: LIDD database.

Whereas most EU countries do not impose formal limitations, they do include substantive limits. Six out of 10 states expressly prohibit the use of the AI on a number of topics. The topic prohibitions vary considerably.

While Poland only prohibits topics related to finances/budget, others, such as Spain and Denmark, have an expansive list of prohibitions that include, *inter alia*, finances/budget, international law, fundamental rights/freedoms, forms of state, and territorial issues. On the other hand, Austria, Bulgaria, Finland, Italy, Lithuania, and Slovenia impose no express topic constraints.

The signature-gathering process also plays an important role, most obviously the number of signatures required. Greece's new constitutional provision for an AI has a signature requirement of over 5 percent of the electorate – a significant hurdle when compared with Bulgaria that has a largely symbolic requirement of just 50 signatures.

On the other hand, Greece does not impose a time limit for the signature-gathering process. A number of other states, such as Estonia, Netherlands, Portugal, and Slovakia, also do not impose a time limit but, unlike Greece, have dramatically lower signature thresholds.

The last three columns of Table 6.3 cover whether there is a territorial threshold, formal ID requirements, and whether e-signatures can be used.

A Subgroup Analysis of Countries with both Agenda Initiative and Bottom-Up Instruments

In this last section of the AI mapping exercise, we address how it is regulated in comparative terms, that is, in relation to the bottom-up citizen-initiated referendum. The analysis focuses on the subset of eight countries satisfying the condition of having both the AI and the bottom-up referendum, and enables us to see whether a particular country treats the two instruments similarly or differently. One would expect the bottom-up referendum to be the subject of greater regulatory constraints than its weaker cousin, the AI. Table 6.4 suggests this intuition is broadly correct.

Table 6.4: Comparison of Features (Agenda Initiative vs Bottom-Up Initiated Referendum).

Country	Formal limits	Substantive limits	Signature requirement	Time limits
Bulgaria	No → Yes	No → Yes	× 5840	90 → 90 (same)
Italy	Yes → Yes	No → Yes	Same	180 → 90 (90 days less)
Latvia	No → No	Yes → Yes	× 15	No limit → 365 days
Lithuania	No → Yes	No → No	× 6	60 → 180 (120 days more)
Poland	No → Yes	Yes → Yes	× 5	90 → No limit
Portugal	No → Yes	Yes → Yes	× 3	No limit → No limit (same)
Slovakia	No → Yes	Yes → Yes	× 34	No limit → No limit (same)
Slovenia	Yes → Yes	No → Yes	× 8	60 → 35 (25 days less)

Source: Own elaboration based on LIDD database.

Table 6.4 focuses on the same three dimensions: the formal, substantive, and sig-nature-gathering requirements. The table shows the difference between moving from one instrument, the AI, to the other instrument, the bottom-up referendum. Across the three dimensions, we can see that for every row (country) there are at least two differences. Starting with the formal limits, five out of the eight have some form of wording requirement for the bottom-up referendum compared with the AI. This is perhaps the least onerous dimension with which to comply.

In terms of substantive limits, three countries (Bulgaria, Italy, and Slovenia) have topic limitations, while the others make no distinction between the two in-struments insofar as the substantive limits dimension is concerned. The signa-ture collection process is different, and in some cases, radically different. The biggest differences relate to the signature threshold. In Bulgaria, it is increased by a factor of 5840. This seems stark, mostly because of the extremely low AI sig-nature threshold in Bulgaria. For the bottom-up referendum, the threshold is 5.8 percent of the electorate. The most dramatic differences are for Latvia and Lith-uania, where the signature threshold for the bottom-up referendum is 10 percent and 12 percent of the electorate, respectively.

Another way in which the signature collection process can be constrained is by time limits. On this dimension, the changes are more variable. For three coun-tries (Bulgaria, Portugal, and Slovakia), there is no distinction between the AI and the bottom-up referendum. For another three countries (Italy, Latvia, and Slovenia), the time limit is more constrained for the bottom-up referendum. In-deed, Latvia imposes a one-year time limit on the bottom-up referendum, unlike its AI instrument that has no time limits. Lastly, there are two cases diverging from the general trend. Lithuania allows an extra 120 days for the bottom-up referendum but with the extraordinarily high hurdle of 12 percent of the electorate. Poland is the least intuitive case insofar as the AI is concerned, as it has a time limit on the AI but not for the bottom-up referendum.

In sum, the AI is well represented as a complementary democracy device, with well over half the EU Member States possessing the instrument. Interestingly, half of the EU countries that possess the AI also provide for the more powerful bottom-up referendum. When comparing the two instruments within the same country, we find that the AI tends to be more lightly regulated than the bottom-up referendum. This is not too surprising given the latter's greater potential impact.

Case Studies: Spain, the EU, and Latvia

We have chosen three AIs to explore in more detail: two at the nation state level and the one existing transnational instrument. Spain offers in its Constitution an example of a long-existing instrument with a view to contributing to a democratic transition which is increasingly invoked but rarely results in legislative action. The Latvian AI, in stark contrast, is a new addition provided for outside the constitutional text, in a small country that already had a little-used citizens-initiated referendum, and where the AI in contrast has been invoked frequently with unparalleled legislative outcomes. The EU also has a new AI. Indeed, it provides a spur for the diffusion of the AI within and beyond the EU. Given the instrument exists in a constitutional organization of some 27 Member States, the EU variant has unsurprisingly been the subject of considerable commentary and is generating much greater awareness of this tool of complementary democracy.

Spain

The short-lived 1931 Constitution of the second Spanish republic was one of the very first constitutional texts to include the agenda initiative, inspired by the 1920 Austrian Constitution. The AI was included alongside a facultative referendum, whereby citizens could initiate a referendum on laws on which the parliament had voted. These bold steps towards citizen participation were expressly subject to an implementing law that could constrain their usage and their very entry into force. That implementing law was never passed and thus neither of these complementary democracy tools came into effect.

The Spanish Constitution of 1978, signaling a transition to democracy following nearly 40 years of the Francoist dictatorship, reintroduced a provision on the AI. However, the citizen-initiated referendum of the 1931 Constitution was not included. The 15 percent signature threshold of the 1931 Constitution was replaced with a much lower threshold, a fixed minimum of 500,000 signatures, constituting roughly 1.5 percent of the then-population. The Italian variant, which helped inspire the 1978 Spanish AI, had a fixed minimum (50,000 signatures), for a larger country, of one-tenth of the Spain model. The minimum threshold therefore demonstrates significant caution from the Spanish constituent assembly. This was combined with wide subject-matter exclusions including international affairs, taxation, and, most importantly, the expansive category of organic laws that includes matters such as fundamental rights and the electoral system.[34] In short, the constitutional text itself rendered much off-limits to the AI and an implementing law could impose further restrictions.

The implementing law emerged in 1984 and among its core provisions were: 500,000 minimum signatures coming from Spanish citizens on the electoral register, thus retaining the link to elections; a six-month signature collection period; a draft legal text with supporting reasons requirement; an organizing committee requirement; an ex-ante admissibility test by the bureau of the lower house, the decision of which can be challenged by the organizing committee before the Constitutional Court; the initiative be published; scope for expenses incurred by the organizing committee during signature collection; and a potential role for the organizing committee to explain the reasons for its initiative before the lower house. The 1984 law also expanded the prohibited issues with its preamble highlighting that historical experiences demonstrate that direct-democratic instruments can serve demagogic manipulation.[35] The restrictive choices made in the constitutional text and implementing law evidenced apprehension with the AI and suggested it would have little role in the Spanish political system.[36]

It was not until 1996 that an initiative met the signature threshold, with fewer than ten successfully managing to reach the threshold by 2005 and only one resulting in legislative action.[37] The implementing law was reformed in 2006 with a view to improving and facilitating usage, notably by allowing electronic signatures, increasing the signature collection period to nine months, and liberalizing the admissibility test. There has been increased activity since these

---

34 Cuesta-López, *Participación Directa e Iniciativa Legislativa.*

35 Simancas, D. (2021) 'Spain.' In D. Moeckli et al. (eds.) *The Legal Limits of Direct Democracy.* Cheltenham: Edward Elgar.

36 Biglino Campos, 'La iniciativa legislativa.'

37 Cuesta-López, *Participación Directa e Iniciativa Legislativa.*

reforms, with the majority of proposed initiatives registered since the 2006 reforms. By March 2021 there had been over 125 proposed initiatives in a wide array of areas, including education, employment, health, social security, pensions, and the environment.[38] Many were linked to civil society organizations, trade unions, or political parties – not much of a surprise, given the significant organizational capacity and backing needed to make pursuit of 500,000 signatures even remotely possible.[39] Over one-third of proposed initiatives failed the admissibility test, and more than another third failed to meet the signature thresholds.[40] Ten of those reaching the thresholds were rejected in a public vote by the plenary of the lower chamber. In over 35 years of operation, only three initiatives have resulted in legislative action, which is less than 3 percent of those proposed and around 4 percent of those registered.

The European Union

Given the much-discussed democratic and legitimacy deficit of the EU, it is unsurprising that an instrument already existing in several Member States would be proposed for the EU. Austria and Italy proposed it at the Treaty of Amsterdam negotiations, but it was not adopted. An EU AI was then a late addition to the draft constitutional treaty produced by the Convention in 2003. The Constitutional Treaty was famously rejected in referendums in France and the Netherlands;[41] however, the 'European Citizens' Initiative' (ECI) was retained in the Lisbon Treaty.

The Lisbon Treaty text on the ECI made some key design choices.[42] First, unlike national AIs, the request for legislation is not to a parliament, but to the European Commission. Second, it determined the minimum number of required citizen signatures at one million, less than 0.2 percent of the EU population when the Lisbon Treaty entered into force. Third, the language of 'inviting the Commission' made it clear that the Commission's nearly exclusive right of legis-

---

38 Fernández Silva, Á. (2021) *La iniciativa legislativa popular en el ordenamiento jurídico español*. Madrid: Centro De Estudios Políticos y Constitucionales.
39 Fernández Silva, *La iniciativa legislativa popular*.
40 Fernández Silva, *La iniciativa legislativa popular*.
41 See Mendez, F. et al. (2014) *Referendums and the European Union: A Comparative Inquiry*. Cambridge: Cambridge University Press.
42 See further, Mendez, F. and Mendez, M. (2017) 'The promise and perils of direct democracy for the European Union.' *Cambridge Yearbook of European Legal Studies* 19, 46.

lative initiative was formally unaffected. Fourth, the more logical interpretation of the treaty text is that initiatives requiring treaty revision were ruled out.

The desire to realize democratic gains from the ECI was highlighted by the European Parliament calling for it to be implemented without delay. The implementing Regulation then rapidly completed the normally laborious EU legislative process. The 2011 ECI Regulation made some crucial AI design decisions. First, an organizing committee comprising at least seven EU citizens, residing in at least seven different EU Member States, would be required. Second, an ex-ante registration test needed satisfying prior to signature-gathering. Third, the treaty text requirement that the initiative be supported by citizens in a significant number of Member States was set at one-quarter (seven Member States). Fourth, a minimum number of signatures required from each of the minimum number of Member States was introduced. Fifth, signatures could be collected electronically. Sixth, the signature collection period was set at 12 months. Seventh, obligations were imposed for initiatives meeting the requisite thresholds, in particular a) the Commission meets the organizers; b) organizers could present their initiative at a public hearing at the European Parliament; and c) a formal response from the Commission would be published, setting out any actions it would take or not take, and reasons for its decision.

Bold and sometimes hyperbolic claims about the contribution the ECI could make to EU democracy were commonplace from the moment this AI was proposed to when the implementing Regulation emerged.[43] Existing literature indicated AIs had limited impact and infrequently generated legislative output,[44] thus providing no support for the kind of polity-transforming potential that some attributed to this EU-level democratic innovation. Its design at the EU level suggested that getting an initiative registered, unlike supporting an existing initiative, would be no small feat for 'ordinary' EU citizens and that meeting signature thresholds would be a rare occurrence without substantial logistical and financial support from organizations.

The ECI came into force in 2012, and in under a decade over 100 initiatives were proposed (Table 6.5). Of the 85 registered, six reached the thresholds and two await signature verification.

---

43 Mendez, M. (2023) 'The European Citizens Initiative: towards a user-friendly, participatory and powerful agenda initiative for the European Union.' In D. Jancic (ed.) *The Changing Role of Citizens in EU Democratic Governance*. Oxford: Hart.
44 See Cuesta-López, *Participación Directa e Iniciativa Legislativa.*, in contrast to Qvortrup, 'The legislative initiative.'

Table 6.5: ECI Outcomes (April 2012–November 2021).

Status	Number	Percent
Registered	85	
Refused registration	22	
Total	107	100
REGISTERED INITIATIVES	85	
Met 1 million threshold	6 (all answered)	7
Collection ongoing	12	14
Insufficient support	39	46
Withdrawn	19	22
Collection closed	4	5
Collection not started	3	4
Verification ongoing	2	2

Source: Own elaboration (based on ECI official register).

Some 40 percent (20) of proposed initiatives until 2014 were refused registration, leading to much criticism from scholars, civil society organizations, ECI organizers, and other EU institutions. However, it has been argued that the vast majority of these refusals flowed directly from the ECI's design.[45]The Commission cannot register initiatives manifestly falling outside its powers to propose legal acts. Therefore, many were obvious non-starters if treaty revision is off-limits, whether that be proposing abolishing the European Parliament, the introduction of EU referendums, singing the European anthem in Esperanto, providing for self-determination of human rights, or stopping Brexit. The rigidity of the registration test was said to have contributed to a marked reduction in proposed initiatives. Legal challenges to registration refusals were frequent, and significant court victories encouraged better-reasoned registration refusals and the possibility of partially registering initiatives, which was originally rejected by the Commission.[46]

The Commission responses in 2014–2015 to the first three initiatives meeting the signature thresholds also allegedly contributed to a reduction in initiatives, due to an absence of legislative follow-up and expressly rejecting legislation in the case of an initiative proposing legislative changes on embryonic stem cell research. This bolstered a narrative of the Commission stifling the ECI. In fact, the Commission's response to the first initiative (Right2Water) indicated that it ac-

---

45 Mendez and Mendez, 'The promise and perils of direct democracy.' See also Daniela Vancic's chapter in this volume.
46 Mendez, 'The European Citizens Initiative.'

tually had legislative impact during the signature-gathering stage and a legislative proposal did emerge, albeit nearly four years after the Commission response, and was duly adopted. While the response to the fourth initiative meeting the thresholds was that there were neither scientific nor legal grounds to justify banning a particular herbicide, the Commission committed to proposing legislation on a secondary aim concerning scientific evaluations, and the legislation was adopted in 2019.

The narrative of the Commission stifling the ECI helped drive a reform agenda that culminated in a new ECI Regulation (2019), barely seven years after the original Regulation entered into force, thus attesting to the political desire to maximize any potential this bottom-up instrument had in order to alleviate the democratic disconnect between the EU and its citizenry. We focus here on some of the more prominent changes.[47] First, the Commission is now tasked with translating registered initiatives into all official EU languages. Second, partial registration of initiatives is now expressly provided for and regulated. Third, Member States can now allow those aged 16–17 to support initiatives. Fourth, organizers now have six months' flexibility after registration of the initiative before the 12-month signature collection period commences. Fifth, the European Parliament is now expressly tasked with assessing political support for initiatives, and it has changed its rules of procedure to provide for a plenary debate on an initiative, following the public hearing, that can culminate in a resolution. This representative democracy tool of Parliament was used for the first time in 2021 following the public hearings for the fifth and sixth initiatives that met the signature thresholds. However, in relation to the fifth (Minority SafePack), the Commission concluded that no new legislative acts or amendments were necessary, rapidly followed by the response to the sixth (End the Cage Age) proposing a legislative proposal to phase out and prohibit use of caged farming by 2023.

Emphasis on the absence or limited nature of legislative outcomes has led to an excessively critical and inappropriately nuanced account of the contribution made by this new transnational instrument of complementary democracy.[48] Citizens across diverse EU Member States have collaborated to form organizers' com-

47 See further: Mendez, 'The European Citizens Initiative.'
48 See Leino, P. (2019) 'Disruptive democracy: keeping EU citizens in a box.' In I. Govaere et al. (eds.) *Critical Reflections on Constitutional Democracy in the European Union*. Oxford: Hart; and Longo, E. (2019) 'The European Citizens' Initiative: too much democracy for EU polity?' *German Law Journal* 20(2): 181–200. For a positive assessment see Greenwood, J. (2019) 'The European Citizens' Initiative: bringing the EU closer to its citizens?' *Comparative European Politics* 17, 940, and Mendez, 'The European Citizens Initiative.'

mittees on scores of occasions. A large majority of their initiatives have been registered, with the result that millions of EU citizens have supported initiatives on topics including agriculture, animal welfare, education, environment, fundamental rights, health, social policy, and trade. Where signature thresholds were met, organizers were received by the Commission and had a public hearing at the European Parliament; privileged deliberative access of some significance even if legislative proposals did not emerge. When thresholds are not met (an expected outcome for the vast majority of initiatives), the cross-national deliberative and participatory aims of the ECI are still being advanced, and such initiatives can still be examined in another EU forum for deliberative listening, namely the European Parliament petitions committee.[49]

Latvia

The 1922 Latvian Constitution borrowed from the 1919 Weimar Constitution by including a range of direct democracy instruments and a very similarly framed bottom-up instrument allowing 10 percent of the electorate to put a legislative proposal on the legislative agenda that could culminate in a referendum.[50] Shortly after the Second World War began, Latvia was occupied by the Soviet Union, and for some years by Nazi Germany before being reoccupied by the Soviet Union. With the collapse of the Soviet Union, Latvia reinstated its 1922 Constitution in 1991. However, until 2010 the Weimar-style bottom-up instrument only resulted in three initiatives that met the high signature thresholds, one of which was adopted by Parliament without recourse to a referendum.[51]

Latvia joined the EU in 2004. The Lisbon Treaty, with its own AI, came into force five years later. It is no accident that the Latvian AI was created in the wake of the ECI. In June 2011, a privately created citizens' initiative platform emerged ('ManaBalss', translated as 'My Voice') to channel legislative proposals, and initiatives began to collect signatures. The government essentially supported this endeavor, such that, through a combination of an amendment to the Law on Submissions in 2012 and new rules of procedure for the Parliament, a 'collective submission' procedure was born. At 10,000 signatures, the threshold is slightly under 0.5 percent of the population, and no time limit is stipulated. Citizens as young as 16 can sign, thus breaking the link with voting age for elections

---

49 The first such initiative to have a petitions committee hearing was *End Ecocide* in 2015.
50 Auers, D. (2012) 'An electoral tactic? Citizens' initiatives in post-Soviet Latvia.' In M. Setälä and T. Schiller (eds.) *Citizens' Initiatives in Europe*. Basingstoke: Palgrave.
51 Auers, 'An electoral tactic?'

(18 in Latvia) that many AIs retain. Signatures can be collected electronically, and the aforementioned online platform ('ManaBalss') plays a central role in this respect. The submission is directed to the Latvian parliament, and a brief justification is required along with details of the natural person authorized (henceforth authorized person) to represent the signatories. Substantive limits on what can be proposed include requests which are clearly unacceptable in a democratic society or are plainly offensive, or undermine values of human dignity, freedom, democracy, equality, the rule of law, and human rights, including minority rights. Compliance with these rules of procedure is evaluated by the Presidium of the parliament within 20 days of receiving the submission, and the authorized person is invited to the Presidium meeting. If the Presidium ascertains non-compliance with the rules of procedure, it provides a reply pursuant to the Law on Submissions.

The Parliamentary Submissions Committee holds a meeting to initially evaluate the submission within a month of the filing, a meeting to which the authorized person is invited and has the right to justify the submission and take part in the debate. Within three months of the filing, the Submissions Committee drafts a report on its evaluation and prepares a draft parliament resolution on further processing of the submission. This can recommend specific action be taken, such as a parliamentary committee be formed and tasked with preparing a draft law, or that the Cabinet of Ministers prepare a relevant concept or draft law, or that the submission be left without consideration or be turned down. The Submissions Committee supervises fulfillment of the tasks in the draft resolution. The parliament's decision regarding actions to be taken cannot be challenged judicially or by any other body.[52]

Up to November 2021, 97 of these submissions have been presented to parliament at a rapidly proliferating rate (over 50 since 2019 alone). Twenty-nine have been rejected, a large number are in the process of being adopted, and at least 18 have resulted in direct legislative changes in areas that include cancer treatment, vehicle roadworthiness tests, medical reimbursements, land privatization, genetically modified crops, taxation (including value-added tax), pensions, electricity tariffs, and higher education.[53] There have been more signatories, over 2.1 million, collected in total than the population of Latvia, which stands at less than two million. The level of activity and legislative impact of this complementary

---

52 Birģelis, M. (2021) 'Latvia.' In D. Moeckli et al. (eds.) *The Legal Limits of Direct Democracy.* Cheltenham: Edward Elgar.
53 Details are provided on the Submissions Committee website: http://mandati.saeima.lv.

democracy instrument in less than a decade has, in comparative terms, been wholly unprecedented.

Conclusion

This chapter has shown that the AI is now a long-established instrument of complementary democracy that has diffused rapidly in recent decades, such that it now exists at the national level in over 40 countries as well as at EU level. It has nonetheless been surprisingly neglected, especially in comparative scholarship in English. We still know too little about these instruments that have long been highlighted as valuable tools for direct citizen participation and increased policy responsiveness in law-making. The AI now exists in the majority of the EU's Member States, usually as one among other instruments of direct democracy. Its regulation varies significantly both across those states and especially relative to the bottom-up referendum that exists alongside it in a number of EU Member States.

Our case-study coverage suggests that the EU-level AI, the European Citizens' Initiative, is positively contributing to the EU's democratic landscape by offering citizens a regularly deployed bottom-up tool to engage with and be heard by the EU, which can achieve legislative outcomes. While we emphasize that AIs can certainly help engage the citizenry and generate deliberative listening even absent legislative outcomes, as the EU example itself illustrates, it is also true that legislative outcomes constitute a tangible measure of their success. And the absence, or scarcity, of legislative outcomes could result in these instruments not having the intended effect of alleviating democratic discontent, but rather bolstering it. The country (Spain) with one of the three oldest functioning national AIs has produced strikingly few legislative outcomes (three) due in part to restrictive design features. The new Latvian instrument, in stark contrast, has already generated over five times as many legislative outcomes (18) in less than one-third of the time of its Spanish counterpart. Design issues partly explain these wildly contrasting outcomes. Ultimately, the less than a decade of experience with the Latvian instrument suggests that AIs can actually have a truly transformative potential in terms of generating citizen participation, deliberative listening, and legislative outcomes.

Daniela Vancic

Transnational Democracy's Quest Across Borders

With global problems requiring increasingly global solutions, democracy calls for transnational citizens' participation. The European Citizens' Initiative is the world's first tool of transnational participatory democracy, which attempts to mend the democratic deficit in the European Union. The instrument, a right of every EU citizen, has now been in existence since 2012 and is inspiring a global tool of transnational democracy at the United Nations (UN) level: the UN World Citizens' Initiative.

Introduction

Previous decades have led to advances in globalization and technological developments never imagined possible. Through our increasingly interconnected world, hard borders have slowly thawed and dissolved, and goods, services, and people have never in history traveled around the world and across borders at the rate and speed they do today. Even communication barriers are broken down as artificial intelligence allows people speaking different languages to communicate with each other in real time, transforming how we experience personal intercultural exchange. Humans have not only been brought closer together over the last decades, but we have also become much more interconnected.[1] Democracy, too, is breaking down barriers and interconnecting people across borders.

The age of information, access to the internet, and greater opportunities for learning and exchange allow people of the modern day to be the most informed voters. Global grassroots movements, prove that citizens are not only well informed, but also well organized. Citizens today are prepared and eager to campaign and assemble on the issues that matter to them, such as, most notably but certainly not limited to, the global climate and environmental movement. The increase of citizen-led movements yields expertise among citizens and ordinary people, where citizens themselves are capable and competent of lobbying for change. Where politicians were once considered experts on several subjects, gov-

---

1 Beaverstock, J. V. and Faulconbridge, J. R. (2009) *Globalization: Interconnected Worlds*, 2nd edn. London: Sage, pp. 331–343.

https://doi.org/10.1515/9783110747331-007

ernments around the world, including the European Union, now conduct regular consultations with citizens in order to gather their opinions and perspectives on various subjects, while politicians fill the role of drafting and debating the legislation. Such regularly conducted feedback-gathering from citizens is not only beneficial for enhanced democratic value, but it is also essential in addressing legitimacy deficits.[2]

While nearly every aspect of our lives has developed and evolved, our democracies have mainly stagnated or developed at a slow pace. At the global level, no real democracy advancement has taken place. An election cycle every four to five years gives leaders the mandate to enter the global stage with anticipated solutions to the many global issues we face. However, global citizens themselves do not have any say on the global agenda.

As presented in the previous chapters of this book, traditional democracy as we know it, is complemented well by supplementary mechanisms of participation. This chapter explores the participatory and direct democratic mechanisms and instruments that empower citizens beyond the nation state. In an increasingly interconnected, globalized, and informed world, democracy, too, begins to transcend borders.

A More Democratic Union

The European Union in itself is an extraordinary concept and democratic project. Nearly 450 million inhabitants, across 27 Member States, speaking 24 official languages, experiencing countless cultures, all combined in one union with dissolved internal borders. Following centuries of war and aggressive nationalism, Europe is a place where people are now can thrive together in peace, led by the first transnational governmental institution in the world without its own territory.[3]

The European Union is also unlike any other union in the world as it grants union citizenship directly alongside national citizenship, bestowing certain rights and freedoms to all EU passport-holders. Perhaps the most well-loved European citizens' right is freedom of movement, allowing a citizen of one EU Member State the right to live, work, study, and vacation in any other EU Member State. Democratic rights also join the list of rights enjoyed by European citizens.

---

2 Alemanno, A. and Organ, J. (2021) *Citizen Participation in Democratic Europe.* Paris: Rowman & Littlefield Publishers/ECPR Press, pp. 3, 14–16.
3 Scheub, U. and Mehr Demokratie e.V. (2018) *The Unfinished Europe Democracy: A Vision for the European Union*, trans. R. Cunningham. Munich: Oekom Verlag.

The right to vote in the election of the European Parliament, the only directly elected transnational Parliament in the world, has been a shared EU right since 1979.

Furthermore, to the list of democratic rights enjoyed by Europeans is a right and participatory mechanism unique in the world: the European Citizens' Initiative, which gives citizens the right to directly participate in setting the legislative agenda of the EU. In order for an initiative to be considered successful, it requires the pan-European support of one million signatures across at least seven EU Member States,[4] making it the world's first and only instrument of transnational participatory and direct democracy. Numerous citizens' initiative mechanisms exist around the world at the local, regional, and national level; however, the European Citizens' Initiative is the only tool in the world that works across borders by operating as a transnational democratic tool in the EU's participatory toolbox.[5]

The European Citizens' Initiative was introduced in the Lisbon Treaty in 2009 as the product of concerted efforts at the Convention on the Future of Europe in the early 2000s. Its inclusion in the Lisbon Treaty was thanks to the campaigning work of direct democracy activists from across Europe and founding members of Democracy International e.V., an NGO based in Cologne, Germany, that was established in 2011 to strengthen direct democracy and citizens' participation at the local, national, EU, and global level.[6] The European Citizens' Initiative finally entered into application in 2012, where, after a revision process, it now functions under the updated Regulation (EU) 2019/788.[7]

Because the European Commission, the institutional body that registers and receives initiatives, is only required to respond to the initiative, and not necessarily accept the initiative in full and submit legislation on the initiative in question, the European Citizens' Initiative falls a mere sliver too short to be considered a true tool of direct democracy. Instead, successful initiatives solicit a written response from the European Commission on whether or not it will take action on the initiative and its reasons for or against it, which certainly upgrades the European Citizens' Initiative from a no-strings-attached petition tool. The

---

4 'European Citizens' Initiative: how it works': https://europa.eu/citizens-initiative/how-it-works_en.

5 Bouza Garcia, L., Cuesta Lopez, V., Mincheva, E., and Szeligowska, D. (2011) *The European Citizens' Initiative: A First Assessment*. Bruges: College of Europe, p. 55.

6 Story of the European Citizens' Initiative: https://www.democracy-international.org/european-citizens-initiative-reform.

7 Regulation of the European Citizens' Initiative as of 2020: https://eur-lex.europa.eu/legal-content/EN/TXT/?qid=1558082143592&uri=CELEX:32019R0788.

binding nature of the European Citizens' Initiative rather lies in its triggering of a mandatory response and detailed explanation from the European Commission, as opposed to a politically binding response that leads to a legal act.

Democracy International promotes and advocates for a more binding and citizen-friendly tool of direct democracy in the EU by making the European Citizens' Initiative a real citizen's initiative right with a real political impact.[8] The NGO has already been successful in campaigns such as increasing the role of the European Parliament in the follow-up to successful initiatives.[9] Successful initiatives are invited to the European Parliament for a public hearing, and now they are followed by a debate in plenary with a possibility of a plenary vote. While this is a step in the right direction for the world's only transnational tool of (near) direct democracy, Democracy International's greatest dream regarding the European Citizens' Initiative is for the instrument to develop and evolve to become a real direct democratic citizens' initiative right that can trigger a binding European-wide vote on the legislative proposal in question.

According to Democracy International, after registration of an initiative, including an eligibility check to ensure that the initiative falls under the EU's competences and that it is not abusive or contrary to EU values, the first step of the initiative should be the collection of one million signatures within one year, across seven different EU Member States. This is currently the case for the European Citizens' Initiative, where the Commission then decides if, and/or how, it decides to follow up with legislative action. In the case of rejection or inaction by the EU institutions, Democracy International proposes that a next step would allow a *second* round of signatures with a higher threshold to be collected. Should this higher threshold be reached, and should the EU institutions decide again not to adopt the proposal, an EU-wide referendum would be automatically be triggered in order to allow the entirety of the European population to accept or reject the initiative. Institutions would have the possibility to add counter-proposals on the ballot in addition to the initiative. A double majority of the EU electorate and majority of the EU Member States may be required for the vote to pass, and, if the initiative is a case for treaty change, higher thresholds may be introduced.

---

8 Democracy International on the European Citizens' Initiative: https://www.democracy-international.org/eu-citizens-initiative.

9 Democracy International press release regarding strengthening the role of the European Parliament in the follow-up to successful European citizens' initiatives: https://www.democracy-international.org/european-parliament-votes-start-interinstitutional-negotiations-revision-european-citizens.

While this Democracy International proposal for a new and improved European Citizens' Initiative would require treaty change in the first place, the Commission should nevertheless establish closer ties with organizers even after its response to the initiative in order to continue the dialogue with citizens. This can and should be implemented and practiced now, as the success of the instrument will depend on the political response it generates.

Nonetheless, the European Citizens' Initiative is one of a kind. It is the epitome of transnational, coordinated, citizen participation and democratic innovation. It allows citizens to connect on pressing issues despite language barriers, cultures, or borders. In the nearly 10 years of the European Citizens' Initiative's existence, European citizens, and organized civil society, have been able to raise awareness of critical issues, establish transnational networks, put their issues on the EU's agenda, and, in some cases, help write European law.[10] While the instrument in its current form leaves much to the imagination, democracy tends to create a demand for more democracy, so its full potential as a direct democratic instrument may be experienced in the near future.[11] It is far from ideal in its current form, but the European Citizens' Initiative is a start to a more democratic European Union – and, possibly, even the world.

A More Democratic World

Over past decades, there has been a stronger sense of global suffering and greater perceived understanding of global-scale issues affecting our individual-level lives. Global issues are rapidly growing in number and importance due to technological advances and the ever-closer global connectedness of all areas of our lives. Extreme weather events, environmental destruction, the global health pandemic, migration and refugee flows, and endless challenges have demonstrated how closely global problems affect us and how they transcend national borders.[12] There is no country on any continent on Earth that is unaffected by climate change, and climate change is certainly not on pause. Once the global economy recovers from the COVID-19 pandemic, greenhouse gas emissions are

---

10 Gerstenmeyer C., Klein, J., Plottka, J., and Tittel, A. (2018) *Study on the Added Value of the European Citizens' Initiative*. Brussels: European Union, pp. 41–49.

11 Matsusaka, J. G. (2020) *Let the People Rule: How Direct Democracy Can Meet the Populist Challenge*. Princeton: Princeton University Press, p. 82.

12 Bummel, A. and Leinen, J. (2018) *A World Parliament: Governance and Democracy in the 21st Century*, trans. R. Cunningham. Berlin: Democracy Without Borders, p. 179.

expected to return to higher levels.[13] Not only are we all sharing the same planet, but we're also all sitting in the same, steadily sinking boat – a boat which no one country or group of countries *alone* can bring back afloat. There is no denying that global issues require global solutions.

The United Nations is the single most important arena to deal with these global predicaments. The Security Council decides on matters of international peace and security, and the General Assembly makes recommendations, launches treaty negotiations, and moderates international agenda-setting. The UN was established specifically to foster global cooperation and undertake concerns of such a scale and magnitude, and unprecedented global challenges critically require democratic participation on the global level now more than ever.

Growing global climate movements such as Fridays for Future and the responses to the recent UN Climate Change Conference (COP26) show that citizens want their governments to take necessary and ambitious decisions on the global stage. Government representatives in international organizations such as the UN must be accountable not only to their national electorates, but also to the citizenry of the world as a whole, since their interests must also be taken into account.[14] Governments, however, are also not always responsive nor quick to react, making global governance a sluggish and passive process. Furthermore, there is no existing mechanism for citizens themselves to bring their concerns directly to the global stage. Citizens merely have to trust governments to do their bidding when it comes to citizens' concerns regarding global issues. The world's only truly universal global organization is an exclusive club of appointed government diplomats, so unless one goes by the name Greta Thunberg there is no room for regular citizens to raise their concerns, set the global agenda, or have any influence on global decision-making matters. The democratic deficit, or rather, total lack of citizen-specific democratic mechanisms of the UN, demands an immediate mechanism to link citizens to global decision-making. Although the UN has at least made efforts to include civil society in some of its deliberations, such as allowing NGOs to be observers at the UN Human Rights Council,[15] individual citizens still remain voiceless at the global level.

'Complex' and 'bureaucratic' are common ways to describe the intricate multilateral decision-making process of the UN, but there are proposals to complement the UN's state-based structure in order to enhance individual voices and

---

13 United Nations Sustainable Development Goals, *Goal 13: Climate Action:* https://www.un.org/sustainabledevelopment/climate-change/.
14 Bummel and Leinen, *A World Parliament*, p. 323.
15 NGO participation in the Human Rights Council: https://www.ohchr.org/en/hrbodies/hrc/pages/ngoparticipation.aspx.

foster its democratic dimension, which is practically non-existent at the current moment. As the UN today faces the democratic crisis that the European Union critically faced years ago, the UN has much to learn from Europe's experience with the European Citizens' Initiative. This is precisely why, after 75 years of existence, the UN is in dire need of a World Citizens' Initiative. A UN World Citizens' Initiative is proposed to be a democratic tool with an aim to close the global democratic deficit and give citizens a say in setting the global agenda. As the European Citizens' Initiative is the world's first and only transnational democratic instrument, a UN World Citizens' Initiative would annex this title to become the world's only mechanism in the global toolbox of democracy. It would expand and revolutionize multilateralism to be inclusive of individual and ordinary citizens on a scale never before practiced on the global level. Taking from the example of the European Citizens' Initiative, the instrument of a UN World Citizens' Initiative would allow individuals who have gathered enough statements of support to table proposals at the UN, where citizens would be able to complement Member States' proposals with issues close to citizens' concerns. UN bodies such as the General Assembly or Security Council would have to place the item on their agenda and give representatives of the initiative the global floor to make their case, such as during the annual general debate of the General Assembly, while heads of state and government were present.[16]

The UN World Citizens' Initiative is one of several civil society proposals to democratize the UN, but it is the one that focuses on bottom-up citizens' participation in particular. Among other proposals are a UN Parliamentary Assembly to foster democratic participation and representation on the global level,[17] and a UN Civil Society Envoy to formalize the partnership between NGOs and the UN and to give civil society a permanent space at the UN.[18] A campaign for more inclusive global governance including these three proposals is run by civil society organizations, Democracy International, Democracy Without Borders, and CIVICUS: World Alliance for Citizen Participation, in addition to being supported by over 200 other civil society organizations including Greenpeace and Avaaz.[19] As well as wide civil society support, citizens also agree: the World Citizens' Initia-

---

16 More about the campaign for a UN World Citizens' Initiative: https://www.worldcitizensinitiative.org.

17 Bummel and Leinen, *A World Parliament*, p. 115.

18 More about the UN Civil Society Envoy: https://www.democracy.community/stories/un-civil-society-envoy.

19 We The Peoples campaign page for more inclusive global governance: https://www.wethepeoples.org.

tive was frequently mentioned by the 1.5 million people who participated in the 2020 UN75 evaluation exercise, as the UN's own report testifies.[20]

While we refer to the European Citizens' Initiative as the basis for a UN World Citizens' Initiative, it is certainly not the only tool for direct citizen participation in the world. Many countries have instruments that allow citizens to put forward ideas for consideration to their government, most notably Switzerland. However, the European Citizens' Initiative is the only transnational tool that grants citizens this right; therefore it is the appropriate tool to build upon and to serve as a basis for a global version. A global citizens' initiative right has the transformative potential to kickstart action on global issues that, until now, have largely been ignored. Citizens would be offered a direct avenue to set the UN's agenda and a real, official channel to organize, mobilize, and professionalize their efforts, making the UN more responsive to tackling many of the challenges we face today.

A Global Participatory Instrument: A Feasible Reality or Merely a Dream?

The campaign for a UN World Citizens' Initiative was launched by Democracy International, Democracy Without Borders, and CIVICUS in 2019 in New York, just across the street from the UN Headquarters, as a stark symbol to the lack of opportunities for transnational democratic citizen participation. The golden question however is, how would it work? In simple terms, the democratic instrument would operate as a petitioning mechanism, which would allow global citizens to sign initiatives and table proposals at the UN, if they could gather enough support. Nonetheless, for such a complex, wide-reaching, and unique proposal, the devil is in the detail. Could a UN World Citizens' Initiative feasibly be implemented, or is it merely a democratic dream?

This is precisely what a feasibility study carried out by Dr. James Organ, an expert on the European Citizens' Initiative, and Dr. Ben Murphy, an expert on the UN system, and both law professors at the University of Liverpool, aimed to answer.[21] The published study serves as the basis for the formation of the UN World

---

20 Press release, Democracy International: https://www.democracy-international.org/un-we-need-key-un-report-includes-calls-world-citizens-initiative; UN75 Report: https://www.un.org/sites/un2.un.org/files/un75report_september_final_english.pdf.
21 A Voice for Global Citizens: a UN World Citizens' Initiative: https://www.worldcitizensinitia tive.org/files/unwci_study.pdf.

Citizens' Initiative, but in order to visualize what a World Citizens' Initiative could look like, one must be somewhat familiar with the functioning of the European Citizens' Initiative. From the early stages of the campaign, the European Citizens' Initiative, as the only transnational democratic instrument in existence today, was regarded as the starting point for the creation of what a real, concrete global petitioning instrument could resemble, in terms of administrative requirements and thresholds. There are a multitude of aspects that require consideration when drafting a global citizens' initiative mechanism, and several frequently asked questions are covered below.

Principally, just like the European Citizens' Initiative, a World Citizens' Initiative will need a committee of citizens to launch the initiative. The European Citizens' Initiative requires seven EU citizens from seven different EU Member States. For the World Citizens' Initiative, the experts recommended a committee of ten citizens that are geographically representative according to the following criteria and which follow the same geographical pattern set out in the non-permanent seats of the UN Security Council:[22]

- five from African and Asian states;
- one from an Eastern European state;
- two Latin American states;
- two Western European and other states.

Another question to consider for an official worldwide petitioning mechanism is which UN body is going to oversee and implement the UN World Citizens' Initiative. It needs administrative oversight and a gatekeeper to ensure that criteria are being met and that there is proper implementation. For the European Citizens' Initiative, it is clearly the European Commission, as this is the executive and legislative body that holds the right of initiative in the EU. For the UN, however, it is recommended that a new organ in the UN is established to deal with these guardianship issues – for example, it could be called the World Citizens' Initiative Administrative Board.[23]

Also critical for imagining a World Citizens' Initiative is giving its signature criteria considerable thought. How much support would potentially be required for a World Citizens' Initiative? The European Citizens' Initiative requires one million signatures in a minimum of seven EU Member States. For the World Citi-

---

22 Murphy, B. and Organ, J. (2019) *A Voice for Global Citizens: A UN World Citizens' Initiative.* Democracy Without Borders, Democracy International, CIVICUS: World Alliance for Citizen Participation, p. 8.
23 Murphy and Organ, *A Voice for Global Citizens*, p. 49.

zens' Initiative, it is recommended that 18 months be given to collect five million signatures. Imperative here, too, is that there is geographical representativeness, which is why it is recommended that the same geographical criteria as mentioned above for the committee of citizens is met. Additionally, the threshold in each country should be 0.5 percent of the population of that country, meaning that each country is considered equally, regardless of national population.[24] This differs from the European Citizens' Initiative as the threshold of signatures in each EU Member State is based on the number of Members of the European Parliament it has, where smaller states are given an advantage, in proportionate terms.

Concerns regarding responses to successful initiatives and their follow-up are perhaps the most controversial. For all matters besides peace and security, the UN General Assembly would be the right forum in the UN to discuss a World Citizens' Initiative. Successful initiatives could either be added to the agenda to be discussed at the debates of the Assembly, where heads of state are present. A successful initiative could also trigger a special session of the General Assembly, or, as a third possibility, it could be discussed in one of the six main committees relating to the subject in question.[25] This aspect is especially significant as the political and legal response to a successful initiative is vital to the instrument's democratic legitimacy. Nonetheless, successful initiatives cannot render a binding response from the UN due to the nature of the Member State composition of the institution. The European Citizens' Initiative itself is also not a fully binding instrument that in every case yields a political and legal response by the European Commission.

The World Citizens' Initiative, like the European Citizens' Initiative in operation today, aims to be an agenda-setting instrument in order to escalate an issue to the top tiers of decision-making, where the initiative might see a political and legal life beyond its campaign. Inspired directly by the European Union, the UN needs to enter into a new, inclusive, and democratic era, and it has the proper window of opportunity as well as proper transnational democratic example to follow.

---

24 Murphy and Organ, *A Voice for Global Citizens*, pp. 51–55.
25 Murphy and Organ, *A Voice for Global Citizens*, pp. 56–61.

Conclusion

As global problems increasingly require global solutions and cooperation, the way decision-making is carried out, too, requires global democratic approaches. This means that democratic infrastructures need to be created in order to address imminent issues that are not foreseeable today. A UN World Citizens' Initiative would allow global citizens to have more impact in a world with growing interconnected dilemmas that require not only multilateralism, but also global cooperation of both states and citizens alike. It will help create a citizen-based global political sphere and provide citizens with the platform to put issues important to them on the global stage. The proposed transnational democratic instrument would serve as a platform for ordinary citizens and civil society to actively use in order to rally around a concern, put forward an issue, and raise awareness about important topics. If the initiative proves to gain popularity among peers, the proposal lands on the desk of high-level decision-makers. The idea would be game-changing for global governance and have transformative potential to overcome blockages in the UN system. It would enable the UN to take swift and effective action, especially on issues that transcend borders, such as climate change, global health crises, and the loss of biodiversity. It will increase transparency and accountability in the UN's work, providing it with the reinforced legitimacy and relevance the institution so desperately needs. And it would give well-deserved recognition to the democratic instruments at the European level that inspired the global movement for greater global governance in the first place.

A proposed World Citizens' Initiative does not claim to have the answer to fully and finally democratize the UN. The European Citizens' Initiative in fact does not solve all of the EU's deeply rooted democratic problems. Still, it is a remarkable start to the ongoing democratization efforts, and it is powerful in itself that such a working instrument is offered to citizens beyond national borders.

To safeguard the significant multilateral momentum that has been built over the last 75 years, which has contributed to peace and prosperity around the world, democracy across borders, too, needs to further evolve and develop. Transnational democratic mechanisms have been in place since 2012 with the European Citizens' Initiative, but they have also been researched and analyzed for feasibility at the global level. Now that transnational democracy at the UN level has been recognized as legally and practically possible, it is merely a matter of when democracy will truly go global.

Roslyn Fuller
Digital Democracy: Past, Present, and Future

What is Digital Democracy?

How digital technology can be used to affect and effect politics has been a point of debate since internet access first became widespread in the 1990s.[1] During his 1992 US presidential campaign, Ross Perot famously advocated conducting electronic town halls, a call that coincided with several experiments in debating and voting on political issues via television. Shortly thereafter, in the early 2000s, Demoex (an internet voting party that started as a school project) fielded successful local politicians for over 10 years in Vallentuna, Sweden.[2]

Since its inception, the idea of digital democracy has proved remarkably enduring. Harnessing technology to facilitate an accountable and human-centred politics has been advocated by progressive thinkers like Buckminster Fuller, Erich Fromm, and Alvin Toffler, while a 1994 American survey found that significantly more people favoured using interactive television for political purposes (85 percent) than for other tasks, such as shopping or game shows.[3]

Unfortunately, much of the public discourse on digital democracy today focuses purely on the adjective 'digital' while neglecting the noun – democracy. Thus, while we have a better understanding of the word 'digital' than ever before, we have lost touch with the essence of what it is, in this context, supposed to facilitate – democracy.

As a result, the term 'digital democracy' has become diluted and its meaning confused. We need to return to the roots of these words in order to gain a clearer insight into the meaning and development of digital democracy today.

---

1 The Declaration of the Independence of Cyberspace is one much-quoted example of the excesses of cyber-utopianism in this regard (Barlow, John Perry (1996) 'A declaration of the independence of cyberspace.' *Electronic Frontier Foundation*, 8 February: www.eff.org/cyberspace-independence.
2 'Information about Demoex': http://demoex.se/en/.
3 Schwartz, Evan I. (1994) 'Direct democracy: are you ready for the Democracy Channel?' *Wired* (1 January): www.wired.com/1994/01/e-dem/.

https://doi.org/10.1515/9783110747331-008

Democracy

Democracy means 'people power', that is, that the people of a nation or other polity have the power to govern their own affairs. This power is exercised both individually and collectively.

In order for this to be true, the following attributes must be fulfilled:
- the institutions of governance must be constructed in such a manner that the polity's members can exercise their power on a free and equal basis without having to obtain permission to participate;
- no subset of the population may possess inherent privileges that can override these decisions or prevent this exercise in power from occurring;
- each member's vote carries equal weight, which as a corollary necessitates majority rule (unless agreed otherwise);
- the people, as the ultimate decision-making power, are accountable for the nation's policies and ultimately bear the benefits and consequences thereof.

Fulfilling these characteristics necessitates mechanisms via which majority will can be formed, measured, implemented, and re-assessed in an iterative process.

Today, these democratic attributes are most clearly expressed in the referendum, which finds frequent use in Switzerland, California, Ireland, and Taiwan, and less frequent use in numerous other states, such as Canada, Australia, Britain, Hungary, and Colombia.

While elections seek to express the same characteristics, they do so in weaker form, as statistical discrepancies arise from electoral voting systems that make it difficult to precisely determine majority will. For example, it is possible (especially in first-past-the-post voting systems) for a party to win an election while losing the popular vote. In addition to this, because electoral politics involves parties bundling issues into a platform, as well as voting for representatives rather than on issues, it is hard to determine why people voted the way that they did, or even what the goal of voting is (is it to choose a candidate or a set of policies?). Add to this the time-lags between elections that reduce politicians' accountability, as well as party apparatuses that seek to engineer electoral outcomes, and we end up with a system that attempts to mirror the will of the people under conditions of political equality, but is subject to several distortions that make this difficult to truly achieve.[4] This can create friction under the best of circumstances, but becomes even more fraught when parties and lobbyists cyni-

---

4 For more on electoral distortions, see Fuller, Roslyn (2015) *Beasts and Gods: How Democracy Changed Its Meaning and Lost Its Purpose*. London: Zed/Bloomsbury, pp. 43 et seq.

cally seek to exploit these various loopholes. The practice of electoral politics or representative democracy is thus, unfortunately, often much different from the theory.[5] Nonetheless, the theory, at least, is there.

In contrast to both the referendum and election (which both involve free, mass participation (people) and clear decision-points (power)), many practices that are commonly referred to as 'digital democracy' are anything but. This is particularly true of social media, which is often conflated with 'digital democracy' in popular discourse.

Although talking, debating, deliberating, and otherwise communicating can elucidate options and help people to form their opinions, discussion does not in itself confer power; neither does it allow for majority will to be accurately measured.

In fact, since participation on social media is a purely voluntary leisure activity, the vast majority of people do not actively take part. When they do, it is often in ways disconnected from politics (e.g. sports, fashion, staying in contact with friends and family). Social media merely demonstrates that the capacity for mass peer-to-peer public communication *exists*; it offers no means of translating this communication into accountable governing power.

The same can be said for online political campaigning, that is, advertising a party or candidate online. This has changed the medium via which some voters receive information, but has not affected how they exercise power (or even whether they do so at all). It would make as much sense to speak of 'lawn sign democracy' because people put up lawn signs supporting candidates, or 'television democracy' when politicians began advertising on television, as it does to speak of 'digital democracy' in the context of social media and online advertising.

People may communicate *about* politics over social media, but politics does not happen on social media. It happens in the institutions of government.

Digital

The term 'digital' simply describes the method used for communication, in this case binary code. Anything that is expressed in 0s and 1s (or 'on' and 'off') is 'digital'. Communication transmitted by waves (e.g. radio, simply speaking) is, by contrast, analogue. Many of the things we term 'digital' today are a combination of digital and analogue, in the sense that digital messages are translated

---

5 This remains true whether one takes a Burkeaen or Rousseauian view of democratic theory.

back to humans in analogue form; if you listen to music on an iphone, you (fortunately) don't hear beeps and silence, but receive the musical output as a wave. Like its forerunner Morse code, digital communication merely serves to send encoded messages long distances, enabling quick, multi-way, extremely flexible communication.

Thus, when we say 'digital democracy', we are really just talking about using a cheap long-distance communication method to make political decisions on the basis of equality.

This is significant, because until recently multi-way communication was only possible on a face-to-face basis. When it came to political decision-making, this required large numbers of people (voters) to delegate physical attendance to a smaller number of people (representatives), which in turn required a method of delegation (elections). Even had they wanted to, the American Founding Fathers and 19th century British parliamentarians could not very well have constructed modern democracy in any other way than as a representative system. Even those political philosophers who saw the disadvantages of delegation, such as Rousseau and Robert Michels, admitted that it would be impossible for all citizens to meet in any one place to conduct politics and that delegation was therefore necessary.[6]

The recent change in technological capabilities opens up new possibilities, challenges, and threats that have never existed before in the modern era, including the possibility of creating a true digital democracy.

Current Examples of Digital Democracy in Practice

Generally speaking, democracy consists of five stages: Ideation (i.e. coming up with proposals), Deliberation and debate (examining those proposals), Decision-making (measuring support via a vote), Implementation, and Re-evaluation. Some digital tools focus on only one aspect of this process, but these steps can also be consolidated into a single end-to-end procedure. The following will discuss some of the most common applications.

---

6 Rousseau, Jean-Jacques (1913) *The Social Contract and Discourses*, trans. G. D. H. Cole. New York: E. P. Dutton & Co.: https://oll.libertyfund.org/title/cole-the-social-contract-and-dis courses; Michels, Robert (1911) *Political Parties: A Sociological Study of the Oligarchical Tendencies of Modern Democracy*. Verlag Wener Klinkhardt.

Pure Voting Applications (Decision-Making)

Digital voting applications are usually intended to replace voting in elections. Therefore, they tend to mirror the electoral system precisely, with no possibility for online debate among participants and with an emphasis on guaranteeing secret, anonymous voting. The most enduring online voting system in the world today is likely Estonia's i-voting system, which has enabled online voting since 2005, and now extends to local, national, and European elections. While i-voting has sometimes faced criticism from abroad, as well as local legal challenges, it has thus far weathered these trials with nearly half of Estonian voters now casting their ballots online.

Estonian i-voting has recently been joined by similar models in other nations. Voatz, a private online voting provider, has been used by several local municipalities in US elections; while Polys, an online voting system developed by internet security giant Kaspersky, was used by Russia's Yabloko party members to vote in primaries, as well as in Russia's 2021 parliamentary elections.

Such systems can also be used for referendums. A cosmonaut cast his ballot on Russia's 2020 constitutional referendums from the International Space Station,[7] while several Swiss cantons have experimented with multiple online voting systems for referendums.[8]

Of course, the biggest concern with online voting of any sort is security, and there are a variety of approaches for achieving this, ranging from E-ID cards (widely used in Estonia for a multitude of purposes); encrypted keys distributed among party officials; blockchain voting; allowing voters to check the validity of votes; and using algorithms and physical checks to flag unusual behaviour and ensure voter identity. Others advocate the use of open-source code as the ideal way to identify and flag vulnerabilities.

These online security measures tend to at least partially mirror the way in which offline elections are secured – party officials generally observe vote tabulations and acquiesce to the final count (which is, due to human error, rarely completely accurate). In addition, unusual behaviour, such as unrealistic voter turn-out or voting patterns that deviate wildly from pre-election polling may attract further investigation.

---

7 'Cosmonaut votes on Putin's reforms from ISS.' *Moscow Times* (30 June 2020): www.themoscowtimes.com/2020/06/30/russian-cosmonaut-votes-on-putins-reforms-from-iss-a70742.
8 Serdult, U., Germann, M., Mendez, F., Portenier, A., and Wellig, C. (2015) 'Fifteen years of internet voting in Switzerland: history, governance and use.' In Luis Teran and Andreas Meier (eds.) *Second International Conference on eDemocracy & eGovernment (ICEDEG):* www.researchgate.net/publication/283878260.

On a fundamental level, security concerns around online voting can be resolved in one of three ways:
- the online infrastructure is deemed satisfactorily secure by the population, parties, and election officials;
- voting is complemented by other activities such as ideation, debate, and the ability to easily re-vote, making it harder to maintain fraudulent results and substantially decreasing the incentive to commit electoral fraud;
- the requirements on ballot secrecy are lowered.

The third option is certainly the most controversial. However, there are some points that speak for it.

The first is that secret ballots stem from a time when voters were required to physically visit a polling place, a circumstance that opened them up to intimidation and bribery should their vote become known. This danger is significantly reduced in an online environment.

The second is that it is relatively easy to maintain a kind of pseudo-secrecy in online voting, whereby voters have a constant but anonymized online identity. In theory, this could be hacked to reveal the identity of a voter, if not immediately then using better technology in the future. However, the dangers to the average voter of potentially having their vote decrypted many years in the future are questionable.

Not only do many voters willingly post photos of their ballots on social media, but parties and candidates already have a good idea of who votes for them. During Barack Obama's second presidential campaign, party members claimed to hold 1,000 pieces of information on each voter and to know the identity of every single person who had voted for their candidate in the previous election.[9] In other nations (e. g. Ireland), parties keep careful tabs on each person who cast a vote, and, while some guesswork is involved, are remarkably accurate at identifying who voted for them.

The difference between online and offline voting secrecy is thus not quite as marked as it seems at first glance, and this remains an underexplored option for dealing with the security issues surrounding online voting.

The impetus to deal with these issues has certainly increased since the coronavirus pandemic renewed interest in distance voting after several elections had to be postponed during the pandemic, and others (particularly in the United

---

9 Issenberg, Sasha (2012) 'How Obama's team used Big Data to rally voters.' *MIT Technology Review* (19 December): www.technologyreview.com/s/509026/how-obamas-team-used-big-data-to-rally-voters/.

States) became mired in controversy due to novel no-contact methods of voting (drop-boxes, ballot collection).

Constituency Representation (Debate/Decision-Making/Implementation)

Even the Burkean philosophy of representative democracy acknowledges that representatives are supposed to act in the interests of their constituents (if not always their un-intermediated expressed will). Canvassing, in the nations where it is practised, *can* give representatives a good idea of voter preferences, but tends to focus on 'getting out the vote', meaning that representatives often disproportionately canvass those people they know are already aligned to their party. This can give them a distorted view of public opinion in their constituency. In addition, representatives can face pressure from their party to vote according to the party line.

According to one political insider, describing the American party system:

> A loyal, time-serving member of Congress could expect easy renomination, financial help, promotion through the ranks of committees and leadership jobs, and a new airport or research center for his district. A turncoat or troublemaker, by contrast, could expect to encounter ostracism, marginalization, and difficulties with fund-raising.[10]

Thus, even if a representative *knows* what their constituents want, it may be all but impossible for them to act on that information.

In order to counteract these issues, a number of people and parties have campaigned on the idea that elected representatives should be bound by constituency-level votes. This often takes the form of Independent candidates, for example Ben Gleib (a comedian who ran for US president),[11] Michael Allman (an American Republican),[12] and myself, Roslyn Fuller (an Independent Irish candidate). Gleib had links with an American application, democracy.space that utilizes blockchain to facilitate online voting on laws,[13] while I elucidated a compre-

---

10 Rauch, Jonathan (2016) 'How American politics went insane.' *Atlantic* (July/August): https://www.theatlantic.com/magazine/archive/2016/07/how-american-politics-went-insane/485570/.
11 'Ben Gleib for President': www.gleib2020.com.
12 Peters, Adele (2018) 'This candidate for Congress will let his constituents decide how he votes.' *Fast Company* (1 February): www.fastcompany.com/40509226/this-candidate-for-congress-will-let-his-constituents-decide-how-he-votes.
13 Information obtained from interviews with the author.

hensive draft platform from my would-be constituents by inviting them to vote using Canadian software Ethelo.[14] Running an independent candidacy is, however, difficult, and perhaps due to this, efforts to involve party members in online participation rather than constituents in general have been more successful.

For example, the Five Star Movement (M5S) in Italy used the online voting tool *Rousseau* for a number of years. This tool allowed party members to vote on policy (e.g. on whether to form a coalition with another party), as well as to select candidates, and interact with representatives on legislation at all levels of government. As the largest single party in the Italian parliament and part of Italy's coalition government for several years, M5S represents one of the most successful examples of digital democracy in the world today.[15] Other examples include the Icelandic Pirate Party, which runs an online policy and development site for members,[16] as well as the Spanish party, Podemos.

While Podemos's online internal democracy has been less utilized than the Five Star process, it did contribute to one very notable vote: whether party leader Pablo Iglesias and his partner should lose their positions for buying a pricey home felt to contravene the party's social direction.[17] While the couple survived the membership vote, it demonstrates that some forms of digital participation can be used by party membership to call elected representatives to account in ways that were previously impractical.

This same logic can be applied to other member-based organizations, such as unions, cooperatives, and even corporate shareholders to further economic democracy.

Petition (Ideation)

Petitioning also lends itself easily to digitalization. This could include gathering signatures to initiate a referendum, or directly petitioning parliament or another authority to pass, amend, or repeal a law, take another measure, or change a pol-

---

14 '2016 fuller democracy – the results': http://fullerdemocracy.com/2016-fuller-democracy-the-results/.

15 McIntosh, Jane (2018) 'Who are Italy's two leading populist parties: Five Star Movement and the League?' *Deutsche Welle* (6 March): https://www.dw.com/en/who-are-italys-two-leading-populist-parties-five-star-movement-and-the-league/a-42838238; for more details on the Rousseau software see: Fuller, R. H. (2021) *SDI Digital Democracy Report:* https://www.solonian-institute.com/digitaldemocracyreport.

16 'Issues to discuss' (*Piratar Kosningakerfi*): https://x.piratar.is/polity/1/topics/.

17 'Spain's far-left leader wins confidence vote after luxury home purchase.' *RTE* (28 May 2018).

icy.[18] Several online petition vehicles have been launched over the last decades with varying degrees of success.

The White House petition platform, launched under President Obama, while initially celebrated, does not appear, at this point, to have had a significant impact on American politics. Although the White House diligently responded to the petitions (including one well-known prank petition to build the Death Star from Star Wars), these responses tended to simply reiterate pre-existing policy.[19]

The British online petition has met a similar fate. The original system, which allowed an MP to take up a petition during 'backbench time'[20] was replaced by a Petition Committee in 2015. Currently, if a petition receives 10,000 signatures, the government will issue a response, whereas if a petition receives 100,000 signatures it 'will be considered for debate in Parliament'.[21] However, these debates (if they occur at all) are usually Westminster Hall debates, which take place in a side chamber and 'give MPs an opportunity to raise local or national issues and receive a response from a government minister'. Such debates can take place with as few as three people present,[22] and tend to end with the Minister giving his or her response on the matter, often a reiteration of government policy. It is unlikely that this is what most citizens imagine under 'a debate in parliament'.

Similarly, the European Citizens' Initiative, possibly the most ambitious and large-scale petition mechanism to date, has struggled with a lack of publicity, as well as technical hurdles, such as a requirement that petitions be officially registered and convoluted rules as to how collected signatures must be distributed across Member States. Perhaps most importantly, however, the initiative also simply results in a 'response' from the European Commission, which is free to reject a proposal as long as it gives reasons for doing so.[23]

---

18 For the purposes of this chapter, 'petitioning' is construed as an umbrella term encompassing both petitions in the narrower sense (a plea to authority to fulfil a certain action) and 'petitioning' in the wider sense, including petitioning for a referendum to be held, even in cases where the authorities lack discretion to deny such a 'petition'.

19 The archives can be viewed here: https://petitions.obamawhitehouse.archives.gov/.

20 See Fuller, *Beasts and* Gods, pp. 125 et seq for a discussion of the previous platform.

21 'Petitions' (UK Government and Parliament): https://petition.parliament.uk/.

22 'Westminster Hall debates' (UK Parliament): www.parliament.uk/about/how/business/debates/westminster-hall-debates/

23 For more on the European Citizens' Initiative, see Athanasiadou, Natassa (2019) 'The European Citizens' Initiative: lost in admissibility?' *Maastricht Journal of European and Comparative Law* (June): https://journals.sagepub.com/doi/full/10.1177/1023263X18824772. It is possible that the involvement of the European Parliament in debating and voting on such initiatives (as it did in the 'End the Cage' petition) may help to revitalize this process.

Thus, while petitioning provides a way for ideas to originate with citizens (rather than top-down), online petitions often lack meaningful follow-through, in contrast to traditional forms of offline petition that are geared towards triggering referendums, for example in California and Switzerland (direct model).

There are, however, examples of online petitions with a greater degree of success in Latvia and Estonia. These processes, like their successful offline counterparts, tend to link directly into the political process in a more meaningful way, rather than just generating 'responses'.

For example, Manabalss in Latvia is an online petitioning site, whereby petitions that receive more than 10,000 signatures must be voted on in parliament (as opposed to merely discussed or answered). In a country with some 1.5 million registered voters this is a relatively low bar (less than 1 percent of the voting population must sign the petition). In addition, petitioners are provided with support to craft their proposals into working legislation (reducing the risk that they are rejected on technicalities) and are allowed to call witnesses in the parliament to support their proposals. A key factor with Manabalss is that it is a separate institution, not run by the government but financed by micro-payments. In this manner, it is able to stand apart from the government rather than being controlled by it and function more effectively as a 'voice of the people'. Similarly, Rahvalgatuus.ee in Estonia uses a low bar to petitioning (1,000 signatures for a discussion in parliament), as well as continuous follow-ups on the fate of proposals to keep citizens engaged in the process.[24]

Because the petition process in Estonia and Latvia is connected to representative democracy (as opposed to direct democracy), the connection between petition and action is not always clear-cut. At times, petitions that receive low levels of signatures are adopted by authorities, presumably because the content accords with the governmental programme. Because the signature barrier is low, there is no compelling case as to why any particular petition should be adopted into law. Some are clearly frivolous and unlikely to enjoy majority support in any event.[25]

However, what distinguishes the Baltic petition sites from the Anglo-Saxon ones is not a different legal approach, but a difference in the quality of follow-through. Successful petitions are often either debated in parliament or passed to the subject-matter committee or department responsible (just as other draft legislation would be). These bodies tend to deal with the matter thoroughly, often in quite technical detail. Rather than avoiding or downplaying the

---

24 Fuller, *Digital Democracy Report*.
25 For past and current Latvian petitions, see: https://manabalss.lv/page/progress.

issues at stake (dysfunctional representative mode), the Baltic approach tends to squarely deal with the issue at hand (functional representative mode).

Participatory Budgeting (Debate/Decision-Making)

Participatory budgeting (or PB as it is often known) was first conceived of as an offline form of participation that allowed residents to allocate public funds for various purposes in their neighbourhood (for a more thorough discussion, see Greta Ríos's chapter in this book). Its first use was in Porto Alegre, Brazil in 1989.[26] Since then, PB has grown exponentially, and is conducted in various forms around the world. Some of these uses (as in Brazil) have been far-reaching in their powers and thus able to deliver meaningful change for participants.[27] Others, particularly those in Western nations, tend to focus on discretionary spending items of more limited importance, such as arts or recreational projects. Although it started offline, participatory budgeting lends itself well to online conversion or hybrid online/offline models.

PB often involves participants initiating proposals for public spending (e. g. improving street lighting; building a childcare centre), and then voting on a number of these proposals. Arranging these proposals online (where they can be supplemented by videos, photos, and other information) can help participants make comparative decisions. This also allows a greater number of people to vote than would likely otherwise be the case, and, where comments are allowed, also lets them make the case for a project to other voters.

Participatory budgeting also serves the purpose of educating participants about costs and planning, often by allocating each of them a fixed amount of money that they can 'spend' on projects that have been costed in a way that is visible to the public.

One of the most long-running examples of online participatory budgeting is Better Reykjavik in Iceland, which has been in use since 2010.[28] South Dublin

---

26 For a more in-depth look at the origins and development of participatory budgeting in Porto Alegre, see an interview with organizer Tarson Nunez (2021): 'Building trust & breaking down complexity: the past, present & future of participatory budgeting.' *Solonian Democracy Institute* (24 November): www.solonian-institute.com/post/building-trust-breaking-down-complexity-the-past-present-future-of-participatory-budgeting.

27 See Wampler, Brian (2012) 'Citizen participation and participatory institutions in Brazil.' International Conference on Public Participation of the Gauteng Legislature.

28 The platform can be viewed here: https://betrireykjavik.is/domain/1/communities, while more information on its creators, Citizens Foundation is available here: www.citizens.is/.

County Council in Ireland and the City of Paris have also run multi-year online or online/offline PB processes.[29]

PB has likely become so widespread because, although it can be run ineffectively, it has few downsides for elected representatives. Although it can curtail corruption and patronage, it also relieves representatives of making decisions on local public infrastructure, such as swimming pools, lighting, or park benches, which inevitably run the risk of pleasing some constituents while displeasing others.

Planning (Debate)

Planning consultations typically take place at community centres in the evening or with plans displayed in libraries or county councils. Such modes of participation have not always kept pace with technology. Time-strapped parents, for example, don't necessarily have time to attend in-person meetings, and the results of the meetings are often indeterminate to the participants, if not the planners. Perhaps just as pressingly, however, fewer people are as conversant with imagining projects from blueprints or sketches as they once were. For some participants, trying to understand things this way is rather like trying to enjoy a silent movie – what was once exciting technology has become a niche interest at best.

By contrast, video animation, 3-D renderings, and even virtual reality can give people today a much better idea of a project plan and even allow them to experimentally try their hand at design.

Canadian software Ethelo (which can be used for many purposes) as well as American provider PolCo have often been involved in local planning on issues from aquatic complexes to community centres.[30] Ethelo, in particular, has the ability to allow participants to design a community centre, park, or other local amenity, subject to in-built constraints (such as total cost, building footprint, etc.). Because participants can weight their votes according to what is most important to them (e.g. sports), this can help planners (and the public) to determine where consensus lies on any given dimension (a dirt-bike track in a

---

29 The South Dublin County Council site can be viewed here: https://haveyoursay.southdublin. ie/, while additional information on the Paris participatory budget can be viewed here: Clement, Megan (2019) 'Pissoirs and public votes: how Paris embraced the participatory budget.' *Guardian* (3 October): www.theguardian.com/cities/2019/oct/03/pissoirs-and-public-votes-how-paris-embraced-the-participatory-budget.

30 Information obtained from interviews with platform providers, as well as usage in combination with local bodies.

park, for example, might attract strong support and dissent, while a conventional bike path might attract more general support).

Consultation (Debate)

Some nations require public consultations to be conducted on a variety of issues from building to arts initiatives. Consultations are generally non-binding, but they also notoriously suffer from being ill-advertised and often lack transparency (the average person frequently does not even know that a consultation has been held, and even people who do know are rarely informed as to what the outcome was or how public participation affected that outcome).

Many nations hold online consultations, but Taiwan's have been particularly innovative over the past few years under the influence of Digital Minister Audrey Tang. In the past, these have included consultations on Uber drivers and alcohol licensing that focus heavily on allowing participants to communicate with each other, while seeking to build a consensus across multiple different aspects of regulation.

Perhaps even more interesting, however, were Taiwan's snap consultations on coronavirus measures at the beginning of the COVID-19 pandemic. Some of these consultations utilized Slido, a simple software primarily used by corporations to facilitate crowd engagement at business events.[31] By allowing people to participate on Slido, the Taiwanese government was able to get an instant idea of where citizens stood on coronavirus measures – unlike most nations which were forced to act in a vacuum as to what their citizens' preferred course of action was. This example shows how digital tools can be flexibly deployed to gain public input even in difficult, crisis scenarios.

Benefits of Digital Democracy

Minimizing Undue Influence

There are two main avenues used to manipulate modern democracy: the first is to influence the process by utilizing the resources of non-human entities (the legal term is 'non-natural persons') that do not have the right to vote; and the second is to use networks to amplify some voices and drown out others. Both

---

31 Information obtained through interviews with providers.

of these problems have plagued direct and representative democracy since their modern, post-Enlightenment inception.

There are many forms 'non-humans' can take: bots, of course, but also corporations, and non-profit organizations (some of which are large enough to spend hundreds of millions of dollars annually). Such organizations can use these resources to try to distort public opinion in multiple ways, but one of the most common is to continuously ensure that they dominate the discussion.

It is also possible for humans who are entitled to vote to form into networks, constantly amplifying a single message and using their followers to drown out others.

Democracy depends on each person using their own reason and knowledge to contribute to the formation of 'the general will'.[32] When a participant fails to do this, they fail to contribute in any meaningful way to political decision-making, and invalidate the reason for their participatory rights to exist in the first place. This domineering behaviour is thus extremely detrimental, although, unfortunately, it is increasingly accepted as a natural fact of existence.

However, using digital tools it is possible to create decision-making institutions that entirely exclude non-human actors, as well as making it impossible for participants to gain influence in the form of followers. This helps to cut down on the distortion of political debate that can be perpetrated by bad-faith actors (e. g. a corporation that forms an astro-turf group in order to prevent industry regulation or a political group that instructs its members on how to discredit people with opposing viewpoints). Indeed, it is not only possible to do this, but it is actually easier to do so than not to, because tightly controlling and verifying participants and starting each exercise afresh help to maintain the security of the online system.

Not only does this help to reduce distortion, but it may also help to reduce polarization of the debate. While different tools take various approaches to discussion (some tools, like PolCo for example, prefer to split comments into 'for' and 'against' columns that prevent the people in each group from engaging with each other directly),[33] almost all platform providers report extremely low numbers of harassing comments, with some reporting none at all, even after years of use.[34]

Part of this may be psychological: perhaps people who are attracted to local civic exercises (and most digital democracy is exercised on the local level) are

---

32 See Rousseau, *The Social Contract and Discourses*.
33 Information obtained via interviews.
34 This information gained from numerous interviews between the author and operators of a large number of civil participation platforms during research between 2017 and 2021.

less likely to be antagonistic to others. It is equally possible that the material often lends itself less to vitriolic comment.

What speaks against this theory as a full explanation, however, is that participants are sometimes blunt, harsh, and critical vis-à-vis the subject matter under debate, but still rarely attack each other.

It is possible that this partially stems from the lack of organization. Political organization, of necessity, involves drawing boundaries and sharpening divisions, often in ways that are intended to endure over years. For a party, the best, and most secure, voter is one who truly hates the other parties.

Professional campaigns of division often require a great degree of organization and a certain amount of money. One has to *mobilize* people. If one excludes non-human actors, however, and strips off the ability of any individual to retain a network of followers, it becomes very hard to mobilize. And since people cannot be mobilized, they have to be convinced. Similarly, with no obvious influencers on the opposing 'side', participants are left without a clear target to 'take down'.

This disincentivizes needlessly antagonistic commenting. Debate may still be acrimonious (and there is no reason it should be conflict-free),[35] but at least this acrimony will not be fuelled to fever pitch by organized forces capable of sustaining long-running conflict.[36]

Efficient and Flexible

Digital democracy can be put into use very swiftly, as evidenced by the Taiwanese consultation at the beginning of the pandemic. In addition, most digital tools are quite flexible – some tools with participatory budgeting capacity, like Ethelo for example, have been repurposed to conduct carbon budgeting instead. Digital tools can be easily scaled for use in small, large, or even specialist groups. For example, Discuto, an Austrian tool, was used by the Consumers' As-

---

35 Residents of Okotoks, Alberta, for example, thoroughly rejected plans to densify their local area in no uncertain terms during an Ethelo exercise. The records are available here: https://okotoks-2080.ethelo.net/page/collective-results.
36 It is, of course, also possible to simply make rules banning hate speech, demeaning words, and stalking, as well as to enable content moderation, either via crowd-sourced moderation or a moderator.

sociation to develop certification criteria for its eco-label,[37] while SkyVote, an Italian tool, is often used at shareholder meetings. At the same time, other tools, like Rousseau or the Estonian i-voting system, can handle hundreds of thousands or even millions of concurrent participants. This is important, as only mechanisms that ensure free and equal participation may rightly be termed 'democratic'. Any technology used to facilitate democracy must thus possess the scale to permit all entitled and interested citizens to participate.

Access

Digital voting has often been supported by groups of overseas voters, who have the right to vote in their home country but no practical ability to do so.[38] More frequent travel and temporary out-of-country work arrangements have increased this issue to the point where the decision to allow or disallow such voting could alter political outcomes.

In addition, digital voting can permit people living with disability to exercise their democratic rights independently, more deeply, and in some cases at all (facilitating voting for the disabled was a key reason for certain American counties to authorize the use of Voatz in elections).[39]

Counteracting Other Uses of Technology

Many uses of digital technology are highly coercive. This can include surveillance, censorship, neurolinguistic analysis of public sentiment, and bots directed at manipulating public opinion. All of these take control away from the user and have the potential to facilitate a totalitarian society. It is imperative that citizens not remain isolated and without a method of using their collective power that equals the threat posed by the coercive potential of technology.

---

37 'Überarbeitung Umweltzeichen Tourismus – Überblick / Ausblick / Anhang' (Discuto): www.discuto.io/en/informationsseite/ueberarbeitung-umweltzeichen-tourismus-ueberblick-ausblick-anhang.

38 Serdult et al., 'Fifteen years of internet voting.'

39 Mearian, Lucas (2019) 'Utah county moves to expand mobile voting through blockchain.' *ComputerWorld* (21 October): https://www.computerworld.com/article/3446836/utah-county-moves-to-expand-mobile-voting-through-blockchain.html.

Concerns Posed for Digital Democracy

We have already touched on some of the most pressing concerns for digital democracy, such as security and the potential for manipulation, above. These are, as we have seen, serious, if likely not insurmountable, challenges. However, here I would like to discuss two often overlooked points: implementation and the digital transition. These are not necessarily technical challenges, but they are perhaps even more serious political challenges for digital democracy.

Implementation

One of the key issues faced by advocates and practitioners of digital democracy is implementation. Just as every decision of parliament must be executed, so, too, every decision made online, whether it be a referendum or participatory budgeting, must also be executed in the real world. Digital democracy can itself serve as a way to pressure for implementation, because it often creates a transparent view of what people want. In situations where there is a high level of participation and a clear majority in favour of a decision, it is hard to see why it should not be implemented.

However, many politicians and civil servants tend to see digital participation as a way to glean insights into voters' minds and behaviour, rather than as a way to let them take the lead. Thus, all too often, what starts as an exercise in 'hearing other voices' or 'listening to citizens' turns into a way to monitor them in order to try to anticipate their behaviour (a favourite here is 'social listening', that is, tracking what people say about you on social media so that you can counteract their messaging). Thus, rather than democracy, there is a tendency towards instituting processes that could better be described as enlightened despotism.

Too often, civil servants and politicians feel the need to comply with buzzwords like 'engagement' without having thought through what that means or why citizens would want to engage. This leads to two kinds of implementation difficulties – the first is with the process itself, which often fails to have clear parameters for participation (citizens are at sea as to why they are participating or what happens to their data), and the second is in producing concrete outcomes. In a successful project, citizens should be able to point to something in their lives and say (whether they agree with it or not), 'that happened because of a consultation, participatory budget, vote' and so on. When this fails to happen, citizens can quickly lose trust in the process and refuse to participate again.

A key example of this in action was the 'Boaty McBoatface' incident. In an early experiment in online democracy the British National Environment Research Council asked the public to name a research vessel. The normal and expected thing to do (as became clear in the aftermath) is to name a ship after a respected person of longstanding public service. Bucking this trend, the public chose to call the vessel 'Boaty McBoatface'. This created something of a mini-scandal at the time, and is sometimes used as an example of the irresponsibility of the masses.[40]

Organizers would do better to think of these moments as a test. The public is (rightly) sceptical as to whether authorities will 'really' follow their instructions, and thus they create 'tests' or 'traps' to validate their assumptions. When organizers fail this test (the ship in question was duly named the *RSS Sir David Attenborough*), participants conclude that such opportunities are not 'serious' and thus not worth their time.

One can only be associated with a 'window-dressing' level of democracy for so long, before it tarnishes one's reputation completely, and this is a real risk for advocates of digital democracy today.

Digital Transitioning

There can be a tendency to see digital democracy as an argument for instantaneous replacement of offline democracy and an end to face-to-face meeting. This is a course of action few, if any, digital democrats endorse. Many digital democracy advocates are also politically active offline, and some of the most successful participatory forms of democracy blend offline and online experiences.

For example, while M5S used Rousseau (and now SkyVote) to facilitate online participation in a number of ways, this was also complemented with offline participation in the form of meetings, candidate question periods, protests, and other forms of engagement. Similarly, many participatory budgeting projects allow for both online and offline ideation phases, as well as voting. People who do not have access to, or do not want to use, the internet should not be obligated to in order to participate. Even in a future that may include a virtual reality Metaverse, this will continue to be the case.

---

40 Boylan, Jennifer Finney (2020) 'Trump and the Boaty McBoatfacing of America.' *New York Times* (28 October): https://www.nytimes.com/2020/10/28/opinion/trump-boaty-mcboatface.html.

There is no reason why digital democracy could or should outpace the adoption of technology for other uses. However, if it lags too far behind, it runs the risk of beginning to seem anachronistic. To make a simple analogy: some professional photographers swear by the superior virtues of film, but it is no longer used by the vast majority of consumers. While it once seemed perfectly normal to wait for one's photos to be developed, it now feels like a ridiculously onerous activity. People tend to take the path of least resistance, rarely engaging in activity that demands more energy than it has to. The plus side of this is that it opens up opportunities to use the surplus energy. People certainly take more photos since they no longer have to pay to have them developed.

Likewise, instant communication has created surplus capacity for democracy today, which should be channelled into constructive uses. Failing to grasp the opportunities presented by digital democracy risks allowing this surplus energy to degenerate into frustration and possibly destructive behaviour. It is thus important that such a transition be managed constructively and proactively rather than just reflexively blocked.

Conclusions

The much-loved comparisons of digital technology to the printing press are not misplaced, as, like the printing press, digital communication has the ability not just to revolutionize our technical abilities, but our sociological ones as well. There are various paths such change could take (as we have seen above) and certainly many very real challenges. However, the progress that has been made along this path is already significant and robust, with many examples of enduring and productive digital democracy existing in the field.

Gil Delannoi
Sortition in Current Democratic Regimes

So, you want to draw a sample of the population? Then, you have to learn the basics of sortition. As a researcher and scholar on sortition, I have heard many diverse questions that have been raised by people from all walks of life. They had divergent interests, different commitments, and were sometimes clear and sometimes contradictory. This chapter aims to summarize and answer these questions.

The issue can be expressed in one sentence: If you want to use the lottery and conduct a democratic draw, these points are necessary to know and follow. Here, sortition is defined as the use of a lottery to select and appoint officials or any other type of member for a function or position to be held in a group smaller than the entire population or body politic. Hence, the word 'sortition' is in most cases interchangeable with 'lottery', drawing of lots, or random selection of individuals. Direct democracy is defined here as popular assembly or referendum, and implies a first and last word given to the people in the political system.

Introduction

On the underlying structure of the following paragraphs, the common thread of the questions is made of two elements: history and theory show that sortition mainly belongs to the category of direct democracy (A), but sortition is always more or less than direct democracy (B).

Different feelings can be justified: sortition has just emerged from near nothingness. I am not the only one, but I can testify personally to the recent aspect of this adventure towards outgoing democracy. At the beginning of the 2000s, a few isolated books provided a start to sortition. I had gathered some of the main authors (not all, but a significant part) for a conference.[1] There was little audience and little echo. A movement was beginning to take place, but it was academic, perhaps not utopian, but eccentric. Since then, sortition has been elaborated and tested in theory and practice.

---

1 Delannoi, G. and Dowlen, O. (2016) *Sortition: Theory and Practice*, vol. 3. Upper Pine: Academic Imprint.

https://doi.org/10.1515/9783110747331-009

In France, sortition as a procedure was mentioned on the political scene by several candidates for the 2017 presidential election.[2] These proposals were one of the many singularities of this 2017 election. They were unprecedented at national level in any other country. During the Socialist primary elections, Arnaud Montebourg proposed that a senator be chosen by lot from the citizens of each French *départment*. In a speech in Frangy, he imagined a Senate designated in three thirds: one-third of citizens selected by lot, one-third of scientists and technicians, and one-third of elected representatives according to the procedure in force, in order to maintain a representation of the territories. Arnaud Montebourg tested sortition locally when he entrusted the task of supervising a budget and local tax increases to a jury of randomly selected citizens.

Jean-Luc Mélenchon's project was not intended to be regular or repeated, since he recommended the lottery as a procedure among others to appoint a Constituent Assembly. This complicated device amounts to leaving the choice of procedure to the electorate. The voter is able either to vote for a representative or to give his or her vote to a drawing of lots that will be carried out afterwards in a particular trade-off between vote and draw.

Last but not least, the candidate Emmanuel Macron announced that sortition would be used during his presidency. After his election, the promises were only partially kept, possibly thwarted by the pandemic. We will look at la Convention Citoyenne sur le Climat (CCC) (see §13).

Material

What is the relationship between sortition and direct democracy? Democracy was born direct. The democratic regime excluded out most indirect procedures. The etymology, the first documented experiment and a regime of quasi-forced participation from Athens via small republics and free cities, has always involved the more or less extensive use of sortition. This fact was still evident to Montesquieu. With very different modalities, very variable intensity, but with consistency, sortition was and remains, on a par with voting, the republican and democratic procedure.

Why is sortition more or less than direct democracy? Summing up, direct democracy in a single formula would come down to this: the people (or any body

---

2 Delannoi, G. and Carson, L. (2017) 'French presidential election and sortition.' Research and Development Note: https://www. newdemocracy. com. au/2017/06/20/french-presidential-election-and-sortition.

politic at any scale) have the first word and the last word in politics, whether on large decisions or the adoption of laws. This corresponds to the initiative to pass a law or vote a decision, as well as the recall of laws for possible censorship by the people, and amounts to collective deliberation as extensive as possible. The etymology of democracy was more direct in the beginning than in its evolution.

When the people have the first and the last word, this does not mean that this applies permanently and on all subjects, but that nothing can prevent the event from happening as soon as a petition – individual or collective – has shown such a will. Any law can be proposed, revised, or censored by the people. Though the use of this absolute right is not systematic, as time and energy are limited, it weighs on day-to-day politics as something potential. This first and last word does not create an obligation but a well-integrated right, a possibility, a more or less frequent practice. Even the choice of making democracy as direct as possible is left to some popular judgment.

Sortition can contribute to direct democracy by being added to the direct voting of decisions and laws, but it cannot be substituted for the vote. Without universal suffrage, the lottery cannot achieve direct democracy on its own and could even stifle any real democratic procedure behind an egalitarian smokescreen. An equal chance of being selected by lot is not democratic *per se*. Being less than vote, sortition also offers more than voting because when well used, it can bring participation, consultation, equality, and impartiality to a higher degree than the popular vote.

Better still, when the direct vote is followed by the random selection of the individuals who will carry out the decisions, it reinforces direct democracy by implicating possible participation and execution by any member of the group.

Why was sortition chosen by democrats and republicans of the now distant past? Strictly speaking, the vote on laws in the Athenian popular assembly was often more than a referendum, sometimes less. That said, a referendum is its anachronistic equivalent, particularly in a larger democracy. The crucial difference with modern democracies, even direct or attempting to be so, is the massive nature of the lottery for the courts and the fact that most of the tasks relating to the execution of decisions are entrusted to colleges of citizens selected by lot. In the modern political world, the first aspect has not disappeared, but it is limited to small juries. As for certain executive colleges of the medieval republics, they did not have the same scope or did not emanate entirely of a lottery.

In the Athenian system, the duty to carry out the joint decision oneself, because there was a chance of having been selected by lot, as an executive strongly interacted with the right to participate in that decision. Those who vote for war, for the most part, will be soldiers. In many ordinary decisions, there will be the chance or risk of being drawn to enforce the laws. Socrates's prison guards were citizens designated by the lottery. Perhaps some of them had also been chosen by lot to be jurors at the trial and had voted for or against his conviction. This strong relation between decision and execution reinforces a sense of responsibility at both stages.

Lapse (Omission and Intermission)

Why was sortition rejected by modern liberal and democratic revolutions? The extension of the vote parallel to the disappearance of sortition corresponds to the transition to representative regimes, whose procedures are inherited from religious institutions, free towns, and certain medieval corporate practices. It is true that modern parliamentary democracies, based on national representation and competition between parties, no longer need the lottery. This is mainly why sortition fell into disuse without having been the subject of controversy. The disappearance of sortition did not produce texts unfavorable to the lottery, nor controversies over the respective advantages and defects of the two procedures as happened in Florence in the Quattrocento, but only a lack of interest. The drawing of lots was no longer in the register of modern political procedures.

Should we oppose sortition and voting? Drawing lots and electing by vote are two inseparable pillars of any known democratic regime in which sortition has been used. No democratic regime has dispensed with voting, whether to elect people, make decisions, or pass laws. A political regime which would have replaced the vote by sortition remains a pure utopia. The most comical version was given by Aristophanes in *Assemblywomen* (*Ekklesiazousai*). The plot amounts to an egalitarian revolution founding every civil or public law on the lottery.

How had sortition subsisted in residual form? Sortition survived in some courts of justice for a small number of jurors and was practiced on a larger scale when a draft was used for military service. In many cases, the lottery was not used in accordance with the democratic principles it was more or less supposed to implement. The drawing of conscripts for military service, as it was practiced in France, lost its egalitarian character. Established in France during the Revolution, conscription was regulated by various forms of lotteries from 1804 until 1905. In this process, sortition turned into trade because the tickets drawn could be sold. Not all the selected individuals of the draw did the service for which they had been selected by lot. The 'winning' ticket could be transmitted, against payment, to a substitute. In fact, numbers were drawn rather than people, and those numbers were marketed afterward. One procedure can turn more or less intentionally into another. One operation can hide another. Once again, every detail mentioned or forgotten in a regulation counts.

The practical details condition the consistency, efficiency, and impact of a procedure, which depends to a much lesser extent on the material and the concrete means of the operation. A procedure is not a general idea but a set of practices. The relevance of these practices can only be measured during the procedure and according to its objective.

Accelerator

How did sortition make a comeback? Since the 1990s, we have been witnessing a return to sortition, remarkable in theory, shy in practice. Some pioneering works put the procedure back on the agenda. As early as 1989, in *Democracy and its Critics*, Robert Dahl suggested supplementing the bicameral system of the United States Congress with a third consultative chamber drawn by lot. Nowadays, some experiences of deliberative or participatory democracy are reverting to sortition after two centuries of silence.[3]

The return of sortition in democratic politics is too recent and timid for any conclusion about its importance in the near future. The present use of the draw is an immense and tiny bridge between an undisputed distant past and a promising but only sketchy future.

Where do we think we are? The idea of sortition now resonates in the political arena and what a long way it has come! says the optimist. The pessimist adds, however, as with the referendum, that what is admitted in theory is often excluded from the normal practice of democracy.

What are the various plausible benefits and possible uses of sortition today? The drawing of lots does not allow anyone to know in advance the persons susceptible to be heirs as in a legacy, nor to exchange arguments and add up wills as in a vote, nor to adjust supply and demand as in a market, nor to measure capacities as in a test or exam, nor to register affiliations as in a party or any other type of association. If sortition has a specific value, it is precisely thanks to its difference from all the other operations and procedures. As Oliver Dowlen aptly analyzes, sortition eliminates all the reasons, good or bad, which interfere in a choice.[4]

---

3 Before 2000: Dahl, *Democracy and its Critics*; Goodwin, Barbara (2005) *Justice by Lottery*, 2nd edn. Exeter: Imprint Academic; and Carson, Lyn and Martin, Brian (1999) *Random Selection in Politics*. Santa Barbara: Praeger.
4 Dowlen, Oliver (2008) *The Political Potential of Sortition*. Exeter: Imprint Academic.

As soon as the bad reasons are likely to count for half or more, the draw becomes very interesting. By eliminating all the reasons, sortition is neither rational nor irrational, but a-rational. It must be noted finally that a-rationality characterizes the choice of options made by the selection (items or people) and not the fact of having chosen selection as a procedure. This earlier choice is part of the argument for the pros and cons of the lottery. Also note in passing that it would be absurd, although possible, to use a lottery to decide whether or not to use sortition. Peter Stone argues that the draw cleanses and moralizes politics thanks to a "sanitizing effect." I would add that the advantage of sortition can be summed up in three words or three effects: impartiality, equality, serenity.

What is at stake right now? What matters above all is not the principle (vote, sortition, auction, test), it is not the 'what' (to draw or not to draw), it is the 'how' and the 'why.' All the effects, from mathematical to political, from sociological to psychological, expected or unsuspected, are all the results of the definition and arrangement of details. They must be examined in the observable consequences of a procedural device.

It is vital to avoid any clumsy and counterproductive use of sortition. Its most fervent supporters must understand that clumsy use would do considerable harm to the reception of the procedure they want to see applied. Any procedure includes one or more material operations. It is an ordered and coordinated sequence. It cannot be reduced to operations, but it cannot be intelligible and coherent without a firm mastery of the instruments.

What are the most promising uses? Sortition may be used for the designation of a consulted group, or a legislative group, or colleges of executives. The first use ranges from surveys and polls: provided the size of the sample is not too small, sortition gives a very representative sample for deliberative consultative democracy. The second use creates a possibility of quasi-parliamentarian democracy based on a descriptive representation, in mirror image of the population, as opposed to an active representation, in which the representatives are persons not in the image of the population who elects them. The third use, although very decisive in any institution (as seen in §3 about Athens), is not on the agenda today.

On what scale? On every scale. From local politics to international cooperation. And in different institutions, not just the political ones.

Which method to follow? In the study of all procedures, everything depends on details. Look at these examples: the result of a show of hands, as a non-secret and public vote, can be totally different whether you began by asking who votes 'yes' or you began by asking who votes 'no.' It's these details that matter, not the general principle. Likewise, when distributing equal speaking time (e. g. 10 minutes to 18 people, that is, three hours), the following four procedures make a significant difference. If someone does not use all their speaking time, we imme-

diately go to the next one, and we start a second rotation of speech when everybody has spoken. If, on the other hand, we speak at a fixed time (everyone is
scheduled every 10 minutes) and someone does not use all their speaking
time, we can discuss in private while waiting for the next one. Third option:
you must use all the speaking time (a rare option). Fourth: the schedule alter-
nates between speaking time and a moment for immediate discussion.

Matrix for Sortition

A/Population: Any use of the random selection of individuals, in the political
field or in another field, presupposes the existence of a population.[5] This population is made up of all the people potentially concerned, capable of performing
the future task, as citizens or inhabitants (of a state, of a country, of a region, of a
city), or even as members or agents of an organization or institution. Examples:
France, Britain, or the city of Marseille, or Turin, or the wine-growing profession
(legally registered), or mathematics teachers in secondary education, or a company, or a university.

B/Base or pool (of the draw): This database is the part of a population legally
retained for the draw. It lists all the qualified people (the pool) from a population
to participate in the operation. The image of the pyramid makes it possible to
visualize this: the top of the pyramid is the result of the draw. This base or
pool can be equivalent to the population when the entire population after
legal verification is listed in the database. By contrast, a restricted base is limited
to a small number of people from among whom the draw is made. This restriction takes various proportions: depending on the criteria, of the order of 90, 50,
10, or 1 percent of a population, or even a few individuals, two being the bare
minimum for any random selection. A base will therefore be equal to or smaller
than the population. Examples: for a jury at a tribunal, only adults are retained.
Among the members of a profession, if a few years of experience are required,
only those with a certain number of years of experience are listed in the database. Likewise, if all the students of a university are selected by lot for internal
functions, the first-year students may have to wait one year or one semester before being included in the pool because they have to become familiar with the
institution. A draw for military service is obviously limited by criteria of age
and physical capacity.

---

5 Delannoi, Gil (2019) *Le Tirage au sort, comment l'utiliser?* Paris: Presses de la Fondation na-
tionale des Sciences Politiques.

C/Qualification: Any definition of a database goes through a qualification procedure. The qualification gives the criterion defining a legal base of people taking part in any lottery draw. There are countless usable criteria, ranging from the simple verification of a population to the skill test. Examples: in a national population only residents may be qualified, whereas non-residents are not because they are too far away or too little concerned. The criterion is nationality. In some cases, the draw may be open to non-national residents, with the criterion being residence. In other cases, the draw may concern all nationals, including non-residents. The criteria can be age: above 18, 30, or 40 years old. Another case: if the skill required by the function to be performed is precise or technical, it would be necessary to be qualified on a prior test and pass it to be included in the database (or pool). Skills are very diverse. The ability of those listed in the base may be related to the writing or mastery of a language or to the knowledge of the elements essential for future functions, which may be more or less technical, more or less easy to exercise. Every qualification has to be adapted to each situation.

D/Application (or candidacy): This designates the act of voluntary registration in a database. The application may or may not be subject to filling in of the qualification. This act takes place before the application form if conditions are required, or after the acceptance of the application form if a test is necessary to qualify the candidates for the draw.

E/Refusal (to be registered in a base): This is the possibility that a candidate might not appear in the base, or might withdraw from it before the draw, either by expressing a refusal prior to any possibility of registration (strong refusal, comparable to abstention), or by asking to be withdrawn from a registration already made by an administration, which can then be done piecemeal or for short or long durations.

F/Withdrawal: This designates the right to resign from one's election after the draw, after the transaction (*ex post*). This withdrawal occurs after the drawing operation and before the appointment for the function. The selected person, by withdrawing, frees a place for a person who has arrived further down on the list of people selected by lot.

G/Selection by lot: The person (s)elected by lot is a person selected by the drawing operation. To study the stages of the procedure, the parallel with voting is essential.

Draw → elements drawn → (s)election
Vote → ballot → election

The word 'election' may be a surprise when it comes to the draw. It is, however, entirely appropriate, if only by comparison with a vote. Both procedures require a population, a base, and then an election operation. What is the difference? Voting proceeds by adding votes on names (or options), whereas drawing is by extraction of names (or numbers). In both cases, the final designation of those elected constitutes the result of the election. Regardless of the operation to be carried out, it does not matter whether this election is the result of an addition of votes or a subtraction of one or more names from among a pool or population. At the end of the process, there are people who are elected or people to whom objects are assigned. And vote indeed can also be used for assigning objects or items to individuals or groups. That said, if the word 'election' is a source of possible confusion among the public, the word 'selection' is just as good.

H/List: This word refers to the extensive nomination of all the people included in a database before the draw (as preparation) and to the final list of the persons chosen by lot (result). There are therefore several lists to be considered in a draw: a listed population, a listed qualified legal base, that of the persons selected by lot, with each going down in size. This last list, if it is ordained (drawn first, second, etc.), constitutes a reserve, making it possible to supplement, if necessary. This reserve serves to replace people in the event of withdrawal after the draw or resignation during the term of office. This list of selected officials (kept secret or published) avoids carrying out a new and partial drawing operation each time a replacement is required.

Menu

The Convention Citoyenne pour le Climat began to meet in October 2019, under the aegis of the Economic, Social, and Environmental Council. It gathered 150 citizens drawn by lot. A report released by CCC members in June 2020 included 149 proposals. Almost all of the proposals are the subject of a legal supplement relating to the creation or transformation of laws linked to existing codes of law: work, environment, consumption, education, research, and energy. A legal committee of six jurists undertook this task.

From October 2019 to June 2020, the convention met over seven weekends. The debates were public and broadcast. Most of the time was devoted to expert interventions, lasting around 85 hours. The CCC's deliberation time remained limited.

The CCC was by no means an assembly in the vein of parliament. Its agenda was limited to one item, "To reduce the French emissions of greenhouse gas by at least 40% compared to 1990, in a spirit of social justice." The members gathered in 'thematic groups,' whose themes were defined by the organizers of the assembly, not its members. The schedule and manner in which assembly members considered all of its issues were highly circumscribed, from the questions asked to the facts and witnesses admitted.

> Without external structure, the CCC would have failed completely. Perhaps a better way to think of the CCC is as a jury, not an assembly, whose purpose was to render a verdict on various aspects of the technocratic consensus. There is one thing missing: an adversarial matchup of different ideological viewpoints. In a courtroom, this would be lawyers from opposing sides. However, for the CCC, all of the structure came from a single source: the French Economic, Social, and Environmental Council. It seems to have done a good job from a substantive point of view, but from a Dahlian procedural perspective, a single technocratic source is unacceptable. What's needed, then, is a way to accomplish this task pluralistically.[6]

The drawing of lots was operated in accordance with six criteria: gender, age, level of qualification, socio-professional category, type of territory, and geographical area. This is less a drawing of lots than an invitation sample on the basis of a lottery before rectification by social criteria and subject to acceptance by the guests. Over 100,000 phone calls or invitations to 150 'elected officials' create disproportion and waste of energy.[7]

It remains to be seen whether this practice is as democratic as a parliament. In every case? Certainly not. The People's Republic of China is more inclined to use such a device than to have a true pluralist parliament. Once again, no procedure is democratic in itself. Any procedure can be turned into a ploy of undemocratic manipulation. This remark does not reject sortition at all. This only means that there is still a long way to go before reaching the democratic port. This safe democratic haven conversely is not a lottery without a qualified base in every case. It is running the risk of bringing together people who have not been selected by the organizers before and after the draw, nor according to their own willingness to participate after the results of the draw. Sortition is more likely to have democratic effects when the procedure superposes right and duty to serve. To ponder over the multiple options available to the organizers, see the Matrix above.

---

6 Kovner, Alex and Sutherland, Keith (2020) 'Problems of Citizens' Assemblies.' *Academia Letters* November.

7 Fabre, A., Apouey, B., Douenne, T., Giraudet, L.-G., Laslier, J.-F. et al. 'Convention Citoyenne pour le Climat: les citoyens de la Convention comparés à des échantillons représentatifs de la population française': https://halshs.archives-ouvertes.fr/halshs-02919695/document.

Students and Academics in a University

We must now better understand sortition as a device, that is to say, face the realities of procedures.

Let's talk about sortition for university bodies (assembly, council, committee). Imagine a council of 50 students selected by lot for a one-year term. The base is a university of 5,000 students. Refusal (to be on the list) is prohibited because all the students are involved as users of the establishment and as members of an academic population. The probability of being selected by lot is one in a hundred (1/100). A withdrawal is allowed after the draw or during the session but a good reason must be given. Participating in the council is a duty as well as a right. The functions are consultation by the administration, proposal of questions to be put on the agenda, publication of reasoned opinions, initiatives, suggestions, petitions, and votes. The discussion and deliberation sessions are public or recorded.

Renewal: several successive elections by drawing lots are authorized for an individual. The probability that a person will be chosen by lot a second time remains low. If that happened, that would be really lucky for this individual, since the total probability of being picked twice before the two draws is a one in ten thousand chance.

Another council of 50: academic council of 50, gathering professors, researchers, and academic equivalents.

Base: 250 people, academic community of this university.

This council is selected for a one-year term.

Refusal: prohibited.

Probability of being selected by lot: one chance in five (1/5).

Withdrawal: prohibited.

Functions: the academic council of 50 has prerogatives comparable to the council of 50 students. The fundamental difference is its effect of rotating academics. For the students, their stay is too short to involve a rotation. It would take a council of 1,000 people at least to achieve this rotation.

Sessions: around ten per year.

Without any need for restriction, the law of probabilities will allow you to serve once, twice, maybe three or four times in your life if you have spent all your professional life at the same university. In this case, the probability of not having been selected is very low.

Council of 15:

Base: 250 people (same base as above).

Subject: board of 15 members.

This board has much work to do. This council contributes to important decisions and their execution. Being part of it is equivalent to a part-time job.

Refusal: due to the burden, the procedure allows the 250 academics concerned to refuse to be on the list for the draw. This possibility of refusal may not be granted indefinitely, however, considering that academics have to accept that at one time or another this honor or chore is an obligation.

Probability of being selected by lot: one in sixteen chance (1/16). No strong rotation.

Sessions: weekly.

Withdrawal: prohibited, since refusal was authorized.

Detail: given the existence of various disciplines, it is conceivable that several parallel draws should be made and that several simultaneous draws in each department be added.

Possible adjustment: in this council of 15, half +1 of the members are drawn (= 8/250) and the other half is chosen by a vote of the faculty (7/250). A tripartite formula is also possible: by approximate 1/3, 5 appointed (by the president of the University, the responsible ministry or other), 5 elected by drawing, and 5 elected by vote.

Likewise, the most appropriate options will be chosen for other examples differing in scale, use, context, and purpose. Provided that each experiment is carefully conducted and scrutinized, it will provide much more knowledge than an endless debate over general ideas about procedures.

Local politics:

A town of 150,000 inhabitants in France. Two institutions: on the one hand, juries, or deliberative assemblies at the level of the municipality; on the other hand, the presence of elected officials on the municipal council. Their roles, which are very different, require different degrees of qualification: a broad qualification for the juries, more restricted for the councils.

Local consultative assembly of 100:

Base: no specific qualification, database identical to that of universal suffrage, all adults in possession of their civic rights.

Subject: a hundred people selected by lot for deliberation and consultation on local political issues.

Refusal (to be registered): authorized. Two options: everyone is warned that they are likely to participate in the draw, unless they refuse to register. This is a passive version of the list. The alternative is that one must show an acceptance of being on the list. This implies that the number of registrants will be a little lower, since an act of acceptance had to be made.

Probability of being selected by lot: this probability depends on the proportion of refusals. If one in two people agrees to participate in the draw, the probability of being elected is around 1/500th in a city of 150,000 inhabitants (the number of adults and voters being lower than the number of inhabitants).

Withdrawal: prohibited, except in the event of incapacity. Acceptance was manifested by the possibility of refusing or agreeing to be registered.

Functions and sessions: public discussion and public deliberation, behind closed doors. Consultation, deliberation, reasoned opinion.

Renewal: authorized, because the probability of renewal by the batch remains low (around 1/500).

Municipal council:

The proportions are clearly restricted in the case of the council. For this, a motivation test is necessary – the application. To this must be added a quorum (minimum number of candidates before the draw) in order to guarantee sufficient participation of the population.

Subject: 10 seats out of 50 for the entire board (20 percent) are allocated by the draw.

Base: the qualification for the application, which allows registration in the database, is assigned by sponsorship to the candidates. These sponsorships are given by current and past members of the board and by the candidates in the present election by vote.

If a less socialized approach is desired, the alternative option is the individual application without sponsorship. This acts as a self-qualification. This is to avoid that the number of entries in the draw is too small. Accordingly, the process is subject to a quorum (2,000 candidates for the draw). For the 40 seats allocated by vote, as usual, there will be several lists, that is to say, 100 candidates divided into several lists. For the draw, you need a higher number. A quorum ensures this by requiring, for example, that at least 2,000 people stand as candidates for election by lot. This number can be higher, but it cannot be lower. The quorum thus makes it possible to exceed the volume of activists or close relatives revolving around the lists.

Refusal: impossible, they are candidates.

Probability of being selected by lot: depending on the number of sponsored candidates. The probability of being selected by lot will be between 1/10,000 and 1/5,000 if the will to participate is clear. It cannot fall below the quorum of 2,000 required for the base (the probability then drops to 1/2,000).

Functions: these 10 people drawn by lot in a municipal council sit among the 50 elected by ballot.

Sessions: regular and over several years (six-year mandate in France in 2017).

Disclaimer: prohibited or limited with rare exceptions. Training could be provided to elected representatives of the draw.

Renewal: authorized. The probability of being elected twice by the lot is low.

Assemblies, councils, or juries meet, generally to address different local issues. Their opinions lead to proposals subject to future legislation or to a referendum.

Provincial politics:

Advisory board or jury of 504 selected by lot.

Base: identical to universal suffrage, all adults in possession of their civic rights.

Refusal (to be registered): authorized, for lack of a positive response to the registration notification. Failure to respond serves as a refusal. In a more constrained version, without manifestation of refusal, the tacit agreement for the draw would be recorded. This strong incentive, however, lends itself to contestation in the event of election by lot. The person concerned may declare, in good or bad faith, that they have not received any notification.

Quorum: requiring a minimum acceptance of the draw seems legitimate, between 10 and 20 percent of the base. For example, for 10 percent acceptance from a potential base of two million, the quorum would be 200,000 people agreeing to participate in the draw. Without this quorum, the procedure would not be continued.

Probability of being selected by lot: in a region of several million inhabitants, assuming 500,000 acceptances, the probability is 1/1,000.

Withdrawal: after the draw or during the session, withdrawal is prohibited, except in very specific conditions and in case of incapacity.

Functions: consultation, deliberation, reasoned opinion, vote. Control of regional legislative activity, recommendations, preparation of texts.

Sessions: concerning the public debate and the internal sessions to prepare the debates, one can envisage either a series of dense and close sessions on a single subject and lasting a few weeks, or sessions spaced and spread over several months, over various subjects and of longer duration.

Renewal: authorized, because unlikely, of the order of 1/1,000.

Last Course

Institutional design in national politics: Let us imagine a French tricameral: National Assembly, Senate, Popular Assembly form a new political system combining voting and drawing in different forms. Two hundred senators elected from the draw on the basis of one million qualified (probability = 1/5,000).

The National Assembly, at the center of the system, is elected by a majority vote as it is today. The Senate remains an upper house and small in size. Its members are selected by lottery after qualification by different institutions and legal organizations (civil society included). The qualified population (in the order of a million) would include people who have proven competence in their field. In doing so, the senatorial aspect (of a certain age and worth) would be retained or strengthened. A Senate of 200 people over 40, as in the example below. Finally, a citizens' jury is drawn among the entire population, on the basis of the right to participate in universal suffrage. At least initially experimental, its operation would be limited to consultation, discussion, and control.

These three extremely contrasting types testify to the very variable potential of the draw. Such a system includes three different and complementary types of representation: active and expert in the Senate, political and partisan in the National Assembly, descriptive and unprofessional in the citizens' assembly.

National Assembly

Center of the system, it is elected by vote, by majority vote by constituency, or by proportional representation, or even according to a mixed system including the two types of ballot. It retains the last word on legislation.

Senate of 200:

Basis: the source is not universal suffrage but a smaller population, on the order of 1–2 percent of the national population. These candidates for the draw are qualified through a process of appointment by different legal institutions (elected or appointed political bodies, universities, associations, professional unions). In short, this one million people over 40 are qualified to have accomplished work or quality work in their field. This is a form of call for candidates, but very broad and watered down. The instances form the basis of the draw by addition. The method of appointment is left to the qualifying bodies: hierarchical appointment, election by vote, or by drawing initially within them. Certain designation procedures are obviously excluded: sale of places in the base, or any opaque or uncontrolled procedure. These designation bodies in the database choose their procedure. The regularity of this is checked from the outside.

Refusal (to be registered): authorized, at the level of each body presenting candidates (we can therefore imagine a different regime depending on these bodies: obligation or possibility of refusal).

Probability of being selected by lot: 1/5,000.

Disclaimer: prohibited.

Functions: legislative and supervisory work typical of an upper house.

Sessions: Senate renewable by half every three years.

Renewal: authorized.

A mixed Senate in its election procedure is conceivable: half of the Senate is elected by vote, the other by drawing (2×100 or 2×150).

People's Assembly of 1,680:

Base: close or equivalent to the base for universal suffrage.

Refusal (to be registered): authorized. Participation is encouraged. Registration in the database is done automatically and does not require any action. Unsubscribing requires a personal process.

Probability of being selected by lot: depending on the acceptance rate to be registered in the database. The probability varies between orders of 1/5,000 to 1/15,000.

Withdrawal: forbidden except incapacity during the session.

Functions: questions to the government, hearing of senior officials and experts, consultative votes, right of initiative in matters of legislation.

Sessions: half of the citizens' assembly is re-elected by drawing every two years (840/1,680). This allows for the transmission of the training acquired and a time to learn internal procedures.

Operation: in addition to plenary meetings, such an assembly can set up parallel bodies of smaller size (3×560; 5×336; 10×168) in order to share the work. It also gives the possibility of forming three bodies working in parallel on the same subject after an internal drawing of lots and of comparing their conclusions. In the event of disagreement, the majority of the sub-assemblies wins: 2 to 1 among three assemblies of 560, 4 to 1 or 3 to 2 if it is among five assemblies of 336.

Remuneration: if the work performed corresponds to a professional half-time and if participation is actually observed, the remuneration would be around three times the minimum wage. It seems preferable that those elected to the citizens' assembly keep a part-time professional activity.

If the person elected by drawing is absent from more than half of the sessions and meetings during a semester, he or she is replaced by the person coming next on the list of the drawings. This list has not been made public. The person replacing her therefore only learns of her election by drawing (old and preserved) shortly before taking office. No representative reservoir awaiting replacement is known to the public.

Renewal: authorized. The probability is tiny. It is not forbidden to simultaneously be a candidate for the National Assembly and the Senate.

A Gift for the European Union

The idea of connecting, anchoring, confronting the bureaucracy of the European Union with samples, councils, or assemblies of citizens remains very elusive in the prospects of the Union, according to its leaders, although such allusions are made from time to time. The forest of academic research barely conceals the European democratic desert. The European Union, by its size, could innovate at different levels: regional, national, European. All the possibilities are offered to the Union, in terms of constitution of bases, of broad or restricted qualification, of functioning by consultation, opinion or decision, on the model of the various preceding examples.

Reasonable Conclusion

The impact of sortition, after 20 years of good discussion and small experiments, causes mixed feelings. There is no reason to despair. Patience, tenacity, nuance, precision, audacity, pragmatism, modesty, development, evaluation, imagination in advocacy, and use of sortition are necessary, capable of producing tangible results, renewed participation, reformed decision-making, which will remain to be measured as democratic.

Donatella della Porta and Andrea Felicetti
Social Movements as Democratic Actors

Introduction

Democracy is evolving and its dynamic configuration makes it difficult to pin down what is complementary, and, by contrast, what is central to it. Actually, much of the recent efforts of social movements can be interpreted as attempts to show that the most vital part of democratic life lies beyond minimalist conceptualization of democracy focusing on electoral accountability and comes from outside the realm of representative institutions. Indeed, activists denounce the political system as basically subservient to the values and interests of the neoliberal economic system, unrepresentative of people and worth their trust. This chapter does not intend to engage in an assessment of these claims, nor do we suggest that representative institutions are losing their prominence in contemporary political systems. More simply, we believe that movements' critiques concur with broader trends in pointing to the erosion of the democratic credentials of the representative system. Like many other scholars, we think democracy needs renewal to fulfill its commitment to freedom and equality in the context of contemporary societies. Virtues of deliberation, such as deliberative listening, can surely help in this direction, though we see them as part of a wider set of behaviors that are needed in democracy. With this in mind, we illustrate some movement ideas and practices that could strengthen the democratic qualities of our institutions and political life. Some of these ideas and practices are already playing an important role in democratic life, even entering institutions. We deem it necessary to strengthen these developments. More than a workable solution to embed ideals in practice, as some would have it, democracy in its minimalist form is rather a specific and problematic way to intend democracy, especially at times of rising authoritarian tides and recurrent crises. The notion of complementarity might thus not be sufficient to capture the central role of social movements in democracy.

In what follows, we will also specify that, even though in the context of a decline in the perceived legitimacy of representative institutions social movements are highly active, this, however, does not automatically translate into a greater democratic legitimacy for the system overall. As movements denounce and expose the limits of representative systems, their mobilizations at the same time reflect and can exacerbate the legitimacy crisis. Additionally, their ability to effectively democratize political systems depends on a variety of fac-

https://doi.org/10.1515/9783110747331-010

tors, one of them being representative institutions' resistance to democratization. In this chapter, focusing on cases in which efforts to affirm democratic practices and ideas are consequential, we aim at learning from and about the challenges that movements meet and the contribution they make when acting in this direction.

In this endeavor, our chapter also provides insights on the notion of deliberative listening. Conceived of as the ability to listen without prejudice, deliberative listening captures only part of what movements do since they strive to bring about change mostly by taking action.[1] Social movements might fall squarely beyond the remit of deliberative listening or deliberation when, for instance, movements are inspired by agonistic ideals, when they are uninterested or unable to engage in deliberation,[2] or when they oppose democracy altogether.[3] When it comes to the more communicative side of their action, however, social movements might, and often do, promote deliberative listening within movement arenas or even deliberative and participatory spaces in societies at large. On other occasions they might, instead, try to affirm the views, beliefs, and interests they have come to develop, usually against those of more powerful actors.

Our discussion here draws from work we have been developing to understand the role that social movements can play to renew democracy in a deliberative and participatory sense.[4] We set our analysis in the context of the political and socio-economic transformations triggered by the crisis that hit the world in 2008 and related political developments that have challenged social, political, and civil rights. This development, that Geiselberger has labeled the Great Regression,[5] has been characterized by the spiraling of social inequalities, declining trust in democratic institutions, rising insecurity, and xenophobic reactions.[6]

---

1 Kim, Seongcheol (2020) 'Radical democracy and Left populism after the squares: "Social Movement" (Ukraine), Podemos (Spain), and the question of organization.' *Contemporary Political Theory* 19(2): 211–232: https://doi.org/10.1057/s41296-019-00343-x.

2 Felicetti, A. (2016) *Deliberative Democracy and Social Movements: Transition Initiatives in the Public Sphere.* New York and London: Rowman & Littlefield International.

3 Castelli Gattinara, Pietro and Pirro, Andrea L. P. (2019) 'The Far Right as social movement.' *European Societies* 21(4): 447–462.

4 Della Porta, D. (2013) *Can Democracy be Saved? Participation, Deliberation and Social Movements.* Cambridge: Polity Press.

5 Geiselberger, H. (ed.) (2017) *The Great Regression.* Cambridge: Polity.

6 Streeck, W. (2017) 'The return of the repressed as the beginning of the end of neoliberal capitalism.' In H. Geiselberger (ed.) *The Great Regression.* Cambridge: Polity, pp. 157–172. See also Bauman, Z. (2017) 'Symptoms in search of an object and a name.' In H. Geiselberger (ed.) *The Great Regression.* Cambridge: Polity, pp. 13–26.

The debate is on as to how many blows democracy can take without breaking down.[7] Yet, mobilizations for 'real democracy' and social justice and, more generally, forms of resistance to the democratic backlash are multiplying.[8]

Democratic theory and social movement studies' research on contemporary democratic life suggest that movements' characterization as contentious actors, struggling in the streets for or against change, is reductive. Social movements have in fact the ability to generate new ideas, as they engage in creating and spreading counter-expertise, new knowledge, and innovative practices. Moreover, through different channels their ideas enter institutions and, depending on various conditions favoring (or hindering) their abilities to do so, they innovate democracy.

Progressive social movements, in particular, envisage innovative forms of democratic life that highlight participatory and deliberative elements, which are widely deemed important to renew democracy. This can be observed in different respects. First, by taking advantage of windows of opportunity offered by extant direct democracy institutions, activists have promoted referendums or turned referendums promoted by political elites in a top-down fashion into forms of direct democracy 'from below'.[9] Second, movement parties on the left have emerged (sometimes in reaction to right-wing populist ones), transforming party systems that were deeply shaken, given growing electoral volatility and the decay of mainstream parties.[10] At the same time, candidates appealing to citizens' participation and social justice have met with unexpected support in old-left parties such as, for instance, Labour in Britain and the US Democratic Party. Third, on several occasions from Iceland to Chile, social movements have engaged in 'crowdsourced constitutionalism,' in attempts to deeply transform the very basis of the social pact on which institutions are built.[11]

---

7 Della Porta, D. and Keating, M. (eds.) (2008) *Approaches and Methodologies in the Social Sciences.* Cambridge: Cambridge University Press.

8 Meyer, D. and Tarrow, S. (eds.) (2018) *The Resistance.* Oxford: Oxford University Press.

9 Della Porta, D., O'Connor, F., Portos, M., and Subirats, A. (2017) *Referendums from Below.* Bristol: Policy Press/Chicago University Press.

10 Della Porta, D., Fernandez, J., Kouki, H., and Mosca, L. (2017) *Movement Parties in Times of Austerity.* Cambridge: Polity.

11 Della Porta, D. (2020) *How Social Movements Can Save Democracy: Democratic Innovations from Below.* John Wiley & Sons.

Movements between Representative Institutions and Alternative Conceptions of Democracy

In the recent past, waves of protest, known as Indignados or Occupy movements, have been organized against austerity measures adopted in response to the financial crisis. These mobilizations reflected and exacerbated a legitimacy crisis and, at the same time, offered possible solutions to redress this situation. The austerity measures, activists claimed, displayed the political institutions' disinterest in the suffering of citizens.[12]

These elements compel us to reflect on what democratic qualities we deem important to democratic systems. As is well known, democracy is an essentially contested concept whose different qualities and practices are understood differently in various conceptions of democracy. As Robert Dahl noted, democracy "has meant different things to different people at different times and places."[13] Over time, the view that has gained centrality is one that sees democracy as accountability through competitive and fair elections and with the political settings of Western polities.[14]

The crisis of democracy, however, has questioned this minimalistic understanding of democracy. A need has emerged to give attention to democratic qualities that include but cannot be limited to electoral accountability.[15] As mainstream democratic conceptions and practices have been targets of contestation, others have gained ground. These include forms of participatory, deliberative, and welfare democracy.[16] Two main features at the basis of representative democracy have seemed most in tension with qualities characteristic of other understandings of democracy. They are, delegation of power and majoritarian decision-making (even in its mitigated forms including degrees of protection of minorities). That movements for democracy find these aspects problematic is not surprising. As Bernard Manin famously argued, representative government embodied a normative commitment to mitigate democratic forms of participation with oligarchic ones.[17]

---

12 Della Porta, D. (2015) *Social Movements in Times of Austerity: Bringing Capitalism back into Protest Analysis*. Cambridge: Polity Press.
13 Dahl, R. A. (2000) *On Democracy*. New Haven: Yale University Press, p. 3.
14 Held, D. (2006) *Models of Democracy*. Cambridge: Polity Press, p. 166.
15 Rosanvallon, P. (2006) *La contre-démocratie: la politique à l'âge de la défiance*. Paris: Seuil.
16 Della Porta, *Can Democracy be Saved?*, ch. one.
17 Manin, B. (1997) *The Principles of Representative Government*. Cambridge: Cambridge University Press.

By placing emphasis on elections, there is a risk of obfuscating the fact that electoral accountability, to be effective, requires critical citizens who hold representatives accountable. As Alessandro Pizzorno argued:

> When the electoral institution is chosen as the institution characterizing democratic regimes the much more important presence of a sphere that is both public and distinct from the regimes is obscured. Deprived of this, deprived that is of open public discourse, and despite being governed by persons regularly elected, such a regime could only misleadingly be called democratic.[18]

Alternative views, participatory democracy in the first place, have long stressed the need for diverse opportunities for participation beyond elections.[19] The latter is too rare, prone to manipulation, offering only a narrow set of choices. Participation, instead, helps foster good forms of citizenship and empowerment. It supports socialization of citizens to different visions of public goods and it also has potential to increase trust and support for institutions. Participatory democrats call for democracy beyond parliaments and governments, in societal organizations, from workplaces to neighborhoods, to public services.

Deliberative theorists, from their end, have highlighted the need for high-quality discursive spaces where citizens can exchange reasons and envisage shared understandings of the public good.[20] High-quality discursive processes are deemed key for legitimate and efficient decisions. Going beyond an aggregative understanding of legitimacy, what is central is the way in which preferences are formed, rather than counted. In deliberative spaces citizens treat each other as equals, seek to understand each other's views, and assess these views on the basis of emerging standards of fairness.

Some scholars at the crossroads between participatory and deliberative democracy have showed the important role that forms of democratic life beyond institutions play in democracy. Jane Mansbridge has discussed enclaves free from institutional power and usually populated by activists.[21] Similarly, Iris Mar-

---

18 Pizzorno, A. (2010) 'Introduzione.' In A. Pizzorno (ed.) *La democrazia di fronte allo stato democratico.* Milan: Feltrinelli, pp. xi–xxvii, at p. xiii.

19 See: Arnstein, S. R. (1969) 'A ladder of citizen participation.' *Journal of the American Institute of Planners* 35(4): 216–224; Barber, B. R. (1984) *Strong Democracy: Participatory Politics for a New Age.* Berkeley: University of California Press; and Pateman, C. (1970) *Participation and Democratic Theory.* Cambridge: Cambridge University Press.

20 Dryzek, J. S. (2000) *Deliberative Democracy and Beyond: Liberals, Critics, Contestations.* Oxford and New York: Oxford University Press.

21 Mansbridge, J. (1996) 'Using power/fighting power: the polity'. In S. Benhabib (ed.) *Democracy and Difference: Contesting the Boundaries of the Political.* Princeton: Princeton University Press, pp. 46–66.

ion Young has highlighted the need for developing "processes of engaged and responsible democratic participation [which] include street demonstrations and sit-ins, musical works and cartoons, as much as parliamentary speeches and letters to the editor."[22] In particular, Nancy Fraser famously highlighted the importance of subaltern counter-publics (including workers, women, ethnic minorities, etc.) that form discursive arenas, parallel to the main one, where counter-discourses can be developed and identities, interests, and needs built and redefined.[23] Unlike minimalist conceptions of democracy that take identities, ideas, interests, and preferences to develop outside of the democratic process, participatory and deliberative understandings highlight the role democratic spaces ought to have in this regard.

Existing democracies, as they have evolved over time, have mitigated the overwhelming reliance on representative democratic ideas and practices and added elements linked to other democratic conceptions.[24] The recognition of the limits of delegation and majoritarianism has made room for participatory practices in schools, firms, and neighborhoods, and through the political recognition of social movement organizations. Further, referendums, once considered a vestige of direct democracy, are increasingly used, as are institutions in which the principle of delegation is rethought, as happens in institutions based on lottery and consensual decision-making. Finally, democratic innovations – from participatory budgeting to citizen assemblies – are spreading in an attempt to restore the connection between citizens and democracy.[25] It is against this background that social movements play their role of promoters of innovation and change in democracy.

Progressive Social Movements as Drivers of Change and Innovation

A quick look at the broad historical dynamics of social movement mobilization suggests that, contrary to the hypothesis of this book, social movement activism does not rise when legitimacy of representative government shrinks. Rather, ad-

---

22 Young, I. M. (2003) 'Activist challenges to deliberative democracy'. In J. S. Fishkin and P. Laslett (eds.) *Debating Deliberative Democracy*. Oxford: Blackwell, pp. 102–201, at p. 119.
23 Fraser, N. (1990) 'Rethinking the public sphere.' *Social Text* 25/26: 56–80.
24 Della Porta, *Can Democracy be Saved?*
25 Font, J., della Porta, D., and Sintomer, Y. (eds.) (2014) *Participatory Democracy in Southern Europe*. London: Rowman and Littlefield.

vances in democratization of institutions favored, and in turn were supported by, social movements. As Charles Tilly has argued:

> A wide correspondence between democratization and social movements. The roots of social movements are found in the partial democratization that moved British subjects and the North-American colonies against those that governed them in the eighteenth century. Throughout the nineteenth century, social movements generally blossomed and developed wherever further democratization took place, decreasing when authoritarian regimes impeded democracy. This path continued during the twentieth and twenty-first centuries; the maps of the development of institutions and social movements widely overlap.[26]

Also, the bulk of democratization, in which movements had a central role, as was the case with labor and women's movements of the past, was about struggle and contestation. Some research has suggested that participatory, mostly, and deliberative elements had a role in the civil rights movements, as well as other 'new' social movements later on.[27]

Departing from a view of social movements as contentious actors, mainly taking to the streets to oppose or spur political change, research pointed at their capacity to forge new ideas, about democratic institutions, among other things. Furthermore, it indicated that social movements do not only stay 'at the gate' of the institutional system, but enter institutional arenas in different forms and follow various channels. Social movements have indeed the capacity to 'take the floor,' creating public spheres and participation.

Of course, not all movements have promoted democracy: some (particularly right-wing ones) are often openly anti-democratic; others (including left-wing ones) have triggered authoritarian turns. Here we focus on progressive social movements. Progressive movements have struggled for an inclusive and just society and for democratic deepening.[28] Following Claus Offe, we consider progressive views as characterized by:

> the liberation (or 'emancipation') of collectivities (for example: citizens, classes, nations, minorities, income categories, even mankind), be it the liberation from want, ignorance, exploitative relations, or the freedom of such collectives to govern themselves autonomously, that is, without being dependent upon or controlled by others). Furthermore, the free-

---

26 Tilly, C. (2004) *Contention and Democracy in Europe, 1650–2000.* Cambridge: Cambridge University Press, p. 125.

27 See della Porta, D. (ed.) (2009) *Democracy in Social Movements.* Houndsmill: Palgrave; and Polletta, Francesca (2002) *Freedom Is an Endless Meeting: Democracy in American Social Movements.* Chicago: University of Chicago Press.

28 Allen, A. (2016) *The End of Progress: Decolonizing the Normative Foundations of Critical Theory.* New York: Columbia University Press.

dom that results from liberation applies equally to all, with equality serving as a criterion to make sure that liberation does not in fact become a mere privilege of particular social categories.[29]

Such movements have certainly been pivotal in pushing for some democratic innovation. In the early days of social movement studies, research on collective behavior by scholars close to the so-called Chicago School showed that collective phenomena do not simply reflect social crises. Rather, they produce new solidarities and norms which drive change, especially in value systems. Students of collective behavior developed these interpretations in looking at movements at times of intense social change.[30]

Rooted in symbolic interactionism, these scholars gave prominence to the meanings actors attributed to social structures, and focused on how institutional behavior was transformed by new norms driving social action.[31]

Similarly, research on new social movements, which focused on macro-level transformations of society, saw movements as main actors of innovation. Alain Touraine, who inaugurated the debate on the emergence of new conflicts,[32] considered social movements as representing the opposition to dominant powers in societies. In contemporary societies, social movements struggle for control of then-emerging programmed societies, in which knowledge plays a special role. Alberto Melucci paid particular attention to movements as norms producers within the context of societies defined by high differentiation, increasingly invested in the creation of individual and autonomous centers of action, but also extending their control over the motives for human action.[33] Thus, rather than focusing only on material gain, new social movements develop 'other codes' to resist state and market intrusion into the everyday lives of citizens. Traditionally associated with disruptive forms of participation, in the Habermasian

29 Offe, C. (2011) 'Rethinking progress and ensuring a secure future for all: what we can learn from the crisis.' *Trends in Social Cohesion* (no. 22): 79–92, at 79–80.
30 See e. g.: Blumer, H. (1951) 'Social movements.' In A. McClung Lee (ed.) *Principles of Sociology.* New York: Barnes & Noble, pp. 199–220; and Turner, Ralph, and Killian, Lewis (1987) [1974, 1957] *Collective Behavior.* Englewood Cliffs: Prentice Hall.
31 Della Porta, D. and Diani, M. (2020) *Social Movements: An Introduction.* Oxford: Blackwell.
32 Touraine, A. (1985) 'An introduction to the study of social movements.' *Social Research* 52: 749–788.
33 Melucci, A. (1982) *L'Invenzione del Presente: Movimenti, Identità, Bisogni Individuali.* Bologna: il Mulino; and Melucci, A. (1989) *Nomads of the Present.* London: Hutchinson Radius.

perspective, movements have a positive role in mobilizing against the invasion of the logics of the system.[34]

More recently, social movements have been considered as 'learning sites.'[35] They have been deemed capable of building knowledge through discursive processes consisting of the "talks and conversations – the speech acts – and written communications of movement members that occur in the context of, or in relation to, movement activities."[36]

Knowledge producers have identified three dimensions of cognitive praxis: a cosmological dimension concerning the "common worldview assumptions that give a social movement its utopian mission"; a technological dimension referring to "the specific technological issues that particular movements develop around"; and an organizational perspective as "a particular organizational paradigm, which means they have both ideals and modes of organizing the production and ... dissemination of knowledge."[37]

Research has found a broad range of knowledge practices of democracy within social movements. These span "from things we are more classically trained to define as knowledge, ... to micro-political and cultural interventions that have more to do with 'know-how' or the 'cognitive praxis that informs all social activity' and which vie with the most basic social institutions that teach us how to be in the world."[38] Actually, social movements are:

> 1) engaging in co-producing, challenging, and transforming expert scientific discourses; 2) creating critical subjects whose embodied discourse produces new notions of democracy; and 3) generating reflexive conjunctural theories and analyses that go against more dogmatic and orthodox approaches to social change, and as such contribute to ethical ways of knowing.[39]

---

34 Habermas, J. (1985) *The Theory of Communicative Action: Lifeworld and System: A Critique of Functionalist Reason.* Boston: Beacon Press.
35 Welton, M. (1993) 'Social revolutionary learning: the new social movements as learning sites.' *Adult Education Quarterly* 43(3): 152–164.
36 Benford, R. D. and Snow, D. A. (2000) 'Framing processes and social movements: an overview and assessment.' *Annual Review of Sociology* 26: 611–639, at 623.
37 Eyerman, R. and Jamison, A. (1991) *Social Movements: A Cognitive Approach.* University Park: Pennsylvania State University Press, pp. 68–69.
38 Casas-Cortes, M. I., Osterweil, M., and Powell, D. E. (2008) 'Blurring boundaries: recognizing knowledge-practices in the study of social movements.' *Anthropological Quarterly* 81(1): 17–58, at 21.
39 Casas-Cortes, Osterweil, and Powell, 'Blurring boundaries,' p. 22.

Knowledge practices can be either formal or informal, and refer to concepts, theories and imaginaries, methodological aspects, or research tools.[40] As self-reflexive actors, progressive social movements acquire and develop knowledge as they move through their activities. Learning can occur during meetings, protest, organizing, and educational activities, as well as in self-reflection on their actions.[41]

Social movement knowledge is seen as situated instead of universal, committed rather than detached, aiming at radical systemic change instead of intervention in the symptoms of general malaise.[42] It aims at providing useful skills; to develop a critical view of agency and power and to connect local and global levels.[43] Knowledge production is embodied[44] and oriented to articulate theory and praxis, starting from concrete realities.[45]

Importantly, in social movements, knowledge emerges not only from abstract theorization but also from action. Movement theorizing is:

> Grounded in the process of producing 'social movements' against opposition. It is always to some extent knowledge-in-struggle, and its survival and development is always contested and in process of formation. Its frequently partial, unsystematic and provisional character does not make it any the less worth our attention, though it may go some way towards explaining why academic social movements theory is too often content with taking the 'cream off the top,' and disregarding – or failing to notice – everything that has to happen before institutionalized social movement theorizing appears in forms that can be easily appropriated.[46]

Furthermore, social movements continuously engage in democratic innovation. They experiment with new ideas internally, prefigure alternative forms of demo-

40 Casas-Cortes, Osterweil, and Powell, 'Blurring boundaries,' p. 28.
41 See: Mayo, P. and English, L. (2012) 'Adult education and social movements: perspectives from Freire and beyond.' *Educazione Democratica* 2(3): 170 – 208.
42 Lange, E., 2001. Mayo, Peter (1999) *Gramsci, Freire and Adult Education: Possibilities for Transformative Action*. London: Zed Books. *International Review of Education* 47(3): 395 – 403.
43 Crowther, J., Galloway, V., and Martin, I. (eds.) (2005) *Popular Education: Engaging the Academy: International Perspectives*. Leicester, NIACE; and Foley, G (ed.) (2004) *Dimensions of Adult Learning: Adult Education and Training in a Global Era*. Maidenhead: Open University Press.
44 Casas-Cortes, Osterweil, and Powell, 'Blurring boundaries,' p. 43.
45 De Molina, M. M. (2004) 'Common notions, part 1: workers-inquiry, co-research, consciousness-raising,' trans. M. Casas-Cortés and S. Cobarrubias: http://eipcp. net/transversal/0406/malo/en.
46 Barker, C. and Cox, L. (2002) 'What have the Romans ever done for us? Academic and activist forms of movement theorizing.' In C. Barker and M. Tyldesley (eds.) *Alternative Futures and Popular Protest VIII: Conference Proceedings*. Manchester: Manchester Metropolitan University, pp. 1– 27, at p. 23.

cratic life, and spread ideas within institutions. Besides policy change, they also address meta-political issues and experiment with participatory and deliberative ideas. In doing this, they have developed innovative ideas and alternative knowledge.

Since the 1970s the 'new social movements' have in fact sought new forms of participation in decision-making, spreading a sort of 'contagion from below.'[47] This change was spurred by dissatisfaction towards centralized and bureaucratic features of representative democracy. In the early 2000s, building upon reflexive practices and the building of deliberative spaces, the global justice movement paid specific attention to knowledge production. In the 2010s, protesters in Tahrir, Porta del Sol, Syntagma Square, or Zuccotti Park, and later in Gezi Park or Place de la République, criticized representative democracy as deeply corrupted but also experimented with other models of democracy featuring in particular participatory and deliberative qualities. As a main protest repertoire and an organizational form, the acampadas – long-term camps in squatted public spaces – have represented a democratic experiment adopted and adapted in a variety of contexts. Learning from past experiences, the acampadas were based on older practices of internal democracy, such as those of social forums.[48] In these activities, participation from below was combined with efforts to develop egalitarian and inclusive public spheres.[49]

In addition, contemporary progressive movements consider transparency, equality, and inclusion as important values. In particular, open-air camps have meant to enhance the publicity and transparency of the process, as well as reclaiming public spaces. Open spaces being the main site of protest enabled activists to emphasize the inclusivity within processes ideally addressing the entire agora.

In effect, participants' heterogeneity is taken as a most positive aspect of the camps.[50] Within the camps, general assemblies strived to mobilize the common people, communities of citizens. The everyday management of camp activities was also run on the basis of alternative practices, including free kitchens, med-

---

47 Rohrschneider, R. (1993) 'Impact of social movements on the European party system.' *Annals of the American Academy of Political and Social Sciences* 528(1): 157–170.

48 Della Porta, D. (2015) *Social Movements in Times of Austerity: Bringing Capitalism back into Protest Analysis*. Cambridge, Polity Press.

49 Della Porta, *Can Democracy be Saved?*

50 Gerbaudo, P. (2012) *Tweet and the Street*. London: Pluto Press, p. 69.

ical tents, media centers, libraries, and information centers for new participants and visitors.[51]

Movements Impacting on Institutions

Some of the democratic ideas and practices mentioned above have been at the basis of institutional innovations seeking to foster participatory and deliberative ideas. Social movements perform their role as carriers of innovation in institutions in different ways and with a variety of results. Social movements do not only engage in claims-making on policy issues, but they also target the way political systems work: their procedures, recruitment, and the informal power configurations.[52] Movements have often attained decentralization of power; opened up processes of consultation with citizens; appealed public administration decisions; allowed testimonies before representative and judicial institutions. Collective action repertoires, once stigmatized and addressed as public order matters, have progressively become legitimate,[53] while direct democracy has increasingly been acknowledged as an additional channel to access representative democracy.[54] Movements have also contributed to creating new arenas of public policy developments, including expert commissions or administrative and political branches, such as ministries or bureaus on women's and environmental issues.

Democratic innovations nowadays generally include participatory processes open to citizens. Particularly at the local scale, there has been the creation of high-quality communicative spaces to empower citizens. Graham Smith has distinguished two main frames: assembleary democracy or forms oriented to the construction of a 'mini-public', usually selected by lot.[55] Social movements have been participating especially in the former, for instance in neighborhood or thematic assemblies, local councils, consultation committees, participatory budgeting, and the like. In particular, participatory budgeting has spread globally from Porto Alegre in Brazil, being recognized by the United Nations as

---

51 Graeber, D. (2013) *The Democracy Project: A History, a Crisis, a Movement*. London: Allen Lane, p. 240.

52 Kitschelt, H. (1986) 'Political opportunity structures and political protest: anti-nuclear movements in four democracies.' *British Journal of Political Science* 16(1): 57–85.

53 Della Porta, D. and Reiter, H. (eds.) (1998) *The Policing of Protest*. Minneapolis: University of Minnesota Press.

54 Della Porta et al., *Referendums from Below*.

55 Smith, G. (2009) *Democratic Innovations: Designing Institutions for Citizen Participation*. Cambridge: Cambridge University Press. See also Chapter Nine of this volume by Gil Delannoi.

one of the 'best practices' globally.[56] Social equality and occasions for empowerment are sought by inviting citizens to decide distribution issues through a structured process of involvement in committees and assemblies.

Institutional outcomes of movements are visible in the ways in which participatory and deliberative conceptions and practices have been presented in constitutional processes, direct democracy, and party politics. Social movements' experimenting with different forms of internal democracy and with institutions shows the porosity of the boundaries between institutional and non-institutional activities. They need to challenge existing institutions, in order to realize the social and political changes which are their aim. When intervening in institutional politics, social movements bring with them attention to policy change, but they also foster the development of participatory and deliberative decision-making processes. Under certain conditions, they might succeed in putting new topics on the agenda, influencing democratic transformations, and in spreading new democratic repertoires.

Crises can be triggers for change. As Altman noted,

> elected representatives do not, by their own volition, give up their exclusive domain over the legislative agenda without a strong reason to do so. The adoption of citizen-initiated mechanisms of direct democracy tends to occur in times of political instability: times when, for one reason or another, lawmakers believe that a new page in a nation's history is being turned.[57]

Social movements have the potential to intervene at different stages of a process of democratic innovation. As we argue elsewhere,

> Social movements, together with other civil society actors, are at times co-producers of citizen-led democratic innovations. Unlike top-down democratic experiments, in which institutions and the interests they pursue are of primary importance, bottom-up ones, which give citizens the central stage, spring from protest and respond to the need for radical democratic reform.[58]

---

56 Allegretti, G. (2003) *L'insegnamento di Porto Alegre: Autoprogettualità come paradigma urbano.* Firenze: Alinea, p. 173; and Greta Ríos in Chapter Three of this volume.

57 Altman, D. (2019) *Citizenship and Contemporary Direct Democracy.* Cambridge: Cambridge University Press, p. 22.

58 Della Porta, D. and Felicetti, A. (2019) 'Innovating democracy against democratic stress in Europe: social movements and democratic experiments.' *Representation* 1–18, at 14.

Even when the results of bottom-up mechanisms of direct democracy fall short of promoters' expectations, there can be positive spillover effects on democracy, both on

> the political game itself (by generating incentives for political consensus, moderating circumstantial majorities, and expanding the political playing field), and [on] the relationship between representative institutions and the citizenry (by augmenting policy congruence, women's empowerment, civic participation, satisfaction with democracy, and broadening the topics subject to popular consideration).[59]

Crowdsourced constitutional processes, particularly in times of crisis, give social movements some capacity to exert constitutive powers. At times of democratic malaise, the direct participation of citizens in re-writing the constitution can restore collective identity. Challenging a vision of constitutional processes as a technical process, a participatory standpoint is oriented towards creating a founding moment. In fact, progressive social movements can trigger constitutional processes including citizens' participation in deliberative spaces to build funding normative agreements.

In Iceland and in Ireland, the initiatives of citizens have led to experiments in constitution-making through citizens' assemblies endowed with instruments to interact with the outside. These constitutional spaces were characterized by civility, inclusivity, mutual respect, publicity, and plurality of information. Movements acquired constituent power when claiming constitutional protection for public goods against privatization, and for recognition of the value of citizen participation in democratic life.[60] In doing so, movements have also created public spheres that, following Habermas, can be considered as public in a threefold way.[61] First, by being open to the public. Second, by acting in public. Third, by being devoted to the discussion of public issues against the retrenchment of the public itself consequent to the privatization trend that dominates within liberal constitutionalism.

Referendums and other direct forms of democracy have also been increasingly used as a reaction to the growing mistrust in representative institutions. The uses of referendums have varied greatly, and so has their democratic quality. Still, social movements have at times stressed the advantages in terms of legitimacy and efficiency of handing the right to decide directly to citizens. In Scot-

---

59 Altman, *Citizenship and Contemporary Direct Democracy*, p. 23.
60 Bailey, S. and Mattei, U. (2013) 'Social movements as constituent power: the Italian struggle for the commons.' *Indiana Journal of Global Legal Studies* 20(2): 965–1013.
61 Habermas, J. (1989) [1962] *The Structural Transformation of the Public Sphere: An Inquiry into a Category of Bourgeois Society.* Cambridge: Polity.

land and Italy, or even in Catalonia, this has happened with respect to highly contested issues such as public services conceptions or national independence. Movements' participation in campaigns of the referendum process substantially increased the number of people involved and boosted the plurality of the arguments, since the public spaces in which the referendums' issues were discussed were multiplied.

In taking part in referendum processes, movements strengthen constitutional safeguards against elected representatives' excessive powers,[62] and contribute to balancing delegation and participation.[63] Activists' mobilizations also help in the formation of the citizens' will, possibly improving the quality of public debate and citizens' considered judgments.[64] Beyond the referendums' results, movements' engagement has at times empowered progressive ideas by helping mainstream some topics that had been previously neglected. Actually, referendums from below, which involve a larger than usual degree of extra-institutional mobilization – either by means of citizen-initiated referendums or by the effective appropriation of state-endorsed ones – are particularly apt to foster participation and deliberation.

Finally, in moments of democratic malaise and in a very short time span, movement parties have emerged and attained vast support. The crisis of political legitimacy triggered within the context of late neoliberalism and the ensuing electoral earthquake opened up spaces for new parties. On the left, movements have contributed in developing parties that represented their claims and were influenced by their democratic conceptions and practices. As center-left parties became centrist and as calls for justice and against inequality spread among citizens, new parties emerged in fact on the left. Not without tension with their initial supporters basis, they developed some capacity to attract disappointed voters from the center-left parties. While increasing skepticism towards representative democracy, movement parties (for instance, in Spain or in Greece) attempted to bring participatory and deliberative ideas nurtured by social movements into representative institutions.

---

62 Qvortrup, M. (2014) 'Referendums on independence, 1860 – 2011.' *Political Quarterly* 85(1): 57 – 64. See also: Qvortrup, M. (2022) *Referendums and Ethnic Conflict*. Philadelphia: University of Pennsylvania Press, Ch. One.
63 Marxer, W. and Pállinger, Z.T. (2009) 'Stabilizing or destabilizing? Direct-democratic instruments in different political systems.' In M. Setälä and T. Schiller (eds.) *Referendums and Representative Democracy: Responsiveness, Accountability and Deliberation*. London: Routledge, pp. 34 – 55.
64 Della Porta et al., *Referendums from Below*.

In several cases, at local or national level, activists of progressive social movements, even when critical of representative forms of democracy, took the chance to occupy an electoral space left empty by the fall of center-left parties. They built support for anti-austerity claims developed during the protest cycle. Through mechanisms of organizational appropriation institutional channels were occupied. Initial electoral victories galvanized activists given that street protests alone were insufficient in obtaining the changes demanded. The political opportunities which movements used were those they themselves contributed to generating, occupying, at the same time, what they perceived as empty spaces in institutional politics.

Having democracies capable of 'self-regulating,' as ideally supply-and-demand logic would do in a market economy, is an interesting idea. Injections of legitimacy from complementary sources – including the ability to generate deliberative listening – whenever that of representative government shrinks would be desirable. Yet, our discussion on social movements leads us to think that different and more complex mechanisms might be at play. As our illustration shows, positive developments can be found in different contexts but not necessarily the ones one would expect. One negative example could be useful here. For instance, Cini and Felicetti took Italy as an exemplary case of a political system with chronic legitimacy issues, only exacerbated by the Great Crisis, in high need of participatory and deliberative developments.[65] Today, the country remains a laggard in terms of deliberative experiments, which are spreading elsewhere across European countries, for instance to try to tackle climate change. Also, the national political system remains impermeable to democratic innovations and demands that movements articulate. There is no evidence of the representative system's shortcomings being met with rising forms of complementary democracy or, for that matter, deliberative listening qualities.

Conclusions

Social movements are fully fledged actors of democratic systems. Their practices and ideas are all the more important and influential as extant representative democracy is challenged by several crises. Far from being only contentious actors, social movements have been carriers of participatory and deliberative views of

---

65 Cini, L. and Felicetti, A. (2018) 'Participatory deliberative democracy: toward a new standard for assessing democracy? Some insights into the Italian case.' *Contemporary Italian Politics* 10(2), 151–169.

democracy that circulate in society and in institutions. Early scholarship recognized the innovation work taking place in movements. Later, attention was also given to their knowledge production properties. More recently, they have also been acknowledged as active contributors to democratic innovations. In particular, we have referred to three ways in which movements' ideas and practices have entered institutions: constitutional processes, referendums, and movement parties. The fact that movements can play these active roles does not mean that they will systematically do so or that they will always succeed. Movements might deliberately stay away from democratic life, organize against it, or be unable to impact upon it. In our view, the best way of thinking about movements is not as a complement to democracy, nor as contributors to virtuous behavior such as deliberative listening, nor as enemies. Rather, democratic movements are to be considered as among the most valuable and readily available sources of democratic renewal necessary for democracies to try to deliver as much as possible on their promises of freedom and equality in the contemporary context.

Selen A. Ercan and Carolyn M. Hendriks

Performing Democracy through Local Protests: The Case of Knitting Nannas Against Gas

This chapter explores the performative activities of local protests and considers their contribution to democracy understood in deliberative terms. Empirical insights are drawn from Knitting Nannas Against Gas (KNAG) – a locally based protest movement against coal seam gas (CSG) mining in Australia. The chapter applies a dramaturgical lens to analyse KNAG's local protests, and examines their performative effects on the public sphere in divided communities contesting CSG. The case analysis illuminates the importance of local identities and 'place' in staging protests with communicative effect. It demonstrates how local protests, such as those performed by KNAG, can play a vital role in public deliberation by: i) opening up public debates to alternative modes of expression; ii) empowering previously excluded voices to enter the debate; and iii) facilitating communication and reflection in the public sphere.

Introduction

Every week a group of residents in the small rural town of Coonabarabran, Australia meet and knit together in a local café as a form of protest against proposed CSG mining in their region. These residents have been meeting since 2014, and today they are part of a broader network of other knitting groups around Australia collectively named Knitting Nannas Against Gas. At their weekly gatherings, KNAG members, who are mostly women, engage in diverse activities; they knit, talk, laugh, and sometimes they sit in silence. They knit black and yellow beanies, tea cosies, and long scarves that are then displayed as protest messages on public streets, gates, roads, or trees. When we asked the Coonabarabran KNAG members why they gather and knit every week at the same café, they explained: "to save the land, air, and water for the kiddies".[1]

This café scene of knitting women is a far cry from the 18th century coffeehouses Jürgen Habermas described in his seminal work on structural transfor-

---

1 Interview #15, 24 November 2015, Coonabarabran.

https://doi.org/10.1515/9783110747331-011

mation of the public sphere.[2] For Habermas, coffeehouses were the birthplace of a vibrant public sphere; they offered spaces where citizens (only men) could come together to engage in rational debate through the medium of talk. In contrast, the KNAG's weekly gatherings are not only more plural in demographic terms (e.g. gender and age), but also in terms of the variety of discursive activities they host. Here, public deliberation is not confined to rational speech acts among gentlemen.[3] Instead, it is enacted by a group of women who express themselves through a variety of verbal and non-verbal performances; they sit, knit, and display colours, objects and symbols in playful ways, and they share their craft and messages with audiences on the streets and online.

There are striking differences between what Habermas originally envisioned as an ideal setting for public deliberation in a democracy,[4] and how it is enacted in contemporary politics.[5] Today, citizens participate in politics and voice their opinions through a rich array of activities in both face-to-face and online settings. They draw on a variety of performances using visuals, sound, presence, and even silence to express themselves. They use social media; tweet messages, upload videos on YouTube, circulate images and stories on Facebook which are creative, humorous, and antagonistic all at the same time.[6] They seek out creative and personally expressive modes of political action to participate in politics and political debates in ways they can, when they can.[7]

Contemporary protests also take many more diverse forms than the classic large social movements featured or assumed in Habermas's account of a working deliberative democracy.[8] The classic image of protesters as an angry crowd holding placards is being increasingly supplemented by more creative and interactive forms of protest activity. Many of these combine the personal and political, as

---

2 Habermas, J. (1991) *The Structural Transformation of the Public Sphere: An Inquiry into a Category of Bourgeois Society.* Cambridge: MIT Press.
3 Balme, C. B. (2014) *The Theatrical Public Sphere.* Cambridge: Cambridge University Press.
4 Habermas, *The Structural Transformation of Public Sphere.*
5 Wahl-Jørgensen, K. (2019) 'Questioning the ideal of the public sphere: the emotional turn.' *Social Media + Society,* July–September: 1–3.
6 Hendriks, C. M., Duus, S., and Ercan, S. A. (2016) 'Performing politics on social media: the dramaturgy of an environmental controversy on Facebook.' *Environmental Politics* 25(6): 1102–1125.
7 Micheletti, M. and McFarland, A. S. (2015) *Creative Participation: Responsibility-Taking in the Political World.* New York: Routledge.
8 Habermas, J. (1996) *Between Facts and Norms: Contributions to a Discourse Theory of Law and Democracy.* Cambridge: Polity Press.

well as the online and offline in highly performative ways.[9] There is also a growing number of studies focusing on the performative aspects of protests that point to the diverse props and artefacts used by contemporary activists, for example distinctive masks, hairstyles, clothing, or symbols, to mobilize diverse publics and challenge dominant cultural codes and practices.[10] Much of this empirical research on performative protests has been informed by studies of large-scale protests, such as the Occupy movement, and how their repertoires of contention travel between contexts and across the globe (such as the global uptake to occupy parks). In this chapter we zoom in on local protests (as opposed to global, large-scale protests) and consider their contributions to democracy understood *in deliberative terms*.

Deliberative democracy is a normative theory of democratic legitimacy based on the idea that those affected by a collective decision have the right, opportunity, and capacity to participate in consequential deliberation about the content of decisions.[11] In line with the systemic turn in deliberative democracy we understand public deliberation as a multifaceted communicative activity that takes place in various differentiated yet linked spaces that go beyond structured forums.[12] Within this broader view of deliberation, protests represent important spaces of expression and contestation, where dominant discourses and practices can be challenged and diverse publics mobilized.[13]

9 Bennett, W. L. and Segerberg, A. (2012) 'The logic of connective action: digital media and the personalization of contentious politics.' *Information, Communication & Society* 15(5): 739–768; Vromen, A. (2017) *Digital Citizenship and Political Engagement*. London: Palgrave Macmillan; and Mundt, M., Ross, K., and Burnett, C. M. (2018) 'Scaling social movements through social media: the case of Black Lives Matter.' *Social Media and Society* (online first): 1–14.
10 McGarry, A., Erhart, I., Eslen-Ziya, H., Jenzen, O., and Umut, K. (eds.) (2019) *The Aesthetics of Global Protest: Visual Culture and Communication*. Amsterdam: Amsterdam University Press; Clifton, J. and de la Broise, P. (2020) 'The yellow vests and the communicative constitution of a protest movement.' *Discourse & Communication* 14(4): 362–382; and Cadena-Roa, Jorge and Puga, Cristina (2021) 'Protest and performativity.' In S. Gluhovic, S. Jestrovic, S. M. Rai, and M. Saward (eds.) *The Oxford Handbook of Politics and Performance*. Oxford: Oxford University Press, pp. 101–117.
11 Dryzek, J. S. (2000) *Deliberative Democracy and Beyond: Liberals, Critics, Contestations*. Oxford: Oxford University Press.
12 Mansbridge, J., Bohman, J., Chambers, S., Christiano, T., Fung, A., Parkinson, J., Thompson, A., and Warren, M. (2013) 'A systemic approach to deliberative democracy.' In J. Parkinson and J. Mansbridge (eds.) *Deliberative Systems: Deliberative Democracy at the Large Scale*. Cambridge: Cambridge University Press, pp. 1–26.
13 Rollo, T. (2017) 'Everyday deeds: enactive protest, exit, and silence in deliberative systems.' *Political Theory* 45(5): 587–609; and Smith, W. (2020) 'Deliberation in an age of (un) civil resistance.' *Journal of Deliberative Democracy* 16(1): 14–19.

Our particular focus in this chapter is on local protests and the diverse ways they employ performative acts for communicative effect. Our discussion is grounded in an in-depth study of the colourful and creative protest activities of the KNAG movement (introduced above), which is just one of many local groups and alliances opposing the development and expansion of CSG mining in Australia.[14] We pay particular attention to the performative dimension of KNAG's protest activities and explore their communicative effect in communities divided by environmental controversies. We use the dramaturgical concepts of staging, casting, and scripting to study the performative protests of KNAG. Our case analysis illuminates the importance of local identities and 'place' in staging effective and engaging protests. We find that the performative protests of local movements like KNAG can play a vital role in public deliberation by i) opening up public debate to alternative modes of expression; ii) empowering previously excluded voices to enter the debate; and by iii) facilitating communication and reflection in the public sphere. The chapter is structured in three sections. First, we consider the value of protests in deliberative democracy, focusing particularly on local protests and their distinguishing characteristics. Second, we offer a dramaturgical analysis of KNAG's protest activities. Finally, we discuss the communicative impact and broader democratic meaning of these protests in small, regional communities divided by environmental controversies such as CSG mining.

The Value of Protests in Deliberative Democracy

The role of protests in deliberative democracy has been subject to various scholarly debates. While earlier work on deliberative democracy depicted protesting and deliberating as mutually exclusive ways of practising democracy,[15] over

14 Kuch, D. and Titus, A. (2014) 'Emerging dimensions of networked energy citizenship: the case of coal seam gas mobilisation in Australia.' *Communication, Politics & Culture* 47(2): 35–59; and Mann, A. (2008) 'The politics of place: networking resistance to coal seam gas mining.' In B. Brevini and J. Lewis (eds.) *Climate Change and the Media*, vol. 2. New York: Peter Lang, pp. 173–184.
15 Young, I. M. (2001) 'Activist challenges to deliberative democracy.' *Political Theory* 29(5): 670–690.

the past decade, especially with the systemic turn in deliberative democracy,[16] scholars have begun to reconsider the deliberative value of protests.

Since the systemic turn, scholars of deliberative democracy have shifted their focus away from studying a single (perfect) site of deliberation to studying multiple (imperfect) sites of public deliberation. A systemic view of public deliberation acknowledges that some sites of democracy are more deliberative (open, inclusive, reason-based) than others, and some have no deliberative credentials at all.[17] On this account each site or activity is judged based on its contribution to the deliberative system as a whole and not in isolation. The idea here is that "[w]hen different parts of a system perform complementary functions the larger system may approach deliberative standards more closely than any of the parts".[18]

Taking a systemic view, empirical studies have shown that protest movements are crucial for the realization of deliberative democracy.[19] These studies have shown that protests can facilitate the creation of new publics and communicative possibilities. Importantly, protests can enable the expression of previously unheard issues and voices in the public sphere, and potentially influence the decision-making in formal arenas.[20] This is true particularly for large-scale protest movements. In fact, when conceptualizing the value of protests for democracy, existing studies focus heavily on and celebrate large-scale protest movements such as the Occupy movement which began in New York in 2011 and spread to over 80 countries around the world.[21] But protests come in different forms and scales (e.g. local, national, global, online). In this chapter, we

---

16 Parkinson, J. and Mansbridge, J. (eds.) (2013) *Deliberative Systems: Deliberative Democracy at the Large Scale*. Cambridge: Cambridge University Press; Elstub, S., Ercan, S. A., and Mendonça, R. F. (eds.) (2019) *Deliberative Systems in Theory and Practice*. London: Routledge.

17 Parkinson and Mansbridge, *Deliberative Systems in Theory and Practice*.

18 Mansbridge, J. (2015) 'A minimalist definition of deliberation.' In P. Heller and V. Rao (eds.) *Deliberation and Development: Rethinking the Role of Voice and Collective Action in Unequal Societies*. Washington, DC: World Bank Group, pp. 27–46, at p. 28.

19 See: Barvosa, E. (2018) *Deliberative Democracy Now: LGBT Equality and the Emergence of Large-Scale Deliberative Systems*. Cambridge: Cambridge University Press; Min, S.-J. (2015) 'Occupy Wall Street and deliberative decision-making: translating theory to practice.' *Communication, Culture & Critique* 8(1): 73–89; Mendonça, R. F. and Ercan, S. A. (2015) 'Deliberation and protest: strange bedfellows? Revealing the deliberative potential of 2013 protests in Turkey and Brazil.' *Policy Studies* 36(3): 267–282.

20 Giugni, M. and Bosi, L. (2012) 'The impact of protest movements on the establishment: dimensions, models, and approaches.' In K. Fahlenbrach, M. Klimke, J. Scharloth, and L. Wong (eds.) *The Establishment Responds: Power, Politics and Protest Since 1945*. New York: Palgrave Macmillan, pp. 17–29.

21 Thompson, D. (2011) 'Occupy the world: the "99 percent" movement goes global.' *The Atlantic* (15 October).

focus on local protests operating with little or no organizational support that draw instead on place-based acts of everyday resistance and contestation.

Local protests have not featured prominently in empirical studies of either deliberative democracy or social movements. This is largely because local protests often lack the kind of accessible data that can be found for larger national or international social movements.[22] Many decision-makers and media commentators often frame local movements as *Not In My Backyard* (NIMBY) efforts to protect parochial or particular interests at the expense of broader collective benefits. However, in-depth scholarly studies reveal that local movements are mostly motivated around broader issues; for example, ecological concerns, procedural injustice, or loss of local amenity and place.[23] Other research has shown how local protesters sometimes engage in complex framing processes beyond 'place' (e.g. by drawing on global discourses and international alliances) in order to mobilize local support against controversial developments.[24]

While local protests vary considerably, research finds they differ in important ways from the kinds of large protests staged by national or international social movements.[25] For our purposes, here we draw attention to three interrelated characteristics of local protests. First, local protests often feature communitarian tendencies; that is, they rely on, and seek to foster, a sense of community within which they are situated. They build on prior commitments to local communities, places, and traditions,[26] and often blend political and social aspects into their protest activities and repertoires of contention. Those joining local protests often do so not solely based on rational calculations but based on social and affective ties and interactions. Emphasizing the communitarian focus of local pro-

---

22 Rootes, C. (2007) 'Acting locally: the character, contexts and significance of local environmental mobilisations.' *Environmental Politics* 16: 722–741; Hager, C. and Haddad, M. A. (eds.) (2015) *NIMBY is Beautiful: Cases of Local Activism and Environmental Innovation around the World*. New York: Berghahn Books.
23 Mann, 'The politics of place.' See also: Eranti, V. (2017) 'Re-visiting NIMBY: from conflicting interests to conflicting valuations.' *Sociological Review* 65(2): 285–301; Hager and Haddad, *NIMBY is Beautiful*.
24 Della Porta, D. and Piazza, G. (2007) 'Local contention, global framing: the protest campaigns against the TAV in Val di Susa and the bridge on the Messina Straits.' *Environmental Politics* 16(5): 864–882.
25 See: Dufour, P. (2020) 'Comparing collective actions beyond national contexts: "local spaces of protest" and the added value of critical geography.' *Social Movement Studies* 20(2): 224–242; Rootes, C. (2007) 'Acting locally: the character, contexts and significance of local environmental mobilisations.' *Environmental Politics* 16: 722–741.
26 Lichterman, P. (1996) *The Search for Political Community: American Activists Reinventing Commitment*. Massachusetts: Cambridge University Press.

tests, some scholars define them as 'social movement communities' – a concept that draws attention to cultural and social dimension of these groups.[27]

Second, local protests often highlight 'locality and place' to mobilize diverse groups and build solidarity (e.g. across class and ideology) against a common enemy (a developer or urbanites).[28] In-depth research on the mobilization dynamics of local protest groups reveals that local identity and everyday affective experiences of movement members have a profound effect on how these groups form, mobilize, and respond to an external threat, such as CSG development.[29]

Third, a less emphasized characteristic of local protests relates to the specific roles they perform or are expected to perform in their respective communities, especially compared with national or international movements. Given their place-based and social connections, local protest groups (especially those with progressive political agendas) often assume a mediator role in communities and promote dialogue among conflicting groups.[30] This is partly shaped by the strong social imperatives in small, local communities, where everybody knows each other and relies on one another, often over multiple generations. In such contexts, there can be social expectations to negotiate disagreements constructively,[31] and for community members to 'hold back' from confrontational communication styles.[32] These local social norms shape the strategies and repertoires of contention that local movement groups use in their protest activities.

Given these characteristics, local protests can contribute to the public discourse in ways that have yet to be fully appreciated by scholars of deliberative democracy. Deliberative democrats tend to focus on the role of protests mainly in opinion formation in the public sphere. They do not consider, for example, how protests might also work to promote 'connection' [33] or 'integration and so-

27 Staggenborg, S. (1998) 'Social movement communities and cycles of protest: the emergence and maintenance of local women's movements.' *Social Problems* 45(2): 180 – 204.

28 Martin, Deborah G. (2003) '"Place-framing" as place-making: constituting a neighborhood for organizing and activism.' *Annals of the Association of American Geographers* 93(3): 730 – 750.

29 Ransan-Cooper, H., Ercan, S. A., and Duus, S. (2018) 'When anger meets joy: how emotions mobilise and sustain the anti-coal seam gas movement in regional Australia.' *Social Movement Studies* 17(6): 635 – 657.

30 Staggenborg, 'Social movement communities and cycles of protest.'

31 Alexander, D. (2015) 'It's not what you know it's how you know: political connectedness and political engagement at the local level.' *Journal of Sociology* 51(4): 827 – 842.

32 Ransan-Cooper, H., Ercan, S. A., and Duus, S. (2018) 'Getting to the heart of coal seam gas protests – it's not just the technical risks.' *The Conversation:* https://theconversation.com/getting-to-the-heart-of-coal-seam-gas-protests-its-not-just-the-technical-risks-107086.

33 Hendriks, C. M., Ercan, S. A., and Boswell, J. (2020) *Mending Democracy: Democratic Repair in Disconnected Times.* Oxford: Oxford University Press.

cial cohesion' in the public sphere.[34] We find that local protests can generate such outcomes through their emphasis on local identities and places, especially in communities tackling environmental controversies or major landscape changes such as wind farms, CSG wells, or other energy infrastructures. For community members tackling such changes, the landscape is not only a "'surface' waiting for a new plan"; it is "loaded with meanings, signifiers, stories and achievements".[35] Therefore, major landscape changes often "trigger people to express their attachment to place and motivate them to become politically active".[36]

In this chapter, we focus on KNAG as an example of a local protest group featuring the key characteristics outlined above. KNAG seeks to "politicise place"[37] by reframing the landscape as not just something to be used or exploited, but as something that carries important local meanings around land, food, and water. KNAG displays these meanings and engages in a place-based environmental controversy in highly performative ways. In what follows, we elaborate on the socio-political context within which KNAG was formed, analyse the performative aspect of their local protests, and consider their contribution to democracy understood in deliberative terms.

The Local Protests of Knitting Nannas Against Gas

The KNAG movement first formed in June 2012 when a small group of women from the Northern Rivers area of New South Wales felt excluded from their local environmental group (Lock the Gate) protesting CSG in their region. Having experienced sexist and ageist attitudes, especially from male activists, these women decided to establish their own protest group and display alternative activism by subverting the traditional carer roles attributed to them. As the founding member of KNAG, Clare Twomey, explains it:

---

34 Fischer, R., Keinert, A., Jarren, O., and Klinger, U. (2021) 'What constitutes a local public sphere? Building a monitoring framework for comparative analysis.' *Media and Communication* 9(3): 85–96.
35 Hajer, M. and Wagenaar, H. (2003) *Deliberative Policy Analysis: Understanding Governance in the Network Society.* Cambridge: Cambridge University Press, p. 93.
36 Mann, 'The politics of place,' p. 173.
37 Mann, 'The politics of place,' p. 173.

It seemed that they would have liked us to do stereotypical things. So, we would have a meeting, and expected for example to bake some cakes for the fundraisers, make the teas, take minutes ... can you do this research, can you print this out. ... So, we decided to form our own group and twist these stereotypes.[38]

KNAG began their peaceful protests by going into the countryside with their knitting, folding chairs, and thermoses to watch and record the activities of mining company, Metgasco. Initially, knitting was something they did to productively pass the time, but it soon evolved into a key repertoire of the group, an effective way of doing environmental activism in communities contesting the development of CSG mining.[39] The group began gathering and knitting in public spaces, and particularly publicly visible places, to draw attention to the negative impacts of CSG mining in their region. Their place-based, performative activities resonated with others in regions also contesting CSG mining. Since 2012, some 40 local KNAG groups (known as 'loops') have formed to protest against CSG in other regions across Australia, and in pockets of the USA and UK.[40]

Before proceeding with the performative analysis of the KNAG's local protests, a brief note on CSG and its politics is useful. CSG is a form of unconventional mining where wells are drilled to extract natural gas from coal seams. Typically, gas and water are held together under pressure, and as the water is extracted it releases pressure within the coal seam, allowing the gas to flow up through the well to the surface. In many countries CSG mining projects are notoriously controversial; they promise benefits such as local employment and economic development but raise objections due to their potential adverse impacts on the health and well-being of local communities, agricultural production, and the environment.[41] In Australia, CSG mining has divided many communities and created difficult conditions for talking and listening about minning gas – particularly among those who hold different views.[42]

---

38 Interview with the founding member, Clare Twomey, 4 October 2018, Lismore.

39 Larri, L. J. and Newlands, M. (2017) 'Knitting Nannas and Frackman: a gender analysis of Australian anti-coal seam gas documentaries (CSG) and implications for environmental adult education.' *Journal of Environmental Education* 48(1): 35–45.

40 Knitting Nannas (2021), 'Knitting Nannas': https://knitting-nannas.com.

41 See: Ladd, A. E. (2013) 'Stakeholder perceptions of socioenvironmental impacts from unconventional natural gas development and hydraulic fracturing in the Haynesville Shale.' *Journal of Rural Social Sciences* 28(2): 56–89; and Metze, T. (2014) 'Fracking the debate: frame shifts and boundary work in Dutch decision making on shale gas.' *Journal of Environmental Policy & Planning* 19(1): 1–18.

42 Arashiro, Z. (2017) 'Mining, social contestation and the reclaiming of voice in Australia's democracy.' *Social Identities* 23(6): 661–673. See also: Colvin, R. M., Witt, G. B., and Lacey, J. (2015)

KNAG is one of several local groups protesting against CSG mining in their communities. In many respects, it shares much in common with other local environmental mobilizations, particularly those that emerge around LULUs (locally unwanted land use). But there are some especially decentred and performative aspects of KNAG that deserve mention. KNAG proudly describes itself as a "disorganisation";[43] a loosely structured movement composed of "a floating pool of participants".[44] Each local loop has its own personality and decides on its own activities.

Notwithstanding local variety, a common element across all KNAG loops is the use of colour. At any KNAG gathering, members typically dress in yellow and black, not only to attract attention, but also to brand their protest activities and facilitate connections across loops. Yellow and black, which are the colours of danger and warning, are strongly associated with the anti-CSG movement across Australia, largely due to the protest activities of the large national alliance group, Lock the Gate. When KNAG sit down to knit they work with yellow and black wool to craft scarves, beanies, or protest triangles (the symbol developed by Lock the Gate Alliance). As part of the performance, street protests by KNAG typically display large yellow and black banners, alongside various yellow and black wool items that they have knitted. The combined visual effect of all the black and yellow is that KNAG protests are highly visible and eye-catching.

Typically, KNAG protests occur in small-scale multiple localities, rather than via large and centralized protest events. In most localities members meet face to face on a regular basis to knit together in locally well-known public spaces or cafés. Mirroring the communitarian tendencies of local protest groups discussed above, KNAG put the community at the centre of their activities. For example, one Nanna we interviewed in Coonabarabran defines her participation in the group as "doing community" and her weekly knitting with others as a way of expressing "belonging in place".[45] While most KNAG members emphasize care and support for the community, they also want their protests to be disruptive. For example, they organize regular 'knit-ins' outside the offices of their members of parliament or the corporations associated with CSG industry. Their gathering

'Strange bedfellows or an aligning of values? Exploration of stakeholder values in an alliance of concerned citizens against coal seam gas mining.' *Land Use Policy* 42: 392–399.

43 Colvin, Witt, and Lacey, 'Strange bedfellows or an aligning of values?'

44 Stops, L. (2014) 'Les Tricoteuses: the plain and purl of solidarity and protest.' *Craft +Design Enquiry* 6: 7–28.

45 Interviewee #16, 24 November 2015, Coonabarabran.

and knitting in these spaces often have a disruptive effect and cause concern for local politicians supporting the CSG industry in the region.[46]

In this chapter, we focus particularly on three different KNAG loops in south-eastern Australia – one based in the small rural town of Coonabarabran, and the other two located in the regional centres of Armidale and Lismore. All three loops have been actively protesting against the same proposed CSG development, namely the Narrabri Gas Project (NGP). This is a controversial gas project being proposed by the energy corporation, Santos, to extract gas from 850 wells across a project area of approximately 1,000 square kilometres near Narrabri in eastern Australia (Santos, 2017). The NGP has been described as the "most protested against gas development" in New South Wales.[47] The public sphere surrounding the NGP within the region is highly polarized between those who oppose the gas project, and others who support it.[48] Those opposed to the NGP include individuals and citizen groups (such as KNAG) who are concerned about diverse issues such as land and water impacts, the safety of extraction technologies, effects on human health, consequences for the social fabric of communities, and implications for global climate change.[49] Some citizens and local groups, such as 'Yes2Gas', support the NGP because it promises positive impacts on local business and employment. It is against this socio-political background that KNAG stages its local protests.

In what follows, we undertake a performative analysis of KNAG protests to unpack the ways the group draws on local identity, community, and place in their protests and their effect in divided public spheres. In our analysis, we draw on the work of Robert Benford and Scott Hunt, who apply dramaturgy to examine how social movements script performances, such as campaigns and rallies, with core narratives, central characters, and audiences.[50] We make use of three dramaturgical concepts:[51] i) *staging* (the management and direction of performance); ii) *casting* (the key characters in the performance); and iii) *scripting*

---

46 Larri and Newlands, 'Knitting Nannas and Frackman.'

47 HuffPost (2021) 'The startling moment 200 farmers and Nannas told a gas company to "frack off"': https://www.huffpost.com/archive/au/entry/pilliga-protest-the-moment-200-farmers-and-nannas-tell-santos-t_a_23062445.

48 Hendriks, C. M., Ercan, S. A., and Duus, S. (2019) 'Listening in polarised controversies: a study of listening practices in the public sphere.' *Policy Sciences* 52(1): 137–151.

49 Ransan-Cooper, Ercan, and Duus, 'When anger meets joy.'

50 Benford, R. D. and Hunt, S. A. (1992) 'Dramaturgy and social movements: the social construction and communication of power.' *Sociological Inquiry* 62(1): 36–55.

51 Adopted from Hajer, M. (2005) 'Setting the stage: a dramaturgy of policy deliberation.' *Administration & Society* 36(6): 624–647; and Benford and Hunt, 'Dramaturgy and social movements.'

(the central message of the performance). These concepts are well suited to studying verbal and non-verbal performative acts in the public sphere,[52] as well as for unpacking the improvised forms of politics, where discursive conditions are in a state of flux.[53]

Our analysis draws data from several sources, including in-depth interviews with the founder of KNAG and with active members of the three local loops; direct observation (between 2015 and 2018) of KNAG protests in the three loops; text and visual analysis of KNAG's website; and material from relevant Facebook sites.

Staging: Gathering and Knitting in Local Places

The dramaturgical concept of staging refers to how the central protest activities and audiences are managed and directed, and where these activities take place.[54] According to KNAG's website, the main protest activities of the group are to "sit, knit, plot".[55] While KNAG welcome many craft forms, knitting plays a particularly important symbolic role in their protests. It assumes a 'voice function' for women who are excluded or unrepresented in the mostly male-dominated controversy over CSG in their region. As one Nanna we interviewed put it, knitting provides women with a "passageway" to voice the concerns they have about the future of their communities, children, or grandchildren. The same Nanna explained that their knitting-based protests offer "an opening that women have been able to move through to have a voice".[56] Similarly, in her insightful study of KNAG, Liz Stops argues that knitting provides "a language" to speak with, and enables people from diverse professions and different political persuasions to develop a collective sense of empowerment.[57]

An important part of the voice function that knitting can assume is that it is performed in public towards targeted audiences. In this sense, a crucial staging

---

52 Ercan, S. A. and Hendriks, C. M. (2022) 'Dramaturgical analysis.' In S. A. Ercan, H. Asenbaum, N. Curato, and R. F. Mendonça (eds.) *Research Methods in Deliberative Democracy.* Oxford: Oxford University Press, forthcoming.

53 Hajer, M. and Versteeg, W. (2005) 'A decade of discourse analysis of environmental politics: achievements, challenges, perspectives.' *Journal of Environmental Policy & Planning* 7(3): 175–184.

54 Benford and Hunt, 'Dramaturgy and social movements.'

55 Knitting Nannas, 'Knitting Nannas': https://knitting-nannas.com.

56 Interview #21, 6 June 2017, Coonabarabran.

57 Stops, 'Les Tricoteuses,' p. 26.

task of KNAG is determining the target audience and then finding a relevant place to reach that audience. This might be near pedestrian streets, in a local café or club, or in front of political institutions.[58] For the most part, the act of knitting on the street is directed at the community with the aim of establishing connections and having conversations with everyday people about CSG in the local region. To this end KNAG set up their knitting protests in public places where they can meet or be seen by local people, for example outside popular cafés or out on the street in public thoroughfares. As they explain on their website:

> The idea is that we get together outside politicians' offices, work sites, rallies and anywhere else we please to show a mild mannered yet stubborn front, where we get out our camp chairs, table (with lace tablecloth if possible), our knitting (of course!) and have a little tea party. If the workers approach us we offer them a cup of tea. … Our presence is to be positive, creative and above all, fun. After the tea party, we settle down and do our thing. We are using knitting for the title, but any other craft form, card games, crosswords, shelling peas …[59]

Some 'knit-ins' are staged to maximize such visibility, for example along a highway. Others are strategically situated to attract the attention of decision-makers opposition groups, such as a local or federal politician. The goal here is to encourage decision-makers to listen, or at least to see them.[60] Sometimes KNAG stage their 'knit-ins' inside formal institutions, such as a public hearing or a council meeting, where the act of knitting might be seen as 'inappropriate'. This provides useful visual material for publicity and popular media coverage, and a possibility of being heard. As one interviewee puts it, by knitting in these local public spaces:

> We want to just put it in people's faces: "We don't want it. We don't like it. We'll sit here and knit till the cows come home". And show you that we can sit it out and we can go right till the end.[61]

The places where KNAG stage their protests play a crucial role in determining the purpose and impact of their protest activities. When staged in parks and directed towards the general public, the KNAG protests appear to be welcoming and non-

---

58 Interview #46, 9 June 2017, Armidale.

59 Knitting Nannas, 'Knitting Nannas': https://knitting-nannas.com.

60 Clarke, K. (2016) 'Willful knitting? Contemporary Australian craftivism and feminist histories.' *Continuum* 30(3): 298–306.

61 Interview #31, 24 June 2016, Narrabri.

confrontational. Their physical presence and silent practice of knitting aim to raise awareness about the mining developments in the region and invite the public to reflect on the potential risks of these developments, especially for future generations. The group's presence in public spaces works to generate alliances among like-minded people. Yet at the same time, they provide opportunities for non-confrontational conversations with those who might have opposing views or with those who might not yet have an opinion on CSG development in their region.

Sometimes the conversations KNAG initiate in public spaces do not involve any discussion on CSG at all. This, however, is not a problem according to many Nannas we interviewed.[62] The key message they seek to convey through their persistent presence is 'bearing witness' to what is being said and not said about particular issues that they care about in the CSG debate: particularly the safety and health of children, future generations, and the fate of their productive land. Even if there is not much conversation going on, just being there – being present at a rally or on the street or in the public eye regularly and repeatedly – is viewed as an important communicative aspect of KNAG activities. Their embodied presence represents an act of reclaiming the public sphere, and care for local communities.

Casting: Characters with Local Community Meaning

Casting in social movements involves constructing the key characters of the performance including the antagonists, protagonists, victims, and audiences.[63] In KNAG, the central protagonist in the performance is the 'trustworthy knitting Nanna', while the antagonist is the "corporations and/or individuals who seek personal gain from the short-sighted and greedy plunder of our natural resources".[64] Unlike many environmental protest movements, KNAG expend little performative effort on demonizing the antagonist – here the CSG industry and its employees. Instead KNAG concentrate on projecting their central 'Nanna' character.

KNAG honour "a firm tradition of older women's knowing and being".[65] They use this 'Nanna' image strategically and creatively in a range of performative activities. The image of old Nanna and her trustworthiness as well as wisdom

---

62 Interview #15, 24 November 2015, Coonabarabran.
63 Benford and Hunt, 'Dramaturgy and social movements.'
64 Knitting Nannas, 'Knitting Nannas': https://knitting-nannas.com.
65 Larri and Newlands, 'Knitting Nannas and Frackman,' 30.

is used to provoke thought and encourage conversations on CSG mining in the region.[66] As one interviewee explained, this strategy works well; KNAG reach out and "bring together a diverse range of community because people can relate to this 'wise old Nanna' image".[67] This almost matriarchical depiction of the Nanna character carries particular resonance, especially in the small rural communities. She speaks to an enduring stereotype in the mass media of Australian rural women as 'heroic saviours' that rescue rural communities through emotional strength and wisdom.[68] As one interviewee explains:

> Nannas are always seen to be someone that has a very considered opinion, so they are considered wise counsel in the community. So, I think to a certain extent it's quite influential in that if our senior matriarchs of the community are standing up against something like this, it sends a very strong message that they've actually galvanized some action, and gone to the extent of protesting for a group that would traditionally be perceived as being quite conservative. This plays a powerful role.[69]

When people see the image of Nannas gathered in local venues they think "soft little Nannas actually being radicalized, or radical ... there's this nice sort of uneasiness there that gets people interested".[70] As one interviewee puts it: "It's the contradiction" that makes these protests effective. "Nobody can walk past and think, 'Oh, what a bunch of rat bags', except without thinking of their own mother or grandmother."[71] The broader message being: "if Nanna is upset about a situation, something must be going on here".[72]

Successful social movement performances also require enlisting and empowering a supporting cast, in addition to central characters.[73] In the case of KNAG, the supporting cast is composed of the images of grandchildren, who are used to draw attention to the consequences of CSG mining for future generations.[74] Interestingly, when talking about future generations, KNAG do not use the word 'children', as one interviewee notes; instead they refer to 'kiddies', which is Australian slang:

---

66 Interview #21, 6 June 2017, Armidale.
67 Interview #19, 24 November 2015, Coonabarabran.
68 Grace, M. and Lennie, J. (1998) 'Constructing and reconstructing rural women in Australia: the politics of change, diversity and identity.' *Sociologia Ruralis* 38(3): 351–370.
69 Interview #21, 24 November 2015, Coonabarabran.
70 Interview #21, 24 November 2015, Coonabarabran.
71 Interview #22, 24 November 2015, Coonabarabran.
72 Interview #9, 7 June 2017, Narrabri.
73 Benford and Hunt, 'Dramaturgy and social movements.'
74 Interview #46, 9 June 2017, Armidale.

They don't use the word 'children'. I think words can be powerful ... it seemed a bit odd at first to call them [children] 'kiddies', ... but I thought actually it's them being natural, using their language and building on their language to add all the other language that goes with the protest.[75]

The Nanna character along with the supporting cast of future generations broadens local understandings of who is potentially affected by CSG, as well as who is responsible for protecting the land and environment. According to one interviewee:

[KNAG] represents a presence to be able to say that "we want to protect our environment for our grandchildren". ... That's why it's really important to show that there's a diverse range from the community all coming together. ... You need to have people, a range that people can relate to so that you're not stigmatized.[76]

KNAG's focus on future generations also resonates with younger members of the group, as one participant explains:

I'm not a nanna, but the naming of KNAG, the namesake of it means we're looking after a younger generation, even if we're not actually Nannas. ... It is about providing for the future, whether it's ours, whether it's the next species of animals or humans, to me it's ... about being responsible for what we leave behind. ... The name attracts people who feel responsibility for the next generation.[77]

Our analysis shows that casting characters with local community meaning can serve as a crucial mobilizing strategy for local protests, and enable non-confrontational conversations on divisive issues, such as CSG mining.

Scripting: Fun and Welcoming Protests

Scripting in social movements is about "the development of a set of directions that define the scene, identify actors and outline expected behaviour".[78] Scripts are not rigid texts; they are partly improvised as actors interact with each other, with their audience, or with antagonists. Yet, most social movements still have a central script which serves to ensure that the movement's activities are in line

---

75 Interview #17, 24 November 2015, Coonabarabran.
76 Interview #19, 24 November 2015, Narrabri.
77 Interview #46, 6 June 2017, Armidale.
78 Benford and Hunt, 'Dramaturgy and social movements,' 38.

with its goals. Characters are expected to exercise "dramaturgical discipline" and remain "on message", while overly zealous actors may need to be reined in.[79] In the case of KNAG the scripting appears to be relatively open. As noted above, each KNAG loop determines its own script and associated activities. What links different loops is a four-paragraph *Nannafesto* (available on the group's website) that lays out KNAG's key concerns and principles:

> We peacefully protest against the destruction of our land, air and water. We want to leave this land better than we found it. ... We sit, knit, plot, have a yarn and a cuppa and bear witness to those who try to rape our land and divide our communities.[80]

Given that one of KNAG's core goals is to mobilize people into action against CSG, it uses a script that makes protesting against CSG seem fun, humorous, and about 'community'. Although contesting a serious issue, KNAG approach their political messaging and protest activities with playfulness. For example, KNAG members dress up in flamboyant outfits on show days; they attach their knitted objects to landholders' gates; they knit very long scarves, protectively wrapping public spaces, objects, and people; they attach a knitted yellow bikini and matching earrings to a full-size poster of a local male politician. In some instances they sing songs and dance as part of their performative protests.

All these humorous playful acts, images, and props seek to "inject levity and smile" into a controversy characterized by serious threats to land, air, and water in CSG-affected communities.[81] KNAG intentionally script their protesting activities as affirming and positive. As one interviewee notes:

> It is important to have optimism and fun and to keep that up because if we don't, if we don't make this activism and these events and the relationships, you know, life affirming, then we'll be worn down by it, and we'll end up just like our enemies. We have to provide a positive alternative.[82]

KNAG's playful script creates opportunities for discussion and reflection on a topic that has polarized local communities across Australia. In many towns and regional centres, local media reports on CSG have pitted angry 'out of town' environmentalists and farmers against pushy mining companies. In some towns that we visited, locals described how they actively avoid talking

---

79 Benford and Hunt, 'Dramaturgy and social movements.'
80 Knitting Nannas, 'Knitting Nannas': https://knitting-nannas.com.
81 O'Keefe, S. and Brown, R. (2013) 'Knitting Nannas': https://vimeo.com/110102248.
82 Interview #22, 6 June 2017, Armidale.

about CSG because it divides families, sports teams, school communities, and workplaces.[83] Within this divisive community context, KNAG script humorous performances that are disarming and non-confrontational. For example, they gather Nannas wearing flamboyant colourful objects, clothes, and accessories to draw public attention to their protest activities and to invite public intrigue and questions for conversation. People walking past see the colour and vibrancy of 'old Nannas' sitting and knitting together, and they start to ask questions, talk, learn, and engage. Humour generates a welcoming and conversational tone to the 'knit-ins', making them fun and enjoyable community activities.[84]

The Communicative Impact of Local Place-Based Protests

What do local performative protests like KNAG's mean for enacting democracy understood in deliberative terms? Based on the above analysis, we argue that KNAG contributes to public deliberation on CSG in at least three important ways.

First, *KNAG's local protests open up the public debate to alternative modes of expression.* In our case, we have seen that KNAG's place-based protests have expanded the way local people contest the proposed gas project in the Narrabri region. This is a politically conservative rural area where people typically express their political views through voting or by contacting their local state or federal member of parliament. In this context, KNAG offer alternative ways to contest CSG in the public sphere – primarily through the playful act of gathering and knitting. They use both verbal and non-verbal forms of political expression to make a political statement, mobilize local support, and effect change. In doing so, KNAG reconfigure the meaning of public deliberation beyond structured and talk-based forums. Public deliberation becomes something far more than a group of citizens coming together in structured public forums or town hall meetings. It becomes a broader communication to which everyday citizens can join through their colourful and creative performative activities in the public sphere. These performances help to bring the "life experience and imagination of local people to the system".[85]

Second, *KNAG's local protests empower and enable previously excluded voices to enter the CSG debate.* These protests expand the dominant ideas about

---

83 Hendriks, Ercan, and Duus, 'Listening in polarised controversies.'
84 Interview #19, 24 November 2015, Narrabri.
85 Matynia, E. (2009) *Performative Democracy.* London: Routledge, p. 6.

'who is affected' by proposed mining projects. KNAG have been particularly successful at injecting the voices of women and children into the public debate surrounding CSG projects. With their casting of the central character 'Nanna', and supporting characters such as 'kiddies', KNAG offer an effective way of representing previously excluded voices such as future generations. This focus on 'future generations' also helps Nannas to leave the political divisions aside, and create a new sense of commonality across different publics. As one Nanna explained: "I might stand here every Friday morning with somebody with no clue of what they vote because it is not about that ... it is about the kiddies."[86]

Third, *KNAG's local protests facilitate communication and reflection in communities divided by environmental controversies.* While most Nannas we interviewed acknowledge the importance of digital platforms such as Facebook for their collective action, they place more importance on being physically and regularly present in public spaces to be able to reach out to, and connect, diverse publics. Their place-based performative activities make ordinary people curious about CSG developments in their region, and encourage them to have conversations about CSG.[87] As one Nanna put it: "by just 'being there' conversations happen".[88] KNAG's presence in local public places brings together individuals with diverse political orientations and enables communication and connection in communities divided by CSG controversy in Australia.[89]

An equally important communicative function of KNAG's local protests is that they induce reflection in the public sphere. While KNAG may not "do something in ways we would like, while we may not agree with them, they represent a cause for reflection".[90] The regular placed-based performances of KNAG open up much-needed spaces for reflection in divided communities and allow actors to express their perspectives, reflect, and learn more about the views of others in creative and personalized ways.[91]

Deliberative democrats, especially those interested in understanding and improving the prospects of public deliberation in the public sphere, are yet to fully appreciate the role of groups like KNAG in shaping the terms of debate and in enabling inclusion, communication, connection, and enhanced reflection in contemporary public spheres. The case of KNAG shows how local, place-based protests can contribute to democracy in important ways. To be clear, our argument

---

86 Interview #50, 29 June 2018, Sydney.
87 Interview #20, 24 November 2015, Narrabri; Interview #46, 9 June 2017, Armidale.
88 Interview #55, 4 November 2018, Lismore.
89 Hendriks, Ercan, and Boswell, *Mending Democracy*.
90 Clarke, 'Willful knitting?' 298.
91 Interview #9, 7 June 2017, Narrabri; Interview #15, 24 November 2015, Coonabarabran.

here is not to suggest that KNAG alone was able to form a healthy deliberative system, nor do we suggest that the deliberative system around the CSG issue was a perfect one. We acknowledge the structural inequalities and power imbalances in the debate surrounding CSG in New South Wales and in Australia, and how these can pose real challenges to the functioning of a deliberative system. Still, the case of KNAG shows that despite these challenges, local protest groups composed of everyday actors can play a significant role in transforming the public sphere.

Conclusion

In this chapter we have sought to explore the role of local protests in democracy understood in deliberative terms. Our in-depth analysis of KNAG, a networked, placed-based movement against CSG mining in Australia shows that local protests can enhance the prospects of public deliberation in important ways, especially when they are staged and scripted in locally meaningful ways. KNAG is an example of how local protests can script their political performances to resonate with a place-based context, meaning, and characters. At the same time, our analysis shows the need to go beyond a narrow understanding of public deliberation, and embrace the creative forms of political expression and contestation, especially in communities tackling divisive controversies.

Andrea Adamopoulos

Democracy as Art

In 2021, the artist Joseph Beuys would have celebrated his 100th birthday. In his honor, there were special exhibitions in museums all over the world that showed his impressive work. What was new was that many museums not only devoted themselves to his drawings and sculptures, but also took up Beuys's statements on the connection between art and democracy. These statements are more relevant than ever, and it is worth exploring the question of whether democracy is about politics or art on the basis of Joseph Beuys's core theses.

In this chapter, which is about the qualitative further development of our democracy, I will explain to what extent we are called upon to fundamentally rethink our understanding of democracy. Especially given the current crisis, in which democracies are being called into question all over the world, it is more important to recognize that a functioning polity is supported by individuals who actively assume their responsibility for the greater good. In any case, people carry responsibility at all times, whether they realize it or not.

This is where the concept of art comes into play. Using the example of the artist Joseph Beuys, this chapter will demonstrate where a traditional understanding of politics needs to be broken down, away from entrenched power structures and towards a living society of self-determined individuals. Beuys was firmly convinced that a profound social revolution is needed to overcome the ecological and democratic crises. A sustainable society needs a stable ecosystem as a basis for life, as well as a well-functioning social cohesion, that is, a vibrant democracy. Beuys's core concern is understood to be that the radical idea of understanding democracy as art, and understanding ourselves as artistically shaping beings of freedom, is the key idea for a profound change in our coexistence. These understandings are undoubtedly necessary in order to be able to face upcoming challenges such as climate change and the global democratic crisis.

In order to bring the connection between art and democracy as an idea to the people, the already world-famous artist Joseph Beuys opened an office for direct democracy in 1971 at Andreasstrasse 25 in the middle of Düsseldorf's old town.

When Beuys was invited in Kassel, Germany in 1972 to the documenta, the largest art exhibition in the world for contemporary art, he packed up his entire office and set it up in the Fridericianum Museum. From that day on, Beuys was present as an artist in this office for the 100 days of the entire documenta in order to talk to the people on site about the question of democracy and the 'ex-

https://doi.org/10.1515/9783110747331-012

panded concept of art' that he coined. That was considered his artistic contribution to the exhibition, which was taken up much later by the equally world-famous artist Marina Abramovic in her project 'The artist is present.'

At first glance, the conceptual pair of democracy and art seems to be a contradiction. We usually ascribe a high degree of freedom to art ('artistic freedom'), since the artist creates a work of art in a highly individual act of freedom, for whose success only the artist bears full responsibility. On the other hand, we are used to seeing democracy as a great structure of compromise in which the individual is subordinated to the interest of the community. How is the idea of freedom to fit into this structure?

Beuys, who experienced National Socialism and was himself a contemporary, distrusted representative democracy as a system that eliminated the individual's power to shape events and that was supposed to protect Germans from themselves by largely limiting direct co-determination in the municipalities and states, and completely excluding it at the federal level. National Socialism had shown Beuys the devastating consequences when man abandons his destiny as a free creature and loses contact with his very own creative urge. Beuys's conclusion from the atrocities of National Socialism was not that people should be deprived of their autonomy by only electing their representatives every four years, who should decide by proxy on all questions of society. For Beuys, this was the wrong way to go. He used his fame to call on as many people as possible, with his pronounced sense of mission, not to settle for this 'election of representatives,' but to become the shapers of their own living conditions in order to express their human dignity.

Beuys was deeply convinced that an overall picture of a coherent community cannot be achieved without involving the creativity of the individual. Casting one's vote in the form of a cross every four years in federal elections and then watching representatives implement this blank power of attorney for four years seemed to him not to be democratic. He called for the introduction of direct democracy in Germany, which would enable people to introduce their own ideas into existing political structures in a three-stage process. Beuys saw humans' destiny in the shaping of their own biography as the starting point for a society made up of free people, as opposed to victims of the system. His statement, "Every man an artist," has become a much-quoted phrase worldwide.

Beuys's offer to speak at the documenta art exhibition was met with very mixed reactions. National Socialism was still very present in people's minds, with Germany being divided at the time, and the socialism of East Germany was the bogeyman of the Western world. Beuys was perceived as a troublemaker, pressing on a wound that had just been treated with a huge bandage. The bandage was called prosperity. The economic miracle in post-war Germany allowed doubts and questions about a coherent social order to fade into the background. With society being stable, many believed there was no reason to complain about the existing conditions. Society went on in an orderly fashion and the image of the enemy was shifted to the other side of the wall. It was into this peacetime that first Beuys, and later the democracy movement around the OMNIBUS for Direct Democracy and Mehr Demokratie e.V., the association founded almost at the same time, launched their demand to further develop the existing representative democracy by introducing direct democracy.

'Go over there!' (to East Germany) is a phrase that the work of a growing democracy movement in Germany was still hearing years later. When the OMNIBUS for Direct Democracy started its work at a documenta in 1987 to publicize the idea of direct democracy in Germany, it was a common response from ordinary people on the street, some of whom were being confronted for the first time in their lives with the idea of being responsible for their own fate and that of their society. After the war, many people in Germany had willingly handed over responsibility for all political issues to representatives. People no longer trusted themselves and had by now become accustomed to the state of disempowerment. The existence of East Germany, where there were no free elections, was cited as proof of how happy one could be about the West German system with its free elections. The democracy movement's criticism of the existing conditions sometimes provoked knee-jerk reactions from fellow citizens. Anyone who disagreed with the system of representative democracy, combined with the capitalist economic system, should go to East Germany.

The OMNIBUS for Direct Democracy continued its work undeterred, touring through Germany as a traveling networking unit and engaging people on the streets in conversation about the need for direct democracy. It appealed to people's ability to take responsibility for their own destinies and thus for society as a whole, and sketched a picture of a society that did not act according to the 'lesser of two evils' (for many, this is still the guiding principle in political elections today), but according to the quality and freedom standards of art.

When the Berlin Wall fell, completely unexpectedly, the OMNIBUS also traveled to former East Germany to talk to people at the so-called 'roundtables' about a Germany on the move. The activists' great hope was that there would be a referendum on an all-German level where the German people would draft a new constitution, in which, according to the activists, referendums should be firmly anchored. The background to this hope was that the authors of the Basic Law at the time had stated in the preamble that the Basic Law was only a provisional arrangement for as long as Germany was divided. When Germany was reunited, the people themselves should draft a common constitution. This process was not wanted by politicians after German reunification as the outcome of such a process seemed too uncertain, so the scope of the provisional law was transferred to the federal states of East Germany.

This process dampened the euphoric mood of the activists, and the issue of direct democracy on an all-German level seemed to be dead for the time being. However, today, almost half a century later, we have come a good deal closer to the matter of direct democracy. Thanks to the continuous work of OMNIBUS and Mehr Demokratie e.V., direct democratic elements have been introduced in a refined way in all federal states and municipalities and have been regularly improved.

Votes on local issues take place throughout the year in Germany's municipalities as well as at the state level. Every vote is an enormous learning process for everyone involved. The success of a vote is not only limited to the result. The social process, the process of awareness-raising, which takes place when people consider the social issues and proposed solutions and exchange ideas about them, is a necessary prerequisite for the desired conditions. The dialogue, the joint debating, the deliberation, the development of a common vision call for skills that we need as people in a vibrant democracy.

The question of whether democracy is art or politics is a question of perspective. By considering an outcome point of view, a voting process is just another way of arriving at political decisions, although it makes an enormous difference whether a decision is directly legitimized by the people or not. This wrestling over concrete substantive issues over several years challenges and fosters a community.

But by considering the process of a vote as an artistic process, a deeper sense of understanding of democracy is gained, which moves away from quantitative standards and towards an image of humanity that places a high value on the individual. Democracy as an artistic process is a question of inner attitude. What value do I attach to my existence in the interplay with all other existences on earth? If I take this question seriously, I naturally place myself not only in a relationship to my fellow human beings, my neighbors, and my fellow citizens on the other side of the globe, but I also ask myself how my creative ideas can interact with all living things, matter, and the cosmos.

To be more concrete: in Germany there is an orchestra, the Stegreif Orchester, which creates a completely new image of our idea of an orchestra. Traditionally, an orchestra is a group of musicians who rehearse and perform a piece of music under the direction of a conductor. The many different instruments and temperaments of the musicians are brought together to form a piece of music thanks to a knowledgeable and charismatic conductor who has the full overview. Tempo, rhythm, volume, and dynamics are set by the conductor, and the orchestra only functions if each musician, under the direction of the conductor, contributes their abilities to this great entity. This is how a musical piece ready for the stage is created.

The Stegreif Orchester usually works without a conductor. In an intensive process, the musicians have learned to listen to each other so attentively, to perceive the impulses of their colleagues, that they do not need a conductor. Because they have a trained perception of each other, this orchestra can move freely on stage during a performance and thus immediately follow the impulses triggered by the music without losing contact with the other musicians. This gesture reaches the audience directly, who do not have to remain motionless in their concert chairs, but can also participate in the musical experience through their own movement. This interaction is intended from the outset.

In both cases, with and without the conductor, the end result is a piece of music ready for the stage. The difference could lie in how strongly the individual participants are connected with their actions. There are many examples of very successful working relationships between musicians and conductors, and that is in no way to be questioned here, but it is a question of responsibility. There have been several scandals in Germany recently involving artistic directors who have been accused of exploiting their power, terrorizing and exploiting staff. If these individuals speak for themselves, it becomes clear that this behavior is a *déformation professionnelle* in a system that largely denies actors, singers, musicians, and other artistic individuals responsibility for the whole and leaves this task of overseeing and shaping to the artistic directors alone. This can succeed under favorable circumstances, but if one looks at the Stegreif Orchester, a different, larger picture of artistic creation opens up. Listening together, perceiving each other's very own artistic impulses, is an image of the fact that individual creative urge and a functioning community are not necessarily mutually exclusive. The Stegreif Orchester sometimes works together with a conductor for a few days at a time, with whom they then further develop what they have already worked on and perhaps also dare to try something completely new again. Democracy should not only be thought of in terms of results; the entire process that leads us to a decision is also part of democracy.

There are many different forms of direct democracy in the world, but these processes have one thing in common: at the end, there is a result that is legally binding. This is a particularly important aspect of direct democracy after a lively phase of opinion-forming. The many non-binding consultative bodies in which citizens are allowed to participate can only lead to a growing inner commitment of the individual to the overall social structure in the short term. If there is no obligation, the human creative impulse gets stuck in one place, which is frustrating in the long run. That is why the term 'deliberation' is not sufficient if one wants to draw a picture of a society in which the human will shape things in a constructive balance of power with political institutions.

A successful voting process includes a legally binding end, preceded by the countless discussions leading up to the vote. This result can only be convincing in its simplicity because it was preceded by an opinion-forming process that showed each participant the arguments and convictions which the other participants contributed. Even if one does not agree with the result of a vote, it is immediately perceptible as the result of a joint struggle of many individuals.

The Brexit vote, as a negative example, has shown how enormously important the 'bottom-up principle' is in a vote. If one compares this vote with the countless votes that take place in Switzerland every year, one finds that it makes a big difference whether an issue crystallizes in the population and is put to a vote according to a firmly defined process or whether, as in the case of Brexit, there is a power struggle at government level and the principle of the popular vote is instrumentalized to reach a decision. In the latter case, there was a lack of time and a lack of the intensive opinion-forming process that is needed to reach a level-headed decision. The conditions for the success of direct democratic procedures can be well illustrated with Brexit, which has been done many times in expert circles.

To conclude, in his theories Joseph Beuys referred to a model that divides all phenomena of human coexistence into three areas: the realm of law, of the mind, and of the economy. This distinction can help clarify, for example, the question of whether there can be such a thing as equality for us humans at all. Humans are much too diverse for the same guidelines to apply to all of us. According to the model of the realm of law, spirit, and economy, our individuality, our difference, is located in the sphere of the spirit. Our individual creativity makes us unique individuals. In the sphere of the spirit, equality has lost nothing. The principle of equality refers exclusively to the sphere of law. Before the law we are equal, and every human being has a voice. Regardless of sex, race, or economic status, in a referendum every vote counts equally. That is the enormous quality of the principle of democracy: we struggle over an issue, we exchange views, we discuss and argue, we enrich each other in our differences. At the end of the day, there is justice, where each person counts for exactly one vote. The quality of democracy lies in the combination of both. In the third area of the model, the sphere of the economy is, in a sense, a connecting link between the spirit and the law. Economy is about mediation between individuals, it is about the principle of solidarity, about 'for each other,' viewed quite rationally, because in the economy, needs meet fulfillment of needs. Economy, law, and spirit are three spotlights on the concept of democracy, each illuminating a different aspect. The fulfillment of democracy may lie in the clear distinction and interplay of these principles.

Daniela Vancic and Matt Qvortrup

Complementary Democracy: Conclusions and the Way Ahead

"Letting a hundred flowers blossom and a hundred schools of thought contend is the policy for promoting progress in the arts and the sciences and a flourishing socialist culture in our land."[1]

We appreciate that it is somewhat unorthodox to cite Chairman Mao Zedong in a book about democracy. After all, the Chinese Communist leader was not exactly a democrat – the reverse, if anything. Nevertheless, we feel that this quote sums up the essence of complementary democracy.

What the contributors to this book have shown in different ways is that there is not just *one* type of democracy and that there are complements to the prevailing system of representative government. All too often, debates descend into dichotomous 'either–or' statements. We do not believe this is a fruitful way forward. We do not think that there is an alternative to a system of government with elected representatives, but neither do we think that this system can stand alone. It needs to be complemented. We need representative government *as well as* other mechanisms, including referendums, mini-publics, participatory budgeting – and (on occasion) also the recall (although the latter institution comes with a health warning, as shown in Yanina Welp's chapter).

Participation may be at the heart of democracy, but not taking part in democracy, too, is a form of democratic expression. Boycotts or opting out of the democratic process as a style of protest are meaningful mechanisms, particularly in unhealthy democracies where fair competition is impossible. While opting out of democracy comes at a high cost which often does not affect the outcome, boycotts often reiterate the lack of legitimacy of the process and outcome. In democracies where there are few to no democratic instruments to voice concern in addition to the traditional election cycle, the practice of non-participation may be vital to democratic expression.

That there are other ways of doing democracy than through elected representatives was once controversial. Many politicians – and a fair number of self-proclaimed members of 'the elite' – have decried the rise of government by the people. Perhaps none more so than the Spanish philosopher José Ortega y Gasset (1883–1955), who, in his book *La rebelión de las masas* (1929) wrote, "In the right ordering of public affairs, the mass is that part which does not act of itself.

---

1 Mao Zedong, Speech in Peking, 27 February 1957.

https://doi.org/10.1515/9783110747331-013

... It has come into the world in order to be directed, influenced, represented."[2] The reason for this was as old as discussion of public affairs itself. Indeed, no less a figure than Plato held the view that "the masses ... perceive nothing but merely sing the tune their leaders announce."[3]

But these assertions do not make them true. Allowing the people to vote directly on laws is as old as democracy itself. Aristotle, recounted how *Council (or boulē)* in Ancient Athens, "submits preliminary ordinances to the people"[4]. Whether this was a good idea – and is a good idea – is the question. The denunciations of democracy may be popular – among elitists – but they are not empirically based on facts. As Matt Qvortrup shows in his chapter, democracies are economically better off than autocracies – and this economic superiority is even more pronounced in countries that have frequent referendums.

These positive effects are not just associated with tried-and-tested forms of complementary democracy, but have also been reported in jurisdictions with *participatory budgeting* (PB). This innovative system, described in this book as "a gift from the global South," has been defined as a "decision-making process through which citizens deliberate and negotiate over the distribution of public resources."[5]

Elitists might see this as a recipe for disaster. This has not been the empirical experience. Indeed, as Greta Ríos writes in her chapter, "indicators as important as child mortality have seen a decrease in communities with PB, while they have stayed the same in communities that are not implementing PB in Brazil."

Once again, we are not here arguing that we need to replace representative government. What we are merely suggesting is that we complement it with other institutions – and, indeed, other practices, and other forms of participation and protest.

And much as there have always been critics of democracy, there have also been those who support it. From Aristotle to Hannah Arendt, there is no shortage of great minds who believed in the collective wisdom of the ordinary people. One of the most celebrated was the French aristocrat Alexis de Tocqueville (1805– 1859), who wrote that "the most potent, and possibly the only remaining weapon to involve men in the destiny of their country is to make them share in its government."[6] Nearly 200 years later – and without the gendered language – the liter-

---

2 Ortega y Gasset, José (1932) *The Revolt of the Masses*. London: W. W. Norton & Company, p. 115.

3 Plato, *Protagoras*, 317b.

4 Aristotle (1891) *The Constitution of Athens*. London: Seeley & Co, 108.

5 Wampler, *Participatory Budgeting*, p. 21.

6 Tocqueville, Alexis de (2003) *Democracy in America*. London: Penguin, p. 276.

ary critic and activist Judith Butler stressed, in a similar vein, that "acting in concert can be an embodied form of calling into question the inchoate and powerful dimensions of reigning notions of the political."[7]

But one of the problems with contemporary politics is that not all views of the people, and not all of their "calling into question" reaches the politicians. We risk missing many ideas if we do not allow pathways into the political system, such as through mini-publics, agenda initiatives, participatory budgeting, and even supranational votes.

All these mechanisms provide additional ways in which citizens can voice their concerns and contribute to better policy-making. Some institutions may seem to offer only marginal benefits, but in democracy, as in other things, every little helps. Some have been skeptical as regards the impact of agenda initiatives (which provide citizens with the opportunity to propose laws, which are then voted on in national legislatures).[8] Yet, as Mendez and Mendez report in their chapter, citing the example of Latvia, "Ultimately the less than a decade of experience with the Latvian instrument suggests that AIs can actually have a truly transformative potential in terms of generating citizen participation, deliberative listening, and legislative outcomes."

And why limit such mechanisms within the boundaries of the nation state? With global issues requiring global solutions, the need for transnational democratic participation is greater than ever. Daniela Vancic states in her chapter that the European Citizens' Initiative is the world's only bottom-up transnational democratic instrument, with which citizens can propose legislation in the EU. The European Citizens' Initiative has led to new EU laws in several cases, and it is inspiring a campaign for the establishment of a new citizens' participation tool at the United Nations level: a UN World Citizens' Initiative.

Mini-publics have also recently seen an increase in popularity and practice, but they are not panaceas. As Maija Setälä writes in her sober assessment of mini-publics, "mini-publics could improve democracy if they facilitate inclusiveness and quality of public reasoning among policy-makers and the public at large." However, "Without proper coupling and institutionalization, the impact of mini-publics on the democratic system remains low."

Most books on political theory make reference to the Ancient Athenians. This is understandable. Few democrats are not moved by Pericles's defense of his city's system of government, as reported by Thucydides: "Instead of looking at

---

7 Butler, Judith (2015) *Notes Toward a Performative Theory of Assembly.* Cambridge Harvard University Press, p. 9.
8 Some of these skeptical arguments are mentioned in Qvortrup, *Democracy on Demand*, p. 194.

discussion as a stumbling-block in the way of action, we think it an indispensable preliminary to any wise action at all … in our enterprises we present a singular spectacle of daring and deliberation."[9] But much as we admire the Athenians' system of government, we often fail to remember that a center-piece of the system was that many of those holding executive office were chosen randomly. Those who read Aristotle's *The Constitution of Athens* will find that "[the citizens] appoint by lot all the offices belonging to the administration."[10] So, might a similar system by so-called 'sortition' work now? Gil Delannoi – in his chapter on this – believes the answer is in the affirmative. As he writes, this system – while not an alternative to the prevailing model – has shown itself "capable of producing tangible results, renewed participation, reformed decision-making." Of course, the Athenians had some elections, especially for military offices. But they were rather more radical than democratic countries today. As we have seen in Yanina Welp's chapter, politicians can occasionally be recalled if they incur the wrath of the voters by failing to deliver on promises. In Athens officers and other elected officials could be ostracized, "where a promise has been made to the people and not performed".[11]

Politics is not just about voting or even discussing. As Andrea Adamopoulos shows in her chapter, the artist Joseph Beuys espoused the "radical idea of understanding democracy as art, and understanding ourselves as artistically shaping beings of freedom." This conception is close to the idea of performativity that has been in vogue in recent years.[12]

But, more precisely, what other forms can democratic participation take if not arguing, discussing, and voting? For some the mere act of gathering is an important way of democratic expression. As Butler has written, "if we consider why freedom of assembly is separate from freedom of expression, it is precisely because the power that people have to gather together is itself an important prerogative, quite different from the right to say whatever they have to say once they have gathered."[13]

This theoretical perspective is supported empirically; as Della Porta and Felicetti found in their chapter: "Crowdsourced constitutional processes, particularly in times of crisis, give social movements some capacity to exert constitutive

9 Thucydides (1951) *The Peloponnesian War*. New York: The Modern Library, p.105.
10 Aristotle *The Constitution of Athens*, 102.
11 Aristotle *The Constitution of Athens*, 103.
12 See: e.g.: Micheletti and McFarland, *Creative Participation*; and Hendriks, Duus, and Ercan 'Performing politics on social media.'
13 Butler, *Notes Toward a Performative Theory of Assembly*, p. 8.

powers. At times of democratic malaise, the direct participation of citizens in re-writing the constitution can restore collective identity."

This view is further exemplified in case studies. Judith Butler wrote that "The gathering signifies in excess of what is said, and that mode of signification is concerted bodily enactment, a plural form of performativity."[14] There are few better examples of this than the KNAGs – 'Knitting Nannas Against Gas' – whose protest was chronicled and analyzed by Selen A. Ercan and Carolyn M. Hendriks. As they write in their chapter,

> Today, citizens participate in politics and voice their opinions through a rich array of activities in both face-to-face and online settings. They draw on a variety of performances using visuals, sound, presence, and even silence to express themselves. They use social media; tweet messages, upload videos on YouTube, circulate images and stories on Facebook which are creative, humorous, and antagonistic all at the same time. They seek out creative and personally expressive modes of political action to participate in politics and political debates in ways they can, when they can.

This book has looked at some of these ways of participating democratically. They are not all equally efficient, but in different ways they complement the existing system of representative government.

According to the *Oxford Learners Dictionary*, "things that are complementary are different but together form a useful or attractive combination of skills, qualities, or physical features." We think these chapters have shown that the institutions and practices of direct democratic participation analyzed form a 'useful and attractive combination of qualities' that make democracy stronger. We have not discussed them all. No doubt there are others – and new ones still to be invented. But the ones analyzed here are all positive contributions to a better system of governance and of government.

So let a thousand flowers of complementary democracy blossom – the more the merrier!

---

14 Butler, *Notes Toward a Performative Theory of Assembly*, p. 8.

About the Contributors

Andrea Adamopoulos is a German business economist. She has been a democracy activist for several years and is affiliated with Mehr Demokratie and OMNIBUS.

Gil Delannoi is a Senior Researcher (FNSP), a Professor of Political Theory at Sciences-Po Paris, and a Fellow of the Centre de recherches politiques. His main interests include political theory, the history of ideas, the history and theory of democracy, institutional design, and literature.

Donatella della Porta is Professor of Political Science, Founding Dean of the Faculty of Political and Social Sciences, and Director of the PhD program in Political Science and Sociology at the Scuola Normale Superiore in Florence, where she also leads the Center on Social Movement Studies (Cosmos). Among the main topics of her research: social movements, political violence, terrorism, corruption, the police, and protest policing.

Selen A. Ercan is Associate Professor of Political Science at the Centre for Deliberative Democracy and Global Governance at the University of Canberra. Her work sits at the intersection of normative political theory and empirical research and explores the prospects of deliberation in various settings.

Andrea Felicetti is Assistant Professor at the Faculty of Political and Social Sciences, Scuola Normale Superiore. He has worked and published extensively on social movements and democracy and the interaction between them.

Roslyn Fuller heads the Solonian Democracy Institute in Dublin, Ireland. A prolific speaker and writer on various aspects of democracy, she is also the author of *Beasts and Gods: How Democracy Changed Its Meaning and Lost Its Purpose* and *In Defence of Democracy*.

Carolyn M. Hendriks is Professor at the Crawford School of Public Policy at the Australian National University. She has published widely on the practice and theory of democratic aspects of contemporary governance, including on community participation, deliberation, inclusion, listening, and representation.

Fernando Mendez is a Senior Researcher at the University of Zürich. He is currently working on an ERC project investigating the limits of direct democracy and is the author of a number of publications in the field of direct democracy and voting behavior.

Mario Mendez is a Reader in Law at Queen Mary University of London, where he teaches constitutional law, comparative constitutional law, and EU law. He is the author of a number of publications in the field of direct democracy, including *Referendums and the European Union: A Comparative Inquiry* (CUP 2014).

Matt Qvortrup is Professor of Political Science at Coventry University. Described by the *Financial Times* as the "world authority on referendums," his recent books include *Death by a Thousand Cuts: The Slow Demise of Democracy* (DeGruyter 2021).

Greta Ríos is a Mexican activist for democracy. She is the founder of Ollin, A.C., an NGO that aims at a Mexico where the rule of law is the only rule. She has been working on direct democracy and participatory budgeting since 2015.

Maija Setälä gained her PhD at the London School of Economics in 1997 and is currently a Professor in Political Science at the University of Turku, Finland. She has published widely on democratic theory, especially theories of deliberative democracy, direct democracy, and democratic innovations.

Daniela Vancic is the European Program Manager at Democracy International e.V. and an expert on the European Citizens' Initiative. She campaigns for better implementation and further development of the world's first transnational democratic instrument. Daniela studied at Michigan State University and the Geneva School of Diplomacy and International Relations and, since 2017, has lived in Cologne, Germany.

www.ingramcontent.com/pod-product-compliance
Lightning Source LLC
Chambersburg PA
CBHW050650270326
41927CB00012B/2952